A Hell of a War

A
Hell of a War

DOUGLAS FAIRBANKS, JR.

ST. MARTIN'S PRESS NEW YORK

Production Editor: David Stanford Burr

Design by Judy Christensen

Library of Congress Cataloging-in-Publication Data
Fairbanks, Douglas.
    A hell of a war / Douglas Fairbanks, Jr.
       p. cm.
    Sequel to: The Salad days.
    "A Thomas Dunne book."
    ISBN 0-312-08807-8
    1. Fairbanks, Douglas, 1909-   . 2. Motion picture actors and
actresses–United States–Biography. I. Fairbanks, Douglas, 1909-
Salad days. II. Title.
PN2287.F32A3 1993
791.43'028'092–dc20
[B]   92–43657
                                       CIP

First Edition: March 1993

10 9 8 7 6 5 4 3 2 1

DEDICATED TO THE MEMORY OF
ADMIRAL OF THE FLEET, THE EARL MOUNTBATTEN OF BURMA,
K.G., ETC.
HERO AND FRIEND AND HONORARY GOD-FATHER
OF MY THREE GRACES,
DAPHNE, VICTORIA AND MELISSA
FOR WHOSE FUTURE I BECAME ONE OF THOSE WHO FOUGHT IN
A HELLUVA WAR.

For the second time I must acknowledge my great indebtedness to Joan Pollack for all she has done to advise and edit this story of another part, *my* part of a war.

D.F., Jr.

Acknowledgments

W<small>HEN REPORTING</small> a particular event or retelling an old yarn I am often tempted, as are more than many others, to garnish it. In the case of this volume I have tried to avoid such a pitfall and to retell some of my martial experiences as accurately as I could. To back up my account of this part of my active duty in the U.S. Navy I have checked through official action reports, formerly classified correspondence and newsful letters sent to family and friends. Although scared witless much of the time I was consoled by the conviction that a few million others—military and civilian, enemy and ally—were as scared as I was. Often, for sure, with better reason.

My family—all of my children, grandchildren, and cousins—were most helpful in having noted conversations and remembered stories told to them in their childhood. And also literally invaluable help came from friends, too, such as Betty Barker, Helen Benckendorff, Lady (Jill Benson) Tomkins, Esmé and Brian Connell (who once wrote a fine biography of me called "Knight Errant"), Joan Pollack, Jane Cushman, Lady Alexandra Metcalfe, Col. Joseph Bryan III, the wartime letters of the late John McLain and the late David Niven, another biographer and collaborator of mine on the "Fairbanks Album," Richard Schickel, my late beloved cousin and "family historian," Letitia Fairbanks-Milner, and finally the U.S. Navy—once called "The Silent Service"—which has been in every way cooperative and helpful.

"The Story So Far . . ."

A FEW YEARS back I wrote the first volume of this memoir, The Salad Days, *and though it did well enough, I realize that many readers coming to this book will not have read it. Hence, this summary of my life leading up to World War II. Those who are familiar with that book are advised to skim or skip these pages. Others may have found their memories aren't what they once were and want to review the material. And then there are those who like to rewind the tape and see the movie from the beginning every time. The choice is yours.*

As I write this, I am what the Bible calls "full of years," having been born in 1909 on the ninth day of December. I have three daughters whose mother was my late second wife and, God help me (and them), eight grandchildren. Five are boys and three are girls, but none carries on the name of Fairbanks—except one who hyphenates it. When he was quite small, my eldest grandson, Anthony Fairbanks-Weston, saw a famous snapshot of my father in a whimsical mood, standing arms outstretched, holding Charlie Chaplin on one shoulder and Mary Pickford on the other. My father is dressed in elegant though casual riding clothes that give him the look of a ringmaster, Charlie wears a white ruffled shirt, black tie and grubby suit, and Mary looks like a little girl with a huge bow atop long golden ringlets, a short skirt, and black Mary Janes. It is 1917 and they are posing next to a broken-down old truck.

Anthony looked puzzled and said, "Grandpa! Who are these people? Are they in the circus?"

My short answer could have been a smirking admission that their world *was* a circus of sorts, but Anthony's question betrayed such profound ignorance of his great-grandfather and his own roots that it seemed much better to take the long-winded way round.

"No, Anthony, they were not circus performers. They were the most famous and popular movie stars ever—certainly of their own day and at least as popular as Madonna and Michael Jackson are today—superstars before there ever was such a word. Douglas Fairbanks, your great-grandfather and my father, was known and loved everywhere in the world as the happy and confident superhero who could jump, climb—nearly fly—win swordfights or any fights better than any other *three* men, and at the end of each story win the hand of the shy maiden whom he has rescued from something or someone unspeakably dreadful. This little girl with the curls was really a grown-up actress called Mary Pickford. The world called her America's Sweetheart, and she was my stepmother. The man on the other shoulder was my father's close friend and business partner, Charlie Chaplin, and though not in the circus, he *was* the greatest clown who ever lived."

Indeed, no face or figure could ever again be as globally recognized and adored as the tiny-mustached, splayfooted, baggy-trousered Charlie. Not only in the developed West, but in the remotest villages of Africa and Asia where few could even read, the names of the Great Trio were spoken. For very little money, uncountable millions found refuge from their particular worlds in magical black-and-white silent films. Mary and Doug and Charlie were the *real* giants of the movies.

But that's not the whole story—indeed, it's not even the beginning. To start, I must go back to 1880, about the time my grandmother, lovely dark-eyed Ella, was married to H. (Hezekiah) Charles Ulman, a lawyer, probably of Jewish origin, who had been wounded during the Civil War. After their marriage he persuaded Ella to leave her genteel life in Atlanta for Denver, where he hoped to find great wealth in those days of the literally Golden West. My father was born there in

1883. He was Ella's fourth son. She had had two previous husbands; the first and greatest love of her life was a New Englander, John Fairbanks. The father of her eldest son, John, he had died cruelly of tuberculosis. The second, with whom she had another son, Norris, was an abusive, alcoholic judge. Ella met H. Charles Ulman when he helped her obtain a divorce from this scoundrel. Ella's third son was my father's older brother Robert, born in 1882.

Ella made no effort to conceal her dislike of the brown parched land around her, always contrasting it with the gentler past from which she had strayed. The fortune that H. Charles expected and so energetically sought eluded him utterly. He had turned his back on his law career, absenting himself from home for weeks at a time, traveling all about, exploring prospective mines. The drain on their once robust finances began to tell.

When H. Charles was at home he delighted in entertaining old theatrical friends from New York—he had always been contagiously stagestruck—who included Denver in their national tours. In fact, Ulman's splendid looks were at one time mistaken by passersby for those of his greatly admired friend Edwin Booth, who was then America's most famous classical actor (and, of course, brother of Lincoln's infamous assassin, John Wilkes Booth). Ulman was such a serious lover of Shakespeare that he has always been credited with imbuing his younger son Douglas with equal enthusiasm for the theater and the spoken word.

Young Douglas had an unusually retentive memory for verse, and began to "ham it up" at about the age of five or six for all who would listen to his childish treble reciting the classics. No doubt H. Charles, had he been present, would have been proud. He had always been a moderate drinker, but now, as his fortunes fell, moderation grew to excess and he made only sporadic returns to the family hearth, leaving behind nothing but empty bottles as evidence of his presence. The mining ventures had collapsed.

Finally, in an attempt to recoup some status and influence, he accepted a position as a professional Republican party campaign speaker for Benjamin Harrison in the presidential election campaign of 1888, and left for New York that summer. Ella had been completely, and nearly silently, abandoned. Her eldest son, John, then fifteen, steady and serious, began a job with a wholesale grocery firm, and shared his wages with his mother. As gracefully as she could in such needy circumstances, she began taking in lodgers.

The two little boys, seven and six, started going to the local public school. They both did well but Robert did better. Douglas was bright, but he lacked concentration. The school's principal reported that he amused everyone by swinging through branches of trees and walking on his hands "around the entire perimeter of the school wall." In fact, when he was younger, he tried (and failed) to fly à la Peter Pan, off the roof. He bumped his head badly on landing and carried the scar of a gash above his left eye all his life.

When Douglas was twelve he was surprised one day to find his father in Denver on business—and looking for him. The boy enthusiastically urged him to come home with him "to see Mother," but the older man demurred. He took his son to the nearest bar and, although already noticeably unsteady, dismayed the boy by downing at least two more shots of scotch. This did, however, give H. Charles the gumption to go home to Ella with Douglas holding his hand. "All hell broke loose" behind closed doors, ending with Ella furiously ordering the stumbling wreck of the once eminent man out of the house.

That was the last Ella ever saw of him. Douglas, however, did see him again in later years. Ulman would quietly come around, "out of nowhere," to his son's dressing room in a theater where he was playing and, as subtly as he could, ask for handouts. Money was always forthcoming, though my father grew increasingly bitter—not only because of H. Charles's weakness, but also because of his own devotion and loyalty to his mother. It was not hard for him to convey this feeling to the old man, who finally just stopped coming around. He died in New York, alone and almost unnoticed in 1915, the year his son Douglas first burst upon the world's motion picture screens.

Up to the time of H. Charles's last brief and calamitous visit home, the two young boys were known as Robert and Douglas Ulman. Then Ella revived, "for solace" she said, memories of her first, beautiful, but ill-starred marriage to John Fairbanks. She scratched around the roots of the Fairbanks family tree and began to drop claims here and there to establish that she was herself a second or third Fairbanks *cousin* to her first husband—a connection she was sure would give her and her boys a stronger foundation, however distant, from which to return to the better world she once knew. Thus from about 1895 on, Robert and Douglas joined their half brother John in the use of the family name of Fairbanks. Ella's second son, Norris, had not come with them to Denver in 1880, remaining a Wilcox in the South with his paternal aunt.

During the next eleven years Douglas attended a surprisingly good (for Denver) drama school, grandiosely called the Broadway Theater Stock Company, was "allowed" to leave the East Denver High School a month short of his sixteenth birthday, spent two years touring the country with a classical theater company, and began getting small parts in a number of Broadway plays. In late 1906 he was cast as the second lead in *The Man of the Hour,* which became an enormous hit. The name Douglas Fairbanks went up in lights on the marquee of a Broadway theater. He was established and in demand.

After the New York run, the play went on a brief tour that included Boston. One matinee was attended by Beth Sully, who, like many of her friends, was stagestruck. She developed a crush on Douglas Fairbanks and, with her father's cautious help, arranged to meet her hero. His response was almost immediate. Young Fairbanks thought the buxom Miss Sully absolutely entrancing. He invited her for a chaperoned tea (which he could ill afford) at the Ritz. One tea date led to another.

Beth Sully, aged nineteen, saw in Mr. Fairbanks, aged twenty-five, the handsome, virile hero of her dreams. She was very shy and managed to call him Douglas only after their fourth meeting. Douglas was flattered by Beth in every way. She was as blond as he was swarthy, as feminine as he was masculine, and she epitomized the upper-class world in which he felt very much at ease, and which his mother had always thought their due. It was only a month or so before Beth and Douglas exchanged declarations of love everlasting. In June 1907 my mother-and-father-to-be were married. It was a grand affair, held at the family's vast summer house, Kenneth Ridge, in Watch Hill, where a year or so before, Beth had enjoyed a great coming-out ball. *"Toute la Rhode Island"* and New York were invited, and all was gushingly reported by the contemporary society pages.

With the help of her father, the extravagant Beth and her equally extravagant actor-husband were able to rent a luxurious apartment in the Apthorp, at a then snob address between Seventy-eighth and Seventy-ninth streets, on Broadway, way uptown. It was there that I was born very early one December morning, weighing in at nine pounds.

I was not a reliably healthy child. Long, robust periods would often be interrupted by fairly severe illnesses. Sometime during my first year I contracted scarlet fever. This led to paralyzed intestines. I had one or two mild pneumonias, my share of pleurisy, bronchitis, too many colds, and a steady collection of such conventional illnesses as measles, whooping cough, and everything else except—thank God!— mumps. Nevertheless, by the time I was about three, I was a dumpling of a boy: fat but not sassy enough, immensely spoiled by an overindulgent mother and mildly ignored by a kindly but preoccupied father whose success took him and sometimes my mother and me all over the country and abroad.

Particularly in the summertime, Beth became torn between being in Watch Hill with me and her parents in New York with my father— between her concentration on her child and her unstated but justifiable anxiety that my father might be out of her sight for too long. He was handsome, contagiously cheerful, and had such a persuasive gift of projecting his ideal self-portrait that he came to believe in it himself. He designed the living of his life, coloring it as he went along. He did it so successfully that his best friends and biographers were seldom able to see him accurately. He had been indulged from childhood, and when he grew up he expected life to continue the custom. And life acquiesced. He dreaded growing old. In his view that was anything over fifty. Except in his romantic and domestic adventures, he rarely had a setback. Most of his dreams came true—with a minimum of struggle.

In public my parents behaved as the ideal couple their world expected, but in the inner family circle they could and often did become violently hot-tempered. Although my mother's heart and eyes were obviously only for her husband, my father was ridiculously jealous. If, when introduced to any man, she failed to keep her eyes modestly downcast, he would accuse her of flirting or being brazen. Sometimes his scolding made her cry. And though Douglas expected absolute, undeviating loyalty from his intimates, he blithely disregarded such expectations of him in return. He did sincerely love and depend upon Beth, but only his mother, Ella, could demand and receive the almost total devotion from him that he insisted on from others. It was a source of wry amusement to his close friends that his possessiveness extended even to his extracurricular fancies, whose numbers, it turned out, were surprisingly large.

One day in the autumn of 1914, as my parents were dutifully giving me a stroll through Central Park, my father was unexpectedly photographed and then interviewed by a motion picture cameraman. This was an unlikely event in those days. However, the film, showing my father walking with wife and toddler, and even vaulting a park bench, was seen by two motion picture executives, the founders and directors of the newly formed Triangle Film Company in Los Angeles. Theirs was a partnership between the master of masters D. W. Griffith, the slapstick producer Mack Sennett, and the famous producer Thomas Ince. As a result of the filmed charisma of this Broadway favorite, Douglas received a handsome offer to appear in one motion picture with an option for a subsequent series of films. However, since he was committed to do two plays, it was unlikely that he could go out to the coast for at least a year.

In the meantime, he and my mother accepted an invitation from the immensely gifted musical star Elsie Janis to a Sunday party at her home in Tarrytown, outside the city. On that Sunday my father stopped flitting from one discreet indiscretion to another and fell in love again. It was an event that would completely change all our lives. It began as a mild flirtation and grew into the most public romance of the next two decades. For among the several guests at Elsie's house that day were the well-known Irish film actor Owen Moore, and his incredibly rich and famous twenty-one-year-old Canadian wife, Mary Pickford.

The mutual attraction between Mary and Douglas became evident to them during a private stroll along a nearby river. Although they would not meet again for nearly a year, neither forgot the other, and neither could really be as deeply in love with anyone else ever again.

Even before that, however, the emotional temperature of our family life had continued to be volatile. My parents' moods ranged from exuberant highs to ominously seething lows and were interspersed with impulsive blowups. All the members of my mother's family had one characteristic in common: a disarming charm that in a flash could be transformed into a demoniacal rage. So common were these explosions, particularly with the Sullys, who reveled in "scenes," that they undoubtedly influenced my evolving personality. Of all these conspicuous tempers, I was most frightened by Mother's. Consequently, moral cowardice was fine-tuned in me by my real terror of Mother's sound and fury. Servants would be fired out of hand for what seemed to me trivial reasons. My father on occasion let fly with a pretty good show of his own anger. But it was always a summerlike thunderstorm followed quickly by grumpiness and then his personal rainbow. Although I doubt he ever knew it, I was frightened of him too—not in the same way I was of Mother, but frightened nonetheless. I kept my own introverted character protectively to myself.

It was sometime in the fall of 1915, after a summer in Hollywood where my father made his first film, *The Lamb,* and our subsequent return to New York, that my parents were invited to a large formal dance, also attended by Miss Pickford. Their spark was rekindled. Dad, however, characteristically deferred making any emotional decisions. Beth truly liked "dear Mary" (as she innocently called her celebrated new acquaintance) and seemed to enjoy the shadow of her radiance. Thus Mary was invited to the Netherland Hotel—where we rented a suite while we were in New York—for tea one day to "meet the family," as my father put it. Although I was surely unaware of the significance of this incident, I do recall it fairly well.

When Mary arrived—"apprehensively," she said later—she was cheerfully welcomed by my parents at the door to our apartment. I remember very clearly sitting on the living room floor playing with a modest set of toy trains. I got to my feet, as commanded, bowed, as taught, and shook the hand that was offered. My father said, "This is Mary Pickford." My mother, with a tactful smile, added, "She's 'America's Sweetheart'!"

Of course, none of this meant anything to me, but I remember thinking to myself, How did such a little girl, only a *little* bit taller than I, get to be so important and go places all alone? Apparently Mary understood my thoughts immediately and, pointing to the floor, asked, "Are those your trains?" I nodded. Mary smiled. "May I play with them too?" To my delight, she knelt down to the floor and joined me. Mary had made another conquest.

A few months before she died, in 1979, I was sitting by Mary's bedside, holding her tiny, frail, skin-and-bones hand. Her voice quavered, weakly, in pleasurable reminiscence, and with one of her lovely smiles she retold this story exactly as I remembered it.

In the meantime, I was most concerned with the constant packing and moving between the east and west coasts and as ignorant of my family's imminent disintegration as ever. There was no particular shock about the news of "the end" for me when it came, because I so often heard of events only after they happened. When I did finally realize that Dad wasn't coming home again at all, I must have been sorry, but I was promised I'd see him often.

I was much more aware of and excited by the war we had just entered in 1917 than by the news that my father was going to live elsewhere permanently. War fervor affected everyone. I remember joining friends playing at marching and war games. Serious concerns were the hoarding and rolling of all the tinfoil we could collect into great balls. They said they were to be used for making bullets. The girls helped make bandages. The connection between the two activities never occurred to us.

For as long as she lived, and in spite of two subsequent marriages, Mother never got over the pain of the loss of my father and his love. But on the whole, I think I was more fortunate than most children of divided parents—particularly of parents who were so conspicuous. Long after their divorce, whenever either one of them had reason to refer to the other when talking to me, it was usually done with warmth and admiration. To this day I remain deeply grateful for that sweet conspiracy.

Over the next five years my haphazard schooling continued. It had begun during our first trip to California with kindergarten at the Hollywood School for Girls (*very* embarrassing), where some of my schoolmates were Agnes, Margaret, and Cecilia de Mille, and the only other boy, Joel McCrea. Later I was entered in an exclusive boys' grammar school, Bovée, a very snobbish New York City establishment that had to hold special committee meetings before deciding whether or not to admit an actor's son. There followed two semimilitary schools, one in New York, which was the oldest school in the city, Collegiate. And then on two afternoons a week to a military drill group (uniforms and all), called The Knickerbocker Greys, wherein I became a lance corporal and delightedly banged a drum in the band as we marched around the 7th Regiment Armory on Sixty-sixth Street and Park Avenue. Then one on the coast, ending with eighth grade at the Pasadena Polytechnic School. The constant transcontinental life of my parents meant countless hotels and rented houses, and I was never in the same school for more than two years (sometimes less).

After the divorce and remarriage of both my parents (Mother on the rebound to an ex-beau, stockbroker James Evans, Jr., in 1919, and Dad to Mary in 1920) Mother and I lived in Paris, where life was infinitely cheaper than in New York, London, or Los Angeles. Her second marriage was not a success. Jim had speculated on the market with Mother's divorce settlement (about half a million dollars) and lost most of it. She quietly began to sell or pawn a few odd bits and pieces she no longer wanted.

I continued my schooling with a series of individual tutors in every subject from French composition to geometry—even sculpture. By the time I was thirteen Mother decided I should have one regular tutor. She settled on Carlton Hoekstra, the brother of a great friend who was part of her intense Parisian social life. He had just graduated from a university in Michigan and was less than ten years older than I. We hit it off right away, and I nicknamed him "Hookie." He didn't patronize me or even treat me as a boy of thirteen. My lessons, unpressured and patiently taught, were in mathematics, English, history, and geography. Hookie joined me and my friends in ball games and tennis and contributed to my growing up more than might have been predicted.

Hookie had not been in Paris more than a month before he fell for an extraordinarily pretty French girl whose name I cannot remember for the life of me. Since neither of them could speak the other's language, Hookie would ask me to walk with them on the afternoons they met so I could start things off as their interpreter. I enjoyed chattering away with her and she was amused by my glib use of rough Parisian argot. Once they had settled on where to go and what to eat and so on, they went off by themselves and I joined my pals. Later, Hookie would return to escort me home.

Hookie's girl was about twenty-two or -three. As I was within two or three inches of my adult height, I made Hookie promise to tell her I was nearly seventeen. For several weeks I had been unable to dismiss from my most private fantasies the idea that it would be a tremendous thing for me to really kiss, not just a girl like one of my California schoolmates, but a grown-up, very pretty French girl. The thought disturbed my days and nights. A Machiavellian scheme hatched when Hookie asked me if I would tactfully ask his girl if she would ever consider taking a weekend sightseeing tour of the châteaux on the Loire with him. I agreed, but said I thought it would be less embarrassing for her if I broached the subject when he was not present. Hookie, more naïve than I suspected, went along with this idea.

On an unusually warm day in late March we were deep in the lovely Bois de Boulogne. With heart pounding and hands clamming, the girl and I strolled deeper and deeper into the thickest part of the woods while Hookie went in the other direction. First, I presented his invitation in my best French. Then under some lovely concealing leaves brought out by the premature spring, I decided the moment had come for me to speak for myself. How I phrased it, I can't remember, but I *did* make myself clear enough. The girl surely sensed I was unpracticed. She giggled sweetly and led me behind a great clump of bushes quite away from anyone's eyes.

And there and then, to my numbed but ecstatic delight, she kissed me! I was in no way prepared for the vigor and enthusiasm with which she went about it. I had never thought of kissing as such a devouring process. Nevertheless, mildly shocked though I was, I enjoyed it thoroughly. The next thing I knew she suggested I stretch out on the grass beside her—a proposal that needed no urging. Of course I had a pretty good idea by then of the conventionally recommended method by which the species is perpetuated. But I was too bewildered to be aggressive and quite content to, as it were, take lessons. Very strange—and strangely agreeable—things were happening to me that I had never heard of before. What on earth was she doing? It wouldn't have occurred to me to protest, but I never in my life so much as suspected that variety could also be the spice of carnal gamesmanship.

And then I became delightfully dizzy and just plain passed out. When I opened my eyes, I realized the girl was trying to revive me, fanning me with her hanky, gently slapping my face, and asking, *"Est-ce-que ça va, mon chou? Tout va bien? Oh, mon pauvre, joli chou!"*

I shakily suggested we go and find Hookie. The girl was gently understanding and, of course, amused by what was clearly the technical end of my innocence. She giggled as she wiped her lipstick off my clown face and reapplied her own.

I was enormously relieved when Hookie proved not in the least angry at my duplicity. He thought it a great joke and actually arranged for me to have several more meetings with the girl. Why she liked me, or seemed so keen on her extratutorial activities, she never said. All I remember was her dark, straight, "Louise Brooks" bobbed hair, and the bright scarlet dresses she always wore.

Eventually this part of my education had to be deferred. Mother complained to Hookie that I was studying much too hard—I looked tired and pale and had dark circles under my eyes. She ordered a brief respite from my studies to take things easy and spend time with my friends. I don't know if Hookie ever saw the girl again. I know *I* didn't.

By now my mother's financial situation had become acute, and when, out of the blue, an offer came for me to do a film, she readily acquiesced. I was delighted with the idea of being in a movie. Paramount Pictures was still angry at the departure of their great stars Mary Pickford and Douglas Fairbanks and their colossal success as independent producers with Charlie Chaplin and D. W. Griffith at the company they had created, United Artists. They saw hiring me as a "sort of minor revenge" on the senior Fairbanks, who would be bound to be embarrassed to have his overgrown son around as an All-American boy with athletic agility.

Just before I was to leave Paris for California, Dad and Mary arrived at the Hôtel Crillon on one of their greatly publicized trips, characterized by enormous mob scenes and glittering receptions by heads of state and other prominent figures. I was "asked" to meet Dad at the Crillon, and when the concierge there haughtily declined to believe who I was or even announce me, thinking I was some young fan trying to crash the great stars' apartments, I almost welcomed the excuse to slink away. But a member of Dad's sizable entourage came by and recognized me before I could leave.

Minutes later Dad and I stood quite alone together on one of the Crillon balconies overlooking the Place de la Concorde. We proceeded to have one of the worst rows of my life. He was anxious for me to continue my schooling—in fact, in time, to go to Harvard and later to Cambridge in England. Mother, on the other hand, had given me strict instructions not to hint that our depleted finances were in any way an influence on "my" decision to make a film. She never wanted him to know that all the money he had settled on her was gone. As we argued back and forth, he became quite angry and I replied stubbornly—even perhaps rudely. In fact, I was more afraid of Mother's reaction if I lost the day than I was of my father's. I was unlikely to see Dad again for some time, but I still had to go on living with Mother. I left under a cloud of solemn, frustrated disapproval, still shaking.

In any event, Paramount's gamble did not come off. The film, *Stephen Steps Out,* was not a success. Although I enjoyed myself for the few weeks the contract lasted, I was unceremoniously dropped the moment moviemaking was finished. I was really too young to care.

These were the years of my father's classic films: *The Mark of Zorro, The Three Musketeers, Robin Hood,* and *The Thief of Bagdad,* the last released in 1924. (*The Black Pirate,* another classic, came in 1926.) With my Uncle Bob's help I managed to visit Dad's studio unobtrusively now and then to watch the spectacular filming in progress. I would go, outwardly shy, but inwardly eager, increasingly absorbed in moviemaking on such a large, serious scale. I wanted to watch my father's dedication to every phase of his job as writer, producer, and star.

*   *   *

In the course of time Paramount called me back to be part of their "stock company." After some tedious weeks of walk-on assignments I was given a movie role in a melodramatic piece of nonsense called *The Air Mail*. Our location was on the outskirts of the then small desert town of Reno, Nevada, on a local excuse for an airfield. Mother was obliged by law to be with me because of my youth, but wasn't required to be on location for the shooting of every scene.

There was, in fact, one bit of the script that Mother didn't know about. It called for me to make a parachute jump from a two-seater biplane, clutching a precious sack of letters in my arms. I was determined to do the jump myself and was secretly reassured by both the pilot and the director. All I had to do, they said, was to jump when told, count to ten, and pull the rip cord ring—at which point my parachute "would open up real wide and safe-like," allowing me to float gracefully down to the desert some four thousand feet below where the film crew would pick me up.

Mother, ignorant of my duties on this cold and windy day, remained at the hotel. A plane was made ready. A camera was secured to the side of the pilot's cockpit. The aim, focus, and aperture were adjusted and since there wasn't room for a real cameraman, the pilot was instructed to keep the plane on an even flight by clamping the joystick tight between his knees while he simultaneously hand-cranked the camera at the correct speed. I was given last-minute advice and off we went. The higher we climbed, the more frightened I became, but it was too late to turn back. When we reached the right altitude, the pilot, well protected from the wind by his helmet and goggles, signaled me to go ahead and jump. I wore only the dirty suit that was my costume, with no helmet or anything around my head. I was, however, wearing blackened tennis shoes so I wouldn't slip on the wing. Gulping down my fear for the moment, I crawled out, clinging to the struts on the port-side wing. I began to wonder why I had ever been so determined to show my mettle. After an age of inch-by-inch creeping and strut-by-strut grasping, I finally got to the tip of the wing from which I was to jump. The pilot began to crank the camera and waved to me to go ahead.

I looked down—*far* down—*way* down. I knew he wouldn't flip me off as that would spoil the shot. But I stalled and stalled. Both my arms clung to that last strut and the stuffed old mailbag. In my mind's eye my hand was ready to pull the parachute ring. I reviewed my instructions: "Jump! Count ten! Pull!" That was it. But I just couldn't let go. Then, suddenly, the fourteen-year-old boy inside me rose to the surface and, damn it, I began to cry. Ashamed of my fear but incapable of conquering it, I crawled back along the wing and into my seat. We turned around, descended and landed. The director met me in silence, except for a terse word to an assistant about the time we had wasted. The "double" originally engaged for the jump got into my suit and again the plane took off. In a few minutes, the chute with the double attached came down safely and the plane landed.

I was so ashamed and angry with myself I wanted simultaneously to hide and to smash something. When Mother heard about the event, she exploded with rage. The bosses said I had insisted on trying it, there was really no risk, and a double *had* been standing by. I then intervened and said I had at first deceived the director, who thought it was the double in the plane, but when he learned it was me, he signaled the plane to return. Then *I* got hell. So much for *The Air Mail*.

Most of the fifteen films I made between 1925 and 1928 were unmemorable. There were two exceptions. I played the rich high-society boy in the first (silent) version of *Stella Dallas*—the fellow Stella's daughter marries at the end. The director, Henry King, decided that tall and athletic though I was, I looked far too young to marry and I was ordered to grow a mustache for the last scene. After a few days I had to confess the obvious: I couldn't. The only solution was to have a fake mustache stuck on with special makeup glue. I withstood the teasing well enough and the film became a huge success.

When I was eighteen I was hired to play Greta Garbo's dissolute younger brother in *A Woman of Affairs*. My character, besotted with debauchery, died young and helped trigger much of the movie's plot. *The Green Hat* by Michael Arlen, the best-selling novel on which our movie was based, had been banned by the Hays Office (the industry's self-censoring board) as immoral. Prohibition was still in force in 1928, so even though my character was supposed to die of drink, no bottle label was allowed to show. The book's hero commits suicide on his wedding night when he finds he has syphilis. In the film, he does himself in because he's been caught out as an embezzler.

*   *   *

At about this time I had the opportunity to do *Young Woodley,* a play by John Van Druten that had been very successful in London and New York. We played the West Coast—six weeks in Los Angeles and six weeks in San Francisco. Opening night was a great social event with many celebrities, including my father and Mary and Charlie Chaplin, in attendance. Joan Crawford, a young starlet just beginning to be known, apparently was so moved by the play that she sent me a fan letter suggesting we meet sometime. Of course I did ring her up and she invited me to her small house in Beverly Hills for tea before the theater one afternoon. I went gladly and giddily. I brought along, at her request, a small signed photograph. It was a nervous, stilted first meeting for us both. I hammed it up, trying to appear an intellectual, and she played the part of an overwhelmingly impressed country girl who saw glamour in her future. After an awkward but pleasant hour, I got up to leave. I asked if I might have a photograph of her in exchange. She produced a large eleven-by-fourteen studio portrait. On it she inscribed: "To Douglas, May this be the start of a beautiful friendship. Joan." For a time it was.

My initial impression of her was of a vital, energetic, very pretty girl, quite unlike anyone I had known before. Her looks were not classic, but her features projected an overall illusion of considerable beauty. Although she barely avoided being pop-eyed, she shrewdly made her eyes up in a manner designed to make them appear even larger. Her mouth was wide and generous—once described as resembling a torn pocket. She put lipstick on with broad, brave strokes. Her cheekbones were wonderful but her jawline was so square and severe that she could sometimes look hard.

Hers was less a talent than a distinctive gift that inclined her to "perform" her passing thoughts as if she were going through a repertoire of characters at an audition. Her speech shifted between a natural and agreeable Texas-Midwest mixture with New York icing and another affected for those times when she tried too hard to be what Noël Coward called "piss-elegant."

Her figure was beautiful! Joan's approaches to me were so flattering I practically melted. I began to wear her like a flower in my young buttonhole and my interest in other girlfriends diminished in direct proportion to my increasing absorption with the glowing glamour girl. Though jobs were intermittent and indifferent and income just barely sufficient for all my responsibilities, life nevertheless began to seem decked in very bright colors, and I became more and more impatient with family apron strings.

As our involvement with each other became more intense, she asked me not to call her Joan anymore. After all, it was only an invented name. Her given name was Lucille (Le Sueur). She preferred to be called Billie by old or close friends. So I called her Billie for the rest of her high-pitched life.

Billie and I were so strenuously preoccupied with each other that I was delighted when stepmother Mary thoughtfully suggested I show her off at Pickfair, called "Hollywood's Royal Palace" by the columnists of the day. We were both nervous but Mary was always the essence of gentle, hospitable charm and did all she could to make us feel at home. My father, on the other hand, let it be known through others (his aversion to direct showdowns was one of his principal legacies to me) that he was not at all enthusiastic about this "overexploited affair." But he was gentleman enough not to show it—not to knowingly hurt a nice young girl with whom his incomprehensible son was involved.

When Mother met "that Crawford girl," she was not nearly so nice to her as Dad and Mary had been. She was correctly polite, but also condescending, as with a soft smile she described Billie to a friend as "my son's current chorus-girl fling."

Our first big family crisis began during one of the evenings when we were invited to Pickfair to see whatever movie they were showing that night. They ran a new film at least four nights a week. Dad, Mary, their guests and often Charlie Chaplin from next door sat on rearranged sofas or large overstuffed chairs. Billie and I shared a well-cushioned chaise for two, pushed far over to the side of the long living room in which the films were projected.

We thought we were being very discreet in the way we expressed our mutual ardor over in our shadowy corner. After all, we only "embraced" when the lights were out and the others were watching the silent movie. But that was my mistake. Apparently we had not been as inconspicuous as our youthful fervor allowed us to think—if indeed we did much thinking at all. Dad, in an angry but controlled voice, let me (not Billie) have it! To this day I can feel the deep scarlet flush on my face. Dad was as angry as he had been at any time since I let slip some wind among company as a small boy. It was some time before we were asked to see a movie at Pickfair again, and we sat well apart from each other when at last we were. But however much we restrained our public behavior, there was no disguising our head-over-heels look.

We didn't think much about the disparity in our ages. Billie successfully kept her true age a secret from press, public, and me for quite a while. She was, I think, about four years older than I: twenty-two to my eighteen. My own age had been public knowledge, but as I began a campaign to make myself a little older, she arranged to slip quietly backward.

The most important contribution that Billie made to my evolving character was her insistence that I break away from home and Mother. The greatest gift Billie gave me (far better than anything I ever did for her) was a ramrod up my backside—the encouragement to be resolute. She made no bones about telling me that I'd never be a real, responsible adult as long as I let myself be controlled by Mother. I couldn't deny that I had become pathologically frightened of family scenes.

Each time I hinted to Mother that I intended to leave home, she became hysterical and threatened all sorts of dire actions. Once, I came back fairly late from Billie's house and found a cryptic note from Mother asking me to look in and say goodnight. I squeaked her door open a bit. Her bed light was on, and there she was, sprawled across the bed as if in a deep sleep, or a dead faint, or perhaps even a coma. A three-quarters-empty bottle of gin was on her bedside table with a nearly empty glass and a spilled bottle of sleeping pills. A rough shake of her shoulders produced no reaction. Horrified, I was about to ring for the police or an ambulance. I picked up the phone and, almost without thinking, took a quick sip from her glass. There was neither gin nor vodka in it—just plain water. I slammed the glass down in sudden anger at this childish, badly executed trick. At that, Mother opened her eyes blearily, and, seeing me, mumbled semicoherently, "Oh, don't call the doctor! I'll be all right. I'll be all right. But look, *look* what you, my beloved son—you and that dreadful girl—have done to me!" And she sobbed hysterically into her pillow.

Unintentionally, I managed to shock Mother into a white fury when, for the first time on another night, I didn't return home from Billie's until morning. Then I was able to pack my bags and check myself into the most modest room a junior member could get at the Hollywood Athletic Club. Mother's reaction was an eerie, melodramatic silence. When I next returned home to face her, to my immense surprise she received me with docility and charm. The signs of her true feelings were the sickly white powder covering her naturally beautiful skin, her wavy hair pulled starkly back in a bun, and her new voice of hollow congeniality much like the kind one hears at a funeral. I felt I'd at last jumped into the icy waters of maturity.

Billie, whose career was developing more spectacularly than mine, was able to wheedle Louis B. Mayer and other friends at his MGM court into advancing her enough money to begin payments on a new house. Bigger than her old one, it was several miles west of Beverly Hills in Brentwood. The house was bought in her name and we called it *Cielito Lindo* (Beautiful Little Heaven) after a popular Mexican song. I began to worry about how and when I could contribute my share.

Billie insisted that everything had to be spotless all the time. Everyone, even her closest friends, had to remove their shoes when entering her all-white rooms. She was also understandably concerned with maintaining her famous figure. She watched her diet and the scales daily and gloried in doing her "daily dozen" exercises. After any strenuous workout she would rub her skin down with hunks of ice, believing this would keep muscles and skin tight. Although she would later deny it, she did worry about ever having a child lest it somehow ruin her figure, and she saw to it that she had none.

I am sure our marriage was psychologically hastened by the opposition of my parents and the embarrassing publicity pouring out of Hollywood. The picture the world saw and gobbled up was the once poor and humble, now bright and beautiful, hardworking, talented little girl from the Middle West and the gifted, worldly "Crown Prince of Hollywood" as an irresistibly romantic couple. The opposition of my family actually had much less to do with the unsuitability of a glamorous movie star as my future wife than did my youth (I was nineteen).

By then Mother had sold her big house on Beverly Drive and replanted herself in New York at the Algonquin Hotel. Although she had moved back with some anxiety, this young fortyish, prematurely white-haired lady was soon flattered to find a number of beaux paying flirtatious attention to her. One evening Mother attended a performance of the hit musical *Hold Everything*. The leading man was Jack Whiting, a handsome redhead, about twenty-seven or -eight years old, with a virile baritone that helped make "You're the Cream in My Coffee" a popular song. Mother apparently developed an immediate crush on him, and despite the difference of over twelve years in their ages, Jack was also very taken with the still pretty Beth.

Mother's new situation no doubt contributed to her marked change of attitude toward Billie and me when, in May 1929, we arrived in New York by train on a trip to get away from it all. She and Jack, with their own hint of romance between them, were witnesses in the chapel of St. Malachy's Catholic Church, known in New York as "the Actors' Church" (because it is in the theater district), when Billie and I were married on June 3.

Not long after the ceremony and to our immense surprise, a long telegram from Dad arrived at the Algonquin where we were all staying. It was full of hearty blessings and so warm and charming that Billie cried with relief on the spot. For two youngsters in over their heads, it was a never-to-be-forgotten day. We were truly married. And we lived happily . . . for a while.

A few weeks later in California we were astonished by a telegram from Mother and Jack, announcing that they had married. But mostly I was relieved. A great deal of Mother's pressure on me would now be lifted. I had a new stepfather—charming, gifted, and only about eight or nine years older than I. A devoted mother's boy, Jack, I imagined, might become both a proxy for me and for my never-forgotten father in Mother's life.

I was always plagued by comparisons with my father—despite all our dissimilarities, we gave many people an impression of being alike. The sharing of the same name was a great ambivalence to us both. How often Dad regretted his decision to pass his name on to his son can only be guessed.

Now that I was nearly twenty and married, it embarrassed him to call me Junior. So he used initials instead and I became "Jayar." Correspondingly, he didn't want to be called Dad or Father and I certainly couldn't call him Senior. I was uncomfortable with Doug, a name he never really liked anyway. "What would you like to be called if you weren't called Doug?" I asked.

"Oh, I don't know . . . Pete, I guess."

So from then on I called him Pete.

I certainly tried as hard as I could not only to avoid looking like my father but also not to be the same kind of actor. For many years I declined offers to act in a swashbuckler film. I was determined to be a serious straight actor in either comedies, tragedies, or melodramas—as different in every way from my father as I could be.

In 1930, without warning, my breaks returned, this time on a par with Billie's. Howard Hawks, then a very good but not yet really famous director, wanted to cast me in the original *Dawn Patrol,* a film about the British Royal Flying Corps, starring Richard Barthelmess. Set in wartime France in 1915, the picture told the story of a squadron of British fliers with only a handful of rattletrap planes to combat the powerful German Air Corps of the day. Rarely do all the British planes return from their forays behind enemy lines, and the squadron commander begins to crack under the strain of sending young men to their death. The film was very strenuous to make, taking many weeks of long, late days and nights in the studio or working round the clock six days a week, out in the cold on location.

The Dawn Patrol became a spectacular, worldwide success and my part was, glory be, acclaimed to the skies. It was, I admit, actor-proof, very sympathetic, and I made the best of it. In fact when the picture was remade in 1938 with David Niven in my part, he agreed it was a fail-safe role.

One of my favorite studio companions of the day was Mervyn LeRoy, a stoop-shouldered but nice-looking young fellow. He made a great success of directing his first picture, *I Am a Fugitive from a Chain Gang,* starring Paul Muni. His next assignment was another hard-boiled picture, Darryl Zanuck's new "trademark" for Warner Brothers where he was what you might call executive boss. The movie was more or less about Al Capone and titled *Little Caesar.* It would star Edward G. Robinson—a young, serious, classical actor—in the title role. This seemed strange casting then, but time has told how successful it was. Poor Eddie Robinson was typecast as a tough guy for years. No gentler man ever walked. He hated being villainous but it paid so well that eventually he was able to acquire an exceptional private collection of modern art.

There was a very good supporting role in *Little Caesar:* a tough young Italian, Ricky, the hit man for the Boss, and his protégé. To my surprise, Merv asked if I'd mind taking a smaller part after a year of leads and the big personal hit of *The Dawn Patrol.* I was dying to play Ricky! I hoped to demonstrate my versatility in this showy part. I affected slick, shiny dark hair, with short, slanted sideburns, like Rudy Valentino's, and a light Chicago gangster accent. I enjoyed every minute of the film.

I was now able to enlarge my share of the contribution to married life so that it would nearly equal Billie's. Life seemed to be puffing up. Our marital rocket was reaching its apex—and would hang there a bit before fizzling and sputtering out. Certainly Billie, whose own early explorations of life had been more varied than mine, turned over a completely new page of personal conduct during our courtship and early marriage. I have no idea when those enormous hungry eyes first locked on to someone else. The uncertain evidence suggests it was at roughly the same time that I began rather aimlessly to wander. The dream went on for a while, but our eyelids were fluttering.

Billie's big professional challenge in 1932 was as one of the all-star cast of *Grand Hotel.* The idea of being in the same picture with her idol, Greta Garbo—though sharing no scenes—was almost too exciting. All her personal idiosyncrasies (except her fanaticism for super-cleanliness everywhere on the set, which made John and Lionel Barrymore wild) were set aside for the duration. In spite of, or maybe because of, the experienced, stellar competition she faced, the Joan Crawford performance in *Grand Hotel* was first-class. Soon after that, to her great

excitement, she was asked to play Sadie Thompson in a remake of
Rain, the classic adapted from W. Somerset Maugham's short story.

One day Billie hinted that we had best make our own plans and
begin to think about an amicable separation. This idea came so suddenly one morning that I was momentarily stunned. And then she was
off to work. Later, without pursuing her comments further, I suggested that when she had finished shooting *Rain* we should get away
on our too-long-delayed honeymoon, preferably to Europe. Her reaction was a weary, condescending smile and a "Perhaps! Perhaps.
We'll see."

Billie wanted no distractions to interfere with her concentration on
Rain. Therefore, would I "and everyone else" just leave her alone on
Catalina Island where the picture would be made? I, too, wanted to
get away from home life for a bit. I did not welcome Billie's preoccupa-
tion with work to the detriment of our personal life. As luck would
have it, my chum Bob Montgomery (Billie's leading man in *Untamed*)
phoned me one day to suggest that if Larry Olivier and I were free and
could find one more friend, we could charter C. B. deMille's sailing
yacht *Seaward* and split the cost four ways. That seemed a marvelous
idea. Larry had been my good friend since he and his first wife, Jill
Esmond, came to New York to do *Private Lives* and then acquired
RKO contracts in California. Now Larry's own domesticity was rolling and pitching toward the rocks and he was relieved at an opportunity to get away from it all. He had only to finish the picture he was
on, charter a putt-putt plane and fly down to join us at a prearranged
anchorage in Baja California, Mexico. A writer friend, Eddie Knopf,
jumped at the idea and became our fourth shipmate.

Bob, Eddie, and I went carefully about victualing the yacht and
borrowing all we would need in the way of deep-sea fishing gear for
our jaunt. And our first days were gloriously uneventful—clear, bright
sun all day, brilliant stars all night, and calm seas with just enough
breeze to nudge our sails along. After about a week we reached a town
near Mazatlán where Larry was supposed to meet us. It was quite
respectable, with several dusty streets and quite a number of ordinary
houses, mostly adobe and tin, but a few of wood. We went ashore

where a group of the curious, having seen our handsome sailing yacht anchor, was waiting, friendly and smiling. A great sweating man in a white suit and very old Panama hat bustled up as the others made room. Obviously he was someone of substance in the town—the mayor, as it turned out. In a mixture of Spanish, English, and gesture we made immediate friends and went with him to his modest house, where we sat on his front porch and drank tequila.

The mayor was clearly impressed by our yacht and we let him think we were a group of rich playboys on a cruise. We asked him where the local airfield was and told him we were awaiting the arrival of a great friend who was joining us shortly by plane from Los Angeles. Who was he?

"Well," said I, deciding to make poor good-natured Larry the butt of one of my whimsicalities, "he is a very important young Englishman on a visit. Let us," I added conspiratorially, "play a joke on him. Could you arrange to have him arrested—just for fun? Just for a short while? He'll wonder what on earth happened."

The mayor's big belly heaved with laughter at the idea, and he immediately ordered the execution of these plans through a nearby subordinate.

Larry's rickety single-engine plane arrived, touched down on the sand-and-rock runway, bounced, and rattled. As he stepped out, he was greeted by four men, all wearing different uniforms. We watched, well hidden, from a distance, and couldn't hear what was said. But we did see poor Larry being taken briskly by the arm and walked to a wood-and-plaster building next to the airport. Later, we heard that they took him to the town jail and put him behind bars. He was, he admitted, both terrified and outraged. "Where," he shouted, "are we going? Where's Montgomery? Knopf? Fairbanks?"

"Never heard, *señor!*" they replied. "But you fined five hundred pesos!"

"Why, for Christ's sake?"

"Because," said the senior policeman, "you are Englissman!"

Larry now panicked. He couldn't get any *reasonable* explanation, so in desperation he said he must contact the British consul.

"We no recognize British, *señor,*" they told him.

Cruelly, we let poor Larry stew for a bit and then the mayor jovially ordered his release. There is no doubt but that Larry O. was the best sport I've ever seen. The moment he found out it was a gag at his expense, his laughter was the most raucous of all. The mayor, like a beardless Mexican Santa Claus, stopped guffawing for only a moment to tell us our friend was lucky his "soldiers" didn't hit him on the head, because, at the time, they didn't know it was a joke!

Larry was all gung-ho the moment he got aboard. He asked what our daily routine was and Bob facetiously told him that, if the ship were anchored, we all began our day by diving into the water from nearly the top of the mast. Of course, none of us dreamed of jumping off anything higher than the deck or perhaps the first rung or two of the ladder up the mast. Larry didn't hesitate. He was so keen to join in everything that, the moment he stowed his gear away and rejoined us on deck in his swimming trunks, he scampered halfway up the mast and dived into the sea. He made a bad splash that nearly knocked him out. Bob and I jumped in to help get him aboard again. Once more, he took it in the best of spirits. He always did.

As part of our morning exercises, we all donned big boxing gloves and sparred with each other for a short while. Once Larry sustained a tiny chipped tooth. For an actor, whose face is, at the least, a valuable part of his future, this could be worrisome. But not to Larry, whose sense of fun and courage helped see him through one serious and painful illness after another in his final years. No wonder that although he was about two years older than I, I always used to think of him as younger. Up to the day he died we were, in his words, "each other's oldest surviving friends."

The cruise was a marvelous success. We never had so much as a choppy day, never so much as a drop of rain. We returned tanned and fit, our heads clearer by far than when we set sail two weeks earlier.

At home Billie had finished *Rain* and to my immense surprise now seemed delighted with the idea of a honeymoon in Europe—especially since our studios—for publicity—would foot most of the bill. To make it even more fun, the Oliviers were leaving at the same time and we decided to sail together on the new German liner the *Bremen*. I reveled in every detail of planning for the trip: the friends and plays we would see in New York, what cabin on the ship to reserve, what to do in London and Paris, and so on. My next film assignment was six weeks off, so that was about all the time allowed us, but I was delighted. The cruise had helped me see things in what I thought was a clearer light.

That June of 1932 was a tailspin of excitement. It began with a phalanx of sirens and motorcycle police escorting us to our ship, docked in Brooklyn—all arranged by New York's Mayor Jimmy Walker—and then a perfect voyage to Southampton. Billie was obviously bewildered by her first ocean voyage and, I'm sure, kept thinking the whole ship was a movie set of sorts and all the other passengers extras and bit players.

Larry went on for years afterward telling how he and Billie competed with Jill and me in the long summer days at Ping-Pong on the afterdeck. If Billie occasionally made a particularly good shot that got by me, and I mumbled an appropriate "Good," she called out in an irritated voice, "Douglas! You *let* me win that! Now, *don't!*" Of course, I hadn't, nor would I have been that chivalrous, and I said so. But she went on insisting until Larry was forced to intervene: "Oh, for Christ's sake, Joan, shut up and play!" The game would continue. Other games, like deck tennis, she preferred to watch, as she feared for her nails. She insisted on being the glamorous Joan for the other passengers and wouldn't just be herself.

Our arrival in Southampton was quite beyond even my optimistic hopes. Over and above the normal crowd was an astonishing number of press and public, plus representatives of MGM and Warner Brothers to greet us, delaying our debarkation by about an hour. The biggest and most complete surprise was Noël Coward, who'd come all the way from London. From there on it was for me one continuous happy haze. Ensconced cozily in the old Berkeley Hotel in Piccadilly, outside we were the objects of hysterical clutchings, clothes rippings, and police protection. But at that time of our lives the limelight wasn't too bad.

The very first night Noël arranged for us to see his sensational patriotic spectacle, *Cavalcade,* at the Theatre Royal, Drury Lane, arguably the most classically beautiful big theater in the world. It was a breathtaking moment when we, followed by Noël, were ushered into the royal box by a splendid old boy in scarlet and gold-braided livery, knee breeches, and powdered hair. The audience rose to its feet and applauded two absolutely numb and unprepared youngsters. An unforgettable experience of tears, laughter, and wonder filled the next three hours.

Over the ensuing days there followed not only the splendid usual tourist sights of London, but also a meeting with a member of the royal family, the young, elegant, and very handsome Prince George (who took a shine to Billie right away), and invitations to the king's (George V) annual Garden Party at Buckingham Palace. The hospitality was so overwhelming we had to divide one weekend between Ivor Novello's house, Redroofs, in Middlesex, and Noël's rambling house, Goldenhurst, deep in the lush county of Kent. In Paris old friend Maurice Chevalier flattered us by attending a reception given in our honor. What a graduation for me only a few years after I'd been a teenager in Europe! Billie and I had our portraits painted. The pace was dizzying and exhilarating. My own enthusiasm obliged me to hope it was all shared by her. So how *did* she like it all? What did she think of the excitement, the beauty and friendliness of London and Paris in early summer bloom?

She hated it all! She put on a brave, well-trained smiling face and said the right words of gratitude, but she was really only peripherally interested. She said she would have been just as content to read about all this—and anyway, the pictures she'd seen seemed better than the real things. She felt so alien it was like a bad dream. All she wanted to do was get home as quickly as possible—*not* to Cielito Lindo, but to Culver City and the MGM studios, to the security of what she could recognize: her work. So home we went—ahead of schedule. She didn't return for years.

Not long afterward I received an offer from RKO to costar in *Morning Glory* with their newest "find," Katharine Hepburn. They surrounded her with two established costars: Adolphe Menjou and me. The script called for a longish dream sequence in which Hepburn and I were to play two or three big scenes from *Romeo and Juliet*. We were about the right age and conscientiously rehearsed these classic scenes for many days before they were scheduled to be shot. Costumes, wigs, and two sets (one with the famous balcony) were designed. Kate was a sensitive, delicate Juliet, dressed in a gossamerlike floating gown. I, on quite another hand, had gasped myself into skintight sheer green tights that stretched right up to my ribcage. They reminded me of how John Barrymore (my first real stage hero) had described himself in a similar costume: looking like "a decadent string bean." With a full blond wig, one earring, and a good deal of makeup, I looked more nearly like the second-prize winner in a transvestite contest. But this is all hindsight. At the time, we were both rather pleased with ourselves.

In fact, an invited audience of friends, associates, and selected outsiders, including my father and stepmother, came to watch us perform the scenes without the distraction of cameras, lights, and sound equipment. We ended up giving performances that were received with surprising enthusiasm. I thought we were both pretty damned good, though Kate has said having Mary Pickford and Doug Senior come to watch "was pretty scary."

Of course, by that time my too susceptible heart had allowed itself to be captured and my sentiments for Juliet, Eva Lovelace (Kate's character in the picture), and for Kate herself were the same. I did succeed in persuading her to dine with me once or twice, but somehow I lost all poise when trying to express my growing feelings for her. I was romantically tongue-tied. For a while I hoped she suffered from too much shyness to admit a similar reaction. My awakening came one night when I delivered her to her door. After a restrained, just-friendly goodnight peck on the cheek (early—we had to work the next morning), I drove some fifty yards down the road in my top-down roadster. Then I pulled over to the side to gaze at the shining sky and sigh over the wondrous Kate. However, something in the rear-view mirror caught my eye. Across Kate's lawn was a car in the street behind her house. I suddenly saw her slim athletic figure bound out of her back door across the grass, hop into someone else's car, and drive off!

My desolation can be imagined, but even though I was stung I didn't mention the episode to her afterward. Rather than risk the breakup of an already valued friendship, I cooled my behavior and became strictly a friend. I was never quite sure who my rival was, but with hindsight it is reasonable to assume it was Leland Hayward.

Our big Shakespearean scene was finally cut out of the picture entirely, since the producers felt it was not only too long, but "the yokels wouldn't catch the lingo" anyway. *Morning Glory* itself proved a smashing success and came at a good time for me. Kate won the Academy's Oscar for the best performance by an actress that year. Now, although we see each other too seldom, we nevertheless remain the warmest and most considerate of friends.

At home, after our return from Europe, things were quite chilly. As I suspected, Billie had taken a cottage in the then unspoiled settlement of Malibu Beach while I had been cruising to Mexico, but she wouldn't tell me exactly where it was or how I could reach her. She declared she had to sort things out in absolute privacy, she needed "personal solitude" to commune with nature and study lines for her next movie. She did keep one private telephone line through which she could be reached, but only for emergency calls from the studio or her agent. She telephoned me at home to get messages, ask about my general welfare, or give household orders to our cook and secretary-cum-chauffeur.

It was hard to find time or reason to be together. We had become familiar strangers. Whatever emotions or thoughts we once had in common had been fogged over and lost. While we both took pains to disarm the inevitable gossip, some whispers were unavoidable. I was aware that a few of her intimates did know where her hideout was and so, out of pride, I pretended to know too.

In later years Billie would tell interviewers that while she was increasingly absorbed in improving her acting technique and furthering her career, I was more interested in developing our social life—aspiring to be an international sophisticate—and so we had less and less in common. This was nonsense. In the end she had me moved out of *our* house in the middle of one night while I was working at the studio on a big storm sequence calling for repeated cold, windy drenchings on the rolling deck of the mock-up of a ship. (The film was *The Narrow Corner*.) My agent suddenly appeared to tell me the news that all my belongings had been moved to the Beverly Wilshire. The next morning on the front page of the *Examiner* there was Louella Parsons's scoop, quoting Billie's announcement of our "amicable separation." When we met to discuss it, of course we were unnaturally agitated. Billie yawed between the teary-eyed wife bravely resigned to the bitter ending of her dreams and the firm-jawed executive of a corporation discussing financial setbacks. I protested too much in far too many ways.

Three close friends eventually let me know quietly what many others had known for some time, but I did not: for almost two years Billie had been having an intense and fully requited love affair with Clark Gable, one of our friends and frequent dinner guests. Her extra-early-morning departures for the studio, even when not filming, and her late returns home were often the only times they could meet undetected by Clark's wife or me. To record that I was surprised must prove one of this book's greatest understatements.

I was additionally astonished to learn that one of Joan's and Clark's favorite trysting places at the studio was the charmingly decorated, very comfortable portable dressing room I had given her as a wedding present—and only recently finished paying for. Actually, Clark was such a nice guy that even in my private distress I couldn't blame him. Had our positions been reversed, I wasn't sure I wouldn't have been equally deceitful.

So Billie and I were officially separated. She would file suit for divorce on April 29, 1933, but it would not become final for another year.

It was decided in a hurry. Pete and I would go to Europe together. It was the first time I had ever taken a trip alone with my father. To an observer he was still the same energetic leader of the pack, but to my considerable surprise for the first time he treated me as if I were his contemporary—no longer a subconscious rival, but a companion, confidant, and teammate. I wallowed happily in this long-wished-for relationship. In a strange way I was the more responsible, even mature, of the two of us. He began to wonder (without expecting me to answer) what to do about Mary. Although close friends and family knew of her problems, he never once mentioned her secret drinking habit, nor her disinclination to share his enthusiasm for travel and people. He confided his wish to keep his cake and eat it as well, but he was not yet prepared for solutions.

In London, Pete took a large, luxurious flat near Marble Arch on the northern border of Hyde Park. I had a small room there; from the start, I made the point with my father that I would pay all my own expenses.

Pete found himself attracted to the wife of a popular young man about town, Tony (Lord) Ashley. I paid little attention to this at the time—I was preoccupied with seeing favorite sights and old friends from my fizzled-out honeymoon. Indeed, at the first opportunity I visited my old teenage crush, Gertrude Lawrence, who was starring in a comedy called *This Inconstancy.* I remember being absolutely recaptivated by Gertie's magic. Suddenly my personal California dramas faded and my whirling emotions flew to this great woman. I was determined to pay her court, in spite of the fact that she was ten or eleven years my senior. At first I kept the extent of my new romantic plans to myself. She was not only a stunning international stage star, but the ex-love of more than one of my father's friends and contemporaries.

Gee Lawrence was an effervescent personality. Although she never seemed to realize when she sang off-key (frequently), she could always carry it off with the charm of her otherwise liquid voice, her grace of movement, and the mocking sensual mouth that ignored the large, unpretty nose above it. Her lithe figure, though fashionably boyish with scarcely a real curve, remained utterly feminine. It was, I believe, for her that Noël Coward invented the term "star quality."

At the time I came on the scene Gee was being wooed by Eric, Earl of Dudley, a handsome, charming, disturbingly rich yet rather stingy older aristocrat. After her spectacular success in two of the *Charlot's Revues* and with Noël in *Private Lives,* Gee thought if only Eric would propose and pay some of her mounting bills, life would be wonderful. She was notoriously extravagant and I was fairly so. The greatest difference between my father's life and mine at the time was that he could afford it and I couldn't. I was living it up, but was luckily usually a guest.

Gee first decided to openly respond to my courting, to "take me up" as it were, in order to make Eric jealous. But little by little I believe my youth and celebrity made her feel younger, and I began to be a real factor in her life. She had a wide circle of friends into which I was hastily drawn. Among the variety of names in her regular group, one might start with Edward, the Prince of Wales (called the Pragger Wagger behind his back); followed closely by his youngest brother, my now chief royal friend Prince George; and also Larry Olivier, John Gielgud, Noël Coward, Ivor Novello, Cole Porter, Bea Lillie, and Fred and Adele Astaire.

Through Gee I got to know Eric's very extroverted and loving family. His younger twin brothers, Geordie and Eddie Ward, were so identical in their twinship that they often swapped girlfriends the very same evening without being caught out. They were both in the RAF Reserve and through them I had some hair-raising adventures. Once, for instance, on a Sunday morning, we decided to buzz very low over Noël's country house in Kent. We knew he had a lot of weekend houseguests and thought it would be fun to wake them all up early after what we assumed had been a thick night. This we did. Two RAF planes, with this American civilian aboard one of them, zoomed and swooped at rooftop height above the Coward house over and over until we could see the household, one by one, coming out on the lawn, shaking fists and making obscene gestures at us. Eventually we spotted Noël, the Master himself, giving orders to the others. Pillows were brought out and placed carefully on the lawn and the many guests arranged themselves in order to spell out, quite clearly for us to see from the air, FUCK OFF! We did.

My cautious wooing of Gee proceeded at an encouraging pace and I was, within a few weeks, almost an equal rival to Eric Dudley, though it was only natural, as Noël pointed out to me, that her long-run interests would be better served as the Countess of Dudley than as the older girlfriend of an American movie star. Meanwhile I enjoyed the excitement.

There was also a business aspect to our trip to Europe. Soon after our arrival a series of meetings was set up by the United Artists office in

London between my father and the great British producer Alexander Korda. To my surprise and pleasure my attendance was also requested at these meetings. A deal was quickly negotiated for Alex to become a partner in United Artists. As soon as the documents were signed and sealed, Alex and UA jointly announced their first film—an adaptation of a French play, *Catherine the Great*. The famous German actress Elisabeth Bergner would play the young Catherine and she had insisted that her husband, Paul Czinner, be the director. The young character actress Flora Robson was cast as the dying old Empress Elizabeth, and one of the giants of the English theater, Sir Gerald du Maurier, agreed to play the small part of the czar's French valet. At first the Korda group wanted Joseph Schildkraut for the quasi-classic part of mad Czar Peter III. However, both Bergner and Schildkraut spoke with heavy German accents and it was decided one was enough. To everyone's surprise, including Pete's, I was the next choice. At that time Alex had no further need to do anyone any favors—particularly his new UA partners. He was in the catbird seat. After tests and interviews I landed the plum job on my own.

I looked nothing at all like the real Peter III. Research reported that he was stubby with a puffy, pockmarked face. I wanted to create a real character in the part, but Dr. Czinner and Alex Korda insisted our story was essentially romantic. I took camera tests with white wig, plucked eyebrows, very white makeup, lipstick, and a few black beauty marks. My costumes were black or white satin suits, lace jabots, and knee britches. Had I not been so in love with my part and delighted with my good fortune in landing it, I might have been more stubborn about my character, but I was afraid they would replace me. One of our electricians described me as "beautifully tarted up." I agreed. The real Peter III of Russia was said to be rather feminine, but it was strictly against the censorship rules of that day to even hint at homosexuality. Thus I was ordered to defy the period and cultivate my mustache—well mascaraed. The result was inauthentic but apparently satisfactory.

I had been assigned one of three star dressing rooms at the studio in Elstree, a London suburb. Miss Bergner and Flora Robson had the other two. When I learned that my great hero, the incomparable Sir Gerald du Maurier, had been assigned one of the smaller rooms down the corridor, I was horrified. Without any ado, I quietly switched rooms and exchanged the names on our respective doors. When Sir Gerald came to the studio, he moved into the big star room without question. We became and remained good friends until he died—and I'm glad he never knew of my switch.

Miss Bergner was charming to work with, full of special mannerisms and meticulously honed tricks of the trade. She timed her scenes to the second and was technically unsurpassed. Young Flora Robson, as the old empress, her first major film role, made it clear she would become one of the finest actresses of the day. Du Maurier, of course, made a glistening mountain peak out of his foothill of a role as the czar's witty French valet.

As for me, I can now see how many things I might have done better had I had more serious experience as a character actor. In retrospect I think some scenes were clearly if subconsciously influenced by my admiration for John Barrymore.

The rest of that year, 1933, and certainly the next two or three, included such a miscellany of happenings as to defy the recording of their precise dates. My now flowering romance with Gee had one particularly worrying aspect. She had become aggressively possessive. A few weeks earlier, when she and Eric had taken leave of each other (temporarily as it turned out), Gee surprised me by suddenly suggesting we marry. The suggestion scared me. The quickest response I could think up was that my divorce from Joan was not yet legally final. Also I needed to catch up on my finances. "But after that . . . !" Inside me was a tremor of panic. There was no question that I wanted to be the man in her life, despite the considerable difference in our age, fame, and finances. My excuses for delay were real enough, but a third remained unsaid. That was my own honest self-appraisal, admitted only to myself, that however smitten I might be by the bewitching Miss L., I had not ever been strictly faithful to anyone.

In the mid-1930s Gee and I starred in two plays together in England: *The Winding Journey* and another, *Moonlight Is Silver*, for which the eminent playwright Clemence Dane was commissioned to write. Neither ran for very long. If our professional life was unsettled, Gee and I were privately getting on very well. This was surprising because like Billie she was a creature of moods. She worried constantly about money, but erupted in self-justification when her extravagances were pointed out to her. One morning when I was a temporary houseguest in her grand new Chelsea mansion, she protested that she could not make all her loose ends meet. I must have ventured an untimely opinion. Vesuvius had no fury like Gee when crossed. She started pitching all manner of china and silver at me from the breakfast table. I ran out the front door in slacks, a house jacket, and slippers with Gee following, bawling expletives like a Billingsgate fishwife. In my cowardice I jumped on a passing bus. Gee tried to run after it in midmorning Embankment traffic.

This scene must have looked like an old slapstick movie. By the time the conductor came for my fare (I had no money) I was quite far from Gee's house. I was escorted off the bus in a South Bank neighborhood where I was totally lost. It was just as well it took me over an hour to return. By then Gee was happily busy at something else and no more was said about the whole silly business.

At another time, when her money problems were particularly distracting, Gee decided she would run off to Majorca for a complete rest—"alone, away from *everyone*!" I agreed she should go and determined that if I couldn't join her, I would at least take a few days off and go as far as Barcelona with her. This did not happen quite as planned.

Gee's night boat left port for Majorca after a day in Barcelona where we attended a bullfight. The following morning, I decided in a flash of romantic impulse that, instead of returning to London immediately as planned, I would take the next boat to Majorca, give Gee a lovely surprise, stay a few days, and then return. When I reached Palma, Majorca, I hired a broken-down old car and a driver to match and asked him to drive me to Formentor, a town on the other side of the island. In those days, it was a bumpy dirt road and took two hours or more. On arrival at the Hotel Formentor I paid off my excuse for a taxi, presented myself to the concierge, and asked if he knew where Miss Gertrude Lawrence's villa might be.

"Ah, *sí, señor!*" he answered, and then proceeded to diagram how I'd go up the hill, turn right, then down a bit, and so on, until I'd find a white house with red tiles. (Almost all the houses were white with red tiles.) I thanked him, took a small, single room to wash and clean up in (the hotel had only saltwater in the bathrooms, which made the use of soap a problem), and then, spic and very span, I trudged up the hill, humming to myself in happy anticipation.

It didn't take me long to find the house. Excited as any ardent young swain can be, I rang the front doorbell. Gee answered it herself. When she saw me, she looked first startled, then horrified. She began to make frantic hand signals, then glancing over her shoulder, she turned back to me and whispered, "You can't come in! *He's* here!"

I couldn't find anything to say. She had made it so clear she planned to be alone that to find she was deceiving me was too much to digest. How in the world did Eric get there? I wondered silently. Then of course I concluded that only Eric was rich enough and interested enough to rent a villa for Gee at a time when her debts were higher than ever. I didn't say a word. I just turned, like a dog slinking off, and made my way back to the hotel, back to Palma, on a night boat back to Barcelona, and finally back to London, poorer and a tiny bit wiser.

By the time Gee returned, we were both so heavily involved in other activities that we kept a distance of sorts from each other for some weeks and never mentioned the incident.

More than a score of years later, I was sitting cozily in a large leather armchair in London's White's Club. Next to me was my old rival, Eric Dudley. We began to reminisce fondly about "dear Gertie," what a loss to the theater and her friends her death had been, and what a mercurial and fascinating star she was. I then recounted the sad story of my brief visit to Majorca where I found him there ahead of me. Eric listened and then turned to me with a look of utter astonishment and said, "But *I* wasn't there at all! *She* told me that *you* were there! Now the dear gel's dead and we'll *never* know who he was!" The sly thing had triple-crossed us both.

By the beginning of 1936 my romance with Gee had almost completely petered out. We had made a film together, a nonmusical adaptation of the opera *La Bohème* called *Mimi*. I had loved the silent King Vidor production with the magnificent Lillian Gish and John Gilbert. Our production was well mounted; only Gee's and my impulsive miscasting of ourselves was a handicap. Gee looked about as tubercular as a slim Brünnhilde and I, in a fancy beige wig, had only a faint resemblance to the dynamic Jack Gilbert. The film quite rightly didn't do well.

My father's romance with Mary Pickford did not exactly come to an end when their divorce was declared final on January 10, 1936. Pete returned home to California in the hope of arranging a reconciliation with Mary just after that. He told Uncle Bob he had "rediscovered" Mary—she was his "one and only love." Virtually every day found him at Pickfair, taking Mary for drives in the hills and doing his tender best to turn their clocks back. But as Mary later said, she had suffered too much public humiliation from his globe-trotting escapades and public infidelities. However warmly she recalled their life together and however deeply she had loved him, she could not continue to let her pride and heart be lacerated. She was determined not only that the divorce remain final, but also that no possibility of a reconciliation be considered. "The Great Romance" was ended forever.

My father returned to England at the end of February and—probably on the rebound—married Sylvia Ashley on March 7 at the American embassy in Paris. Sylvia, by now divorced from Lord Ashley, was tall, willowy, and golden-haired. In fact, she had once been a model and later a Cochran girl, the London equivalent of a *Ziegfeld Follies* girl. Their romance had begun three years earlier when Pete and I first came to London together. A year and a half after Dad and Mary's final breakup, Mary married the charming Buddy Rogers, her leading man in a movie made in 1927, *My Best Girl*.

During the thirties Marlene Dietrich was second only to Garbo in glamour and beauty. Some thought her even sexier, though probably not so great an actress. Others thought her aura of mystery, her knowing eyes in a sculptured face, her highly publicized perfect legs, and her suggestion of simultaneous sacred and profane sex were all a role she played. But the most important element of her public personality was that she genuinely grew to like the part, and she played it perfectly.

She equally enjoyed dropping the mask to become her other unconventional self—the cultivated *Hausfrau* who loved cooking, games, and children. However, Marlene made little effort to hide the fact that she and her husband Rudi Sieber, a Roman Catholic, were very close and devoted friends, though they lived their lives well apart. For years Rudi shared his separate household with a good-natured German lady nicknamed Tami. Marlene was more cautious about her own irregular romances, at pains to let all rumors remain unproven but constantly suspected.

At the time we met, her most publicized *grand amour* had been with the late Jack Gilbert, who had also been Garbo's ardent lover. He took to the bottle when his career began to slide with the advent of sound pictures, which coincided with the end of his affair with Garbo. He was quickly married and divorced and married again. Then he fell harder than ever for Dietrich. At first she pitied him, but then fell in love and tried to keep him away from the booze that was clearly destroying him. She failed. One night he died in a drunken convulsion. Dietrich was as inconsolable as if she had been his real widow. Wherever she went she now kept small votive candles burning constantly in front of his photograph on her bedside table.

I had met Marlene very casually once or twice in California. When we met again in London, it was at a couple of dinner parties Alexander Korda gave for her. One evening, making chitchat, I asked her to join me and other friends at a small dinner the following week. To my surprise she accepted. There was no word in any gossip column about it afterward and all went very pleasantly. She must have been in her early thirties at the time. I never knew her age for certain, but I had heard she was born in 1901.

My growing infatuation with Marlene soon began to show signs of reciprocation when I became her most favored companion. We spent almost all our free time in each other's company and weekends at various friends' country houses, most often at Dickie (Lady Morvyth) and Con (Constantine) Benson's in Shawford Park, Hampshire. There she made instant and permanent friends by donning an apron, tying her hair back with a hand towel, and preparing fabulous meals from Friday through Sunday night for whole house parties of sometimes as many as ten people. I also took her to meet the Kents—Prince George and Princess Marina of Greece—at Coppins, their country house in Buckinghamshire. They fell for her as immediately as she did for them. (This royal connection delighted Marlene, whose Prussian family had brought her up to be a staunch monarchist.) I still found it difficult to be broad-minded about the embarrassing votive candle burning in her Claridge Hotel bedroom. But I was careful to keep silent and repress my jealousy.

Since we were both anxious to soft-pedal our new relationship, I devised a plan to minimize any gossip by altering my method of leaving her suite at Claridge's in the early morning hours. Instead of taking the lift down to the lobby, I would slip unseen down the hotel fire escape, which could be let down into a deserted cobblestone mews at the back of the hotel. On my first attempt at this route, I tied up my full-dress tailcoat (in those days we wore white tie to the theater and dinner almost every night), turned up my coat collar to cover my tie and winged collar, quietly tiptoed to the fire escape, and let myself down. It was one of those deliciously fine, short summer nights and dawn was breaking as I cautiously touched the ground. I quickly turned down my collar, untied my tails, and turned around, preparing to hail the first taxi I could find. I nearly jumped out of my skin *and* tails when I saw a bobby standing before me with a broad smile on his young face.

He saluted me in a most friendly fashion and said, "Good morning, Mr. Fairbanks! Trying out a new trick for your next film? Good idea now, with nobody about! Good morning, sir." Then he turned and strolled off in the opposite direction.

I could only respond with an embarrassed "Morning . . ." I turned in the opposite direction, hopped into a taxi, and rattled away a few hundred yards to my Grosvenor Square flat.

Marlene gradually did away with Jack Gilbert's bedside picture and the votive candle. Although I sensed, with pleasure, that I was now the man in Marlene's life, I tried to arm myself against future disappointment by thinking of our affair as only her passing fancy. But she gently managed to push any apprehensions out of my defensive mind. I couldn't possibly say I was really in love at the time, but it was certainly a relationship of more sophisticated intensity than any I had so far experienced.

One day I reported to her that a flat in my new Grosvenor Square building on the floor below my recently acquired penthouse was available. She dashed over and promptly took a lease on it for the duration of the movie she was filming (*Knight Without Armour*). Within a day or two her maid had moved her, bag and baggage, to her new flat, set up as a sort of superior townhouse dressing room. We used both my own large living room and roof gardens above as a place to have friends for drinks and sometimes dinner.

Dushka is a Russian term of endearment. Whether Marlene first heard it in a line from her film or because it was the name of the Kents' German shepherd I don't know, but she made it her secret romantic alias. When she left London for California, she—generous to a fault—gave me and my penthouse various gifts (such as a gold wristwatch) inscribed *"Dushka,"* behind which her identity could be hidden. Reassurances of our early reunion were made and away she sailed.

My own career problems resumed their usual place at the forefront of my attention. In 1934 I had started my own company, called Criterion Films, Ltd. From the start we had inadequate financing, though in time United Artists gave us a formal distribution contract for four pictures. I agreed to play in two of them, *The Amateur Gentleman* and *Accused,* both released in 1936. In the end only three films were made. *When Thief Meets Thief* (released in the U.K. as *Jump for Glory*) came out in 1937 and by then Criterion had begun to crumble. I was dissatisfied with the way the business of the company was being managed and resigned.

My next professional decision was not long in coming. Early in 1937 I had a call from David Selznick in California. He announced that he was planning to remake the old classic *The Prisoner of Zenda* with Ronnie Colman playing the star dual role. He wanted to assemble as nearly an all-star cast as he could and offered me the part of Count Rupert of Hentzau, last played in the old silent film by Ramon Novarro. It was clear that Selznick had chosen *The Prisoner of Zenda* as a thinly disguised reference to the Duke of Windsor's recent abdication of his throne and the approaching coronation of George VI in June. Both situations could be related to the *Zenda* plot.

Although I was greatly cheered by having an offer of any kind, the recent setback at Criterion had not altogether discouraged me and I was reluctant to take a featured or supporting part to *anyone*—even so fine an actor as Ronald Colman. I told David this and also assured him of my gratitude.

"Well, think about it some more, old boy," shouted David on the phone. "I won't even consider anyone else—at least for a while."

The next morning a cable from Marlene was delivered, obviously inspired by David, urging me to accept *Zenda* and hurry to California since it was "a marvelous part." But I was still resentful of what I interpreted as a professional demotion.

My preoccupied father was in his house on Park Lane getting ready for his and Sylvia's return to California, and it wasn't the best of times to ask for serious business advice. Nevertheless, he listened attentively and burst out with the conviction that I *had* to accept. Why? "Because not only is *The Prisoner of Zenda* one of the best romances conceived in a hundred years, Rupert of Hentzau is probably one of the best villains ever written. He is witty, irresistible, and as sly as Iago. That part is known to be actor-proof! Nobody has ever played Rupert and failed to steal the show. Rin-Tin-Tin could play the part and walk away with it!" *That* convinced me!

The problem of billing was solved when it was agreed to leave my name off the list of featured actors coming just after the title and put "With Douglas Fairbanks, Jr., as Rupert of Hentzau" in big letters, right at the bottom of everything.

When I reached the coast and was first asked to Pete and Sylvia's Santa Monica beach house, they told me that Merle Oberon lived in the house just north of them. They asked if I knew her young British boyfriend, just out of the British army, who had come to California hoping to break into movies. His name was David Niven. We were soon to become very close friends and I was delighted when he landed the small but sympathetic part of Fritz von Tarlenheim in *Zenda*.

David Selznick and I hit it off famously—but only after I got over the first week of trying to impress everyone with their good fortune in having me to support Colman. It took just a few days for David to patiently make it clear to me that I was not nearly as knowledgeable as I thought and that as a producer I had been very small fry indeed. Furthermore, I was by no means a star of the same magnitude as

Colman. In a word, I really was damn lucky to have this chance to reestablish myself at home after a spotty few years abroad.

Before shooting began, there was some discussion about my appearance. In contrast to Ronnie I decided to have curly hair (even though it meant an extra hour each morning in the makeup department). The plan for costuming was that all the men were to be dolled up in the grandest of Balkan uniforms. However, I recalled my father telling me long ago never to wear anything too distracting around the neck. A loud or large-figured tie always detracted from one's facial expressions. Each of Ronnie's two roles required showy uniforms. There were many elaborate characters, such as the splendid and ever so serious Ray Massey playing the main villain; C. Aubrey Smith, the epitome of the British raj; and also dear Niv. Gorgeous Madeleine Carroll and the great beauty Mary Astor were both fabulously gowned. The lesser parts and the crowds were so fancifully costumed, it made one think this deliberately black-and-white picture was being shot in Technicolor. All this aided my pleas that I should only wear basic black uniforms with an absolute minimum of trimming. Indeed the relative simplicity of my dark costumes was more menacing and also more conspicuous.

During shooting I had more days off than I expected and I spent many of them reading and scribbling at Marlene's house or, weather permitting, by her pool. On Sundays Marlene entertained a number of her European friends. Their talk was about cultural, artistic, and often political matters. They were all passionate anti-Nazis; some were socialists and there was an occasional half-baked communist. One of the most amusing of these intellectuals, who became my good friend, was the great German director Fritz Lang. I remember once being in a fury because Marlene occasionally swam in the buff. She enjoyed having her beauty appreciated. Fritz gently mocked me for my lack of sophistication and reassured me about her "basic fidelity."

One of the high points of *Zenda* was a long saber fight between Rassendyl (Colman) and Rupert (me). The script required a witty dialogue all through the exciting and exacting duel that carried us all over the old castle of Zenda. Selznick rewrote this sequence several times to make it as amusing and thrilling as possible. He also engaged Ralph Faulkner, the best saber teacher in Hollywood, to train and rehearse Ronnie and me.

For the first time I had broken my antiswashbuckling rule. It had been ten years since my father had last swashed a heroic silent-movie sword, so my apprehensions were eased—particularly as I was playing a villain. I was intent on making the fight as realistic as possible. My early training and fencing competitions in my youth helped, but Ronnie had little or no background in the sport. It was therefore necessary for Faulkner to double for Ronnie in most of the medium and long shots. In the end, the time and sweat we all expended proved worthwhile. It turned out to be one of the screen's classic swordfight sequences. *The Prisoner of Zenda* was a whopping success. Suddenly, just as predicted, I was swamped with offers.

Alas, my lovely liaison with Dietrich was not destined to survive much longer. It was too high-powered and sophisticated for me. It was not only the more assured and intellectual German author Erich Maria Remarque who brought our relationship to an end; my own sudden jealousy was also to blame. Quite by accident, while searching Marlene's desk for writing paper, I came across some intense love letters (from someone I'd never heard of) to Marlene. Although I had no idea of their date or circumstances, I blew up in a jealous rage. Marlene's reaction was justifiable anger with me for going through her private papers in the first place. One word led to another, and our waning romance fizzled out then and there. After an interval, wc became lifelong friends.

One day Cary Grant, a remarkable guy with an agile mind (which *he* said was replete with complexes) and a treasure of a friend, asked me if I wanted to play in something called *Gunga Din*. He explained that such scripted plot as existed so far had been inspired by two Rudyard Kipling poems, "Gunga Din" and "Soldiers Three." There had been a number of scriptwriters: Ben Hecht, Charlie MacArthur, and Joel Sayre, with some rewriting by William Faulkner. At first I stalled and said I'd have to read whatever treatment there was before I could give an answer. I wondered even more about where and how I could fit in. Except for those playing Hindus, I would be the only American in our otherwise all-British cast—and furthermore I would be obliged to speak with a semicockney accent.

When an overlong, very rough draft of the script arrived, I read it.

I could see at once what a boisterous, exciting, and funny picture it *could* be. Victor McLaglen had just been hired and I thought he would be ideal as the tough, experienced sergeant in the British Indian Army of the 1890s, but I had no clue as to which of the other two younger sergeants Cary would play and which I would play. They were about equal in importance. One was the romantic who, after numerous exciting adventures, falls in love and gets the girl. This would be Joan Fontaine's first role as a leading lady. The other sergeant was his mate, an engagingly brave, funny young cockney. These two, with the older one, shared the adventures fairly equally.

When I asked Cary which part he intended to play, he answered, "Whichever one you don't want! I want us to be together in this so badly—I think the two of us, plus old McLaglen as our top sergeant, McChesny, will make this picture more than just another big special." I have never so much as *heard* of another actor (usually considered a congenitally selfish breed) who made to a contemporary colleague, in some ways a rival, so unselfish a proposal. I later came to learn that such gestures were typical of Cary. We finally settled the matter by tossing a coin! That was how I became Sergeant Ballantyne, who wants to leave the army for Miss Fontaine, and Cary became the ebullient, funny cockney, Sergeant Cutter. Until he died, Grant and I always addressed each other as Cutter and Ballantyne—from that film of 1938!

George Stevens was quite unlike the conventional, overassertive director. He appeared always to stroll about with a lazy sailor's swagger instead of walking like other people. One's first impression was that he was vague, dreamy, and inefficient, but actually this was an effective mask behind which his creative brain ticked at the speed of light. His producers were often led to believe one thing when he really had something quite different in mind. He would look at you with a sort of dopey solemnity, only to break into a broad grin a moment later and call for a can of beer.

It turned out to be a fine cast and company all around. Chief among them was Sam Jaffe, a splendid serious actor who played the title role. Another was close friend Bob Coote, an English comedian who played still another sergeant, the "silly ass" one.

We spent many weeks in the California desert at Lone Pine, several hours' drive from Los Angeles, close to the base of the Sierra Nevada. According to the technical directors, the setting was much like India's Northwest Frontier. It took at least a month to build a tent city for hundreds of us to live in. Every day we worked in temperatures that sometimes rose to 110 degrees in the shade.

Cary, Bob, Vic, and I always tried to be careful with our language and manners when Joan Fontaine was near. We had many miserable daytime hours when the hot desert winds would blow such volumes of sand and dust as to make filming temporarily impossible and cause Joanie to suffer recurrences of severe sinus headaches and flooding eyes. We all sweated like stevedores, drank gallons of bottled water, and gulped daily rations of salt pills. Costumes were binding and hot and even worse for the women, who had to have their makeup patched every few minutes so they would look cool and comfortable for their scenes.

Apart from these discomforts, Joan's general manner was so shy and maidenly that we all became models of chivalrous behavior in her presence. It was only many years later that she confessed, and indeed recorded in her autobiography, that while we were being so very proper and protective, she was having an intense affair with George. They would take turns creeping into each other's tents very late when everyone else had gone off to sleep.

In one of the picture's spectacular climactic action sequences, we three sergeants are seen standing behind a set representing the battlements of an old fort, trying to hold off the attack of hundreds of maddened Thugs until we are rescued just in time by units of Scottish Highlanders and the Bengal Lancers. The day the scene was shot was even hotter than usual. The timing of the movements of several hundred extras, as well as the dozen cameras shooting from different angles with different types of lenses, took several hours of rehearsal to perfect. Our thirst was quenched by many weak beers (all the studio would allow), brought up to us by the prop man. Finally, Stevens announced over his mike that all was set and the scene must be shot then or the right degree of light would be gone for the day. Vic, by now tight as a tick with all inhibitions melted away, decided that as the beer had gone through him too quickly and none of us could leave our positions high up in this tower behind a rampart, there was no alternative to lessen his intense discomfort but to unbutton his uniform and relieve himself *during the scene!* Cary and I didn't know whether to laugh or be furious. Stevens, not knowing of our "martyrdom," later congratulated us on the spirit of furious defiance we had shown in the scene—which he could discern even from a distance.

Although the romantic character I played became, over the years, one of the public's three or four favorite and best-remembered of my roles, I cringed whenever anyone compared my quite routine stunts in the picture with my father's improbable athletic fantasies (he hated having them called "acrobatics"). In *Gunga Din* I probably did have a little more fistfighting and jumping about (from rooftop to rooftop and other odd places) than in other films, but reports that *Zenda* and now *Gunga Din* marked my entry into the movie swashbuckling fraternity were highly exaggerated. Nevertheless my acquisition of two broken fingers, a cracked rib, a bad twist of my already torn knee cartilege, and three knife scars in the line of duty in *Gunga Din* were matters of pride. Had my parents given me another name, the inevitably odious comparisons would be as minimal as they had been for, say, Ty Power and Errol Flynn when they first began to make costume-action pictures.

The growing threat of war in Europe was being reported daily on every front page. The Roosevelt administration sympathized with our old allies but had established a policy of strict neutrality. Without more strength of their own and outspoken support from us, the British and French felt obliged to back down whenever Hitler screeched his new demands. It was during one of these retreats that *Gunga Din* finally opened in February 1939 at Radio City Music Hall in Manhattan, where it broke every record. The picture's theme glorified the British "Tommy" fighting courageously against heavy odds. Once the film opened elsewhere what was originally intended as a big exciting yarn with an exotic background became not only an enormous hit, but also an effective boost for goodwill toward the British at that uncertain time in international affairs.

The end of 1938 found me living in New York City. As my interest in government, business, and world affairs grew, I received my first taste of public mocking for my naïveté and for "stepping out of line." Some of the press thought movie stars shouldn't be involved in politics and noted for the first time that I "consorted with" such members of the literary establishment as Robert Sherwood. In addition to play-writing, Bob was now acting as adviser and speechwriter to President Roosevelt, joining cronies like Harry Hopkins in evening sessions at the White House or weekends at the Roosevelt country estate, Hyde Park. And there was Herbert Bayard Swope, the former publisher of the New York *World*, whose nightly "gab sessions" in his Park Avenue apartment or Long Island home engendered some of the most stimulating talk on the East Coast. I elbowed my way among an increasing number of interested and interesting folk from many spheres.

For New Year's Day 1939 I accepted an invitation to go out to Herbert Swope's country house on Long Island. It was a cold, dampish afternoon when I arrived at the Swopes' just before tea time. The snow of a few days earlier had melted except for partly iced-over puddles. As usual I was greeted as a contemporary. Herbert was an expansive and dominating talker. He had short gray hair and a red face, with pince-nez spectacles atop a longish nose. Maggie (as Mrs. Swope was to be addressed only after a trial period) was very quiet and serious, and when she chose she could be far more formidable than Herbert.

Someone took my bag and I was asked to come in and sit down. Herbert said the rest of the house party were so "done in" by the previous night's carousing they had gone to take naps and were nowhere to be seen. He then proceeded to run through a list of the guests: a friend of my father's and his wife, Swope's son, and two or three others. "And then let's see," bellowed Swope, "There's 'Hunt' Hartford's wife—little Mary Lee. They're separated so she's here on her own. You'll like her—lots of fun, pretty and very bright. It's mostly for the young." Herbert drew a breath, then said, "Want to get some fresh air, go for a walk? We can chat as we go." Such questions from Herbert were accepted as orders. So I got all rebundled up and ready to face the raw chill outdoors.

Suddenly into the hall bubbled a very small brown-haired girl with large, shining dark eyes and a full, beautifully carved red mouth that seemed to smile even in repose. When it widened into a laugh or grin—which was often—she lit up her immediate vicinity with a cheery display of white-white teeth that were just uneven enough to be fetching. She was young—I guessed somewhere in her early twenties. Furthermore, she seemed to have a considerable talent for easy laughter and bright talk, with just an echo of a southern accent. My quick summary glance noted her exceptionally tiny waist.

Herbert put on his greatcoat and introduced us. We shook hands and I burbled something like, "I know your husband Hunt; we were in Bovée School together as kids . . ." Herb interrupted to say we were going for a "walk-and-talk" before tea and asked if she would like to come along. He wouldn't stop to let her change into more sensible shoes than the silly Indian moccasins she wore, but simply herded us both out the door.

Although my new acquaintance was a minute sample of instant bewitchment, I privately preferred to be alone with Herbert. I had too many serious—to *me*—matters to talk about without being accompanied by a third party I had just met—especially such an attractive one. But she came along anyway. Herbert and I talked almost as if she weren't there.

We took long, fast strides as I rambled on about my recent trip abroad (during which I'd hand-delivered a "very private" letter from Swope to Winston Churchill) and my more recent one to Canada (which touched on the possibility of a visit to the White House by King George VI and Queen Elizabeth). I reported on whom I had seen, what I had said and done, and how I had reacted to people, at the same time trying to answer Herbert's well-targeted questions.

Mrs. Hartford kept paddling along, about two steps to our one in her moccasins, listening attentively. Ever the inveterate strutter, I could not resist showing off a little for her—overstating everything and throwing names about like grains of rice at a wedding—trying to impress Herbert in one way and the delectable little nuisance, Mrs. Hartford, in another.

Something positive must have happened because when we returned, somewhat chilled and chattery, Herbert excused himself and left us alone together in a cozy library with hot tea for Mrs. H. (who insisted I call her Mary Lee at once) and a scotch and soda for me. At the end of an hour of behaving like a human peacock displaying its feathers in flirtatious preening and chitchat, I had damned near over-played my hand (*both* hands, no doubt). Mary Lee decided I'd gone far enough and, suggesting she had better join the others before changing for dinner, got up from the couch we had been sitting on. As gallantly as anyone I'd ever seen in the movies, I pulled myself to-gether, straightened my tie, and went to open the door I had surrepti-tiously shut when we first came in. *Most* unfortunately the damned door was stuck. All my then fairly rugged strength went into the effort to force it. It wouldn't budge. Panic began to set in. How *could* she explain and expect anyone to believe her? I wouldn't have expected anyone to really believe *me*. But Mary Lee had an impeccable private reputation. After an interminable time our shouts and banging on the door aroused the whole house party, and with an assist from the butler the door finally gave way. The poor heroine had been saved from a fate only somewhat better than death. The true story of the door—I *hadn't* locked it—and our really innocent small talk behind it were never quite swallowed by the others, nor did they let up their teasing for years.

I persuaded Mary Lee to lunch with me the following week, then to dine, then go to the theater, and then to accompany me to one or two parties given by mutual friends. The better I got to know this small shining girl, the more serious about her I became.

Mary Lee had a very luxurious life-style (a splendidly useful word that was not then in vogue). She lived in a large, superbly appointed apartment uptown on Fifth Avenue, near the Metropolitan Museum of Art. She went about New York in an enormous Duesenberg limou-sine, driven by a liveried chauffeur. In addition she had been endowed with a lovely pastoral patch of Virginia in an Appalachian valley, between Hot Springs and Warm Springs. Called Boxwood Farm, it was a small gem—a real colonial showpiece, presumably built in the early to mid-eighteenth century. Though she herself had been born in Keystone, West Virginia, she and her family felt intensely southern.

Mary Lee's clothes, jewels, matrimonially shared yachts, and much more were a part of the many material benefits accruing from the Hartford family's ownership of the great A & P chain of grocery stores, the precursors of supermarkets. Until that fateful New Year's Day, I was able to meet my romantic attachments on fairly equal financial grounds—at least grounds not involving such a conspicuous disparity as to make me fear to appear to be a fortune hunter. In many ways I was a very old-fashioned young man. The thought of being actually *married* to someone who could call the financial domestic tune very nearly put me off. On the other hand, Mary Lee had little money *or* possessions of her own. Her family, including her late father, a noted oral surgeon, boasted a number of distinguished, but not wealthy, doctors.

She and Hunt had met at Harvard when she was nineteen and in defiance of parental objections had eloped. Their relationship soon became a *mariage de convenance*. Hunt, though generous and kindly, was not truly domestic by nature. Mary Lee had loyally kept up appearances, but there was nothing onerous or cruel about their marriage; it conformed to the social strictures of the day. However, on the very day that *we* met, Hunt had rung up and announced that he would now like to end their existing arrangement and have a real divorce. He very much wanted to marry someone else. Mary Lee had agreed, readily and cheerfully. The following week she sought out the services of a noted legal firm in New York whose senior partner was the brilliant and popular Maurice "Tex" Moore. He warned us that in order to protect Mary Lee, we must either not go out at all or avoid conspicuous places.

All my anxieties about Mary Lee's money were only exacerbated as Tex announced every fresh detail of the divorce agreement that Hunt was hurriedly making. First of all Hunt decided to make a settlement of more than a million dollars on Mary Lee. A seventy-five-foot yacht, and several fine works of art together with jewels, fine furniture, and on to dizzying further on—including lovely Boxwood Farm and its herd of black-faced Hampshire sheep—had already been outright gifts. We both did feel some guilt as Tex Moore announced the long list of settlements because at this time it was doubtful that Hunt knew of *our* romance. There was no reason to think he really would have cared since he was too anxious to follow his own romantic destiny, but Tex thought it might give the Hartford family and their legal advisers reason to balk.

One would naturally assume that since I had only recently got into and out of a variety of complicated romances, I would not be so foolish as to become involved again quite so soon. This time I *knew* it was solid and realistic. This time I *knew* I had really and truly fallen. And head over heels at that. There was no theatrical resonance because Mary Lee was so patently *un*theatrical in looks, manner, and views. She seemed in all ways self-reliant, with no affectations, a heretofore unknown kind of woman whom I knew *I* needed for my life. I had just about decided that at age twenty-nine it was time to devote my thoughts and energies to *caring* for one person—for the rest of my days.

Sometimes when we found absolutely no place to meet alone and unobserved, we took what now seem very embarrassing steps to amend the situation. I would ask Mother if we could meet for a "private chat" at the Whitings' apartment. Mother, of course, had always adored being privy to secrets, and she quickly sympathized with our situation—especially since she took a fancy to Mary Lee right from the very moment they met.

Mary Lee was as intrigued about the movie world as she was ignorant of it. In fact, she blushed and said she felt "obliged to confess" she had never seen me in a movie. This was a cue for me to swagger a bit, so I suggested a small private screening of one of my films. She jumped at the idea, but admitted she didn't know the names of any of my pictures. I proposed the now two-year-old *Prisoner of Zenda*. Mary Lee was delighted, and I arranged for her to invite eight or ten chums to come along to a United Artists screening room on upper Broadway. On the day of the screening, several of her bubbly friends trooped in and sat down in the great, stuffed leather chairs. Mary Lee was shaking with excitement at this facet of her newly discovered, and possibly *next,* life. The room darkened and the picture began.

I was nervous as well—hoping to show my wares to best advantage in this setting. The film had been running for about fifteen minutes. We actors had all established our characters and the plot was clearly on its way. I had just finished a long and amusing scene in which I first encounter Ronald Colman when Mary Lee grabbed my hand and whispered in a very distressed voice, "Oh, dear! Isn't it *terrible!* I hate to admit it, but I've just now realized *I've seen this before*—and *loved* it! *I just forgot you were in it!*"

Though not an auspicious way to flatter a not yet fully trapped lover, I got over it in time, and it has been a favorite family yarn ever since.

I returned to California to start a new film, *Rulers of the Sea,* and Mary Lee and I communicated as often as discretion allowed. We went ahead with transcontinental telephone plans for our marriage and agreed that a ceremony could take place in California as soon as she had obtained her divorce and I had located a Protestant church that would agree to marry two divorced people. I rented a charming, not very big, two-story, California-Spanish house from Charles Boyer. It was in Pacific Palisades, with a small but pretty garden and a modest swimming pool.

I went over a list of my closest friends in a vain effort to decide whom I should ask to be my best man. No one really fit the part on conventional lines. I was an unintentional loner. I was a good and trusted friend to several, but few ever got very close to me. I wasn't distant or aloof, but I was unable to completely confide in any single person. Finally I thought of asking my father if he would mind the unusual duty of being his son's best man. To my surprise and pleasure, he agreed and *seemed* pleased. In fact, at a party given for him and Sylvia in New York soon after Mary Lee and I had met, he said to his host, "Who is that girl with Jayar?" When he was told, he said, "I bet he will marry that girl."

The Big Day, April 22, 1939, arrived at last. Like so many grooms before me, I went through most of the ceremony in a sort of daze. My most vivid recollection is that my voice sounded detached, as though it belonged to someone else, like a recording emanating from a remote source. Mary Lee's voice was strong and clear. She wore a short beige silk dress and the silliest hat, with funny little flowers and stems that shot upward. It was wonderfully attractive.

Pete, always conscious of being shorter than I (I didn't realize that was one of the reasons he usually preferred me at a distance), stretched himself to the limit all day. But he remained in fine spirits. Mother was at her most appealing: warm, plumply pretty, and dripping with the charm she could always bring out in abundance.

I was not at all sure I merited the rewards of that memorable day and the other beautiful ones we planned to accrue, with luck in years to come. We happily identified with Mrs. Pat Campbell's often-quoted comment after her own wedding day: She was said to glow as she purred about the "peace and quiet of the marriage bed after the hurly-burly of the chaise longue."

Then in August 1939 Hitler and Stalin announced the Russo-German nonaggression pact to a staggered world. Less than a month before, such a thing would have been inconceivable. It was hard to credit this Dark Ages alliance which so cynically ignored the democratic world's views.

Mary Lee and I had slipped easily and happily into our new life in our little stucco and red tile house on Monaco Drive. Within our more personal world, there was surprising but happy news that blotted out any other worries—for the moment anyway. Mary Lee had learned to her delight that she was pregnant. I suppose I reacted like other young fathers-to-be. I gulped to swallow my heart, which was trying to escape through my throat. Almost certainly it would not have been me if I did not suddenly tear up. But having been taught since childhood that it was unmanly to blub even a little, I hid my head behind Mary Lee's as I embraced her.

This was a time when with a new wife, a child on the way, and an imminent new movie (Safari), I nonetheless felt I could devote even more time to writing and speaking against the spreading threat of militarism and the lack of an effective political or economic antidote. My greatest failing has been to bite off a greater variety of things than I can possibly chew, and I was now becoming conspicuously noted for it.

Each day's news made us all so tense that Mary Lee and I decided to charter a fair-sized but not luxurious yacht, get a few pals to share the cost, and take the forthcoming Labor Day weekend as an excuse to sail over to Catalina Island. Our passenger list included Larry O. and Vivien Leigh, and as they weren't yet married and needed to make a hypocritical nod in the direction of morality for the sake of the Hollywood gossips, Vivien's boring, troublesome mother came along

to chaperone. Niv and Bob Coote were among the others aboard. The mood was one of somewhat forced merriment.

Washington was quiet. The world seemed hushed in dread anticipation. Hitler had again disavowed an older nonaggression pact, this time with Poland. Suddenly he blasted his way through that country's western front while Stalin, by prearrangement, rolled over Poland's eastern border. Great Britain and France warned them both that they would honor their guarantees to Poland unless the invaders withdrew immediately. An answer was expected by the morning of the third of September. On that day our little yachting party had slowly been gathering on deck in silence, grouped around the radio, spirits cringing.

The radio suddenly broadcast Big Ben's deep chimes. Then a solemn BBC voice announced, "The prime minister, the Right Honorable Neville Chamberlain." Calmly and briefly Chamberlain reported the situation and said that by the deadline a reply from Hitler had not been received. Therefore, as of 11:15, Greenwich Mean Time, "This country is at war with Germany."

No one spoke. No one could. However apocalyptic our thoughts, we could not have envisaged the horror of the next five years or that they would record the deaths of over *fifty million* human beings as a result of World War II.

We began to drink—lightly. Then more. A very stupid way to cope. But we were fairly young, and probably stupid too. Within a couple of hours we were hiding our utter despondency behind brave talk. Larry, however, was the only one who got really and truly drunk. More than that, he was plainly *pissed*! No longer mixing with the rest of us, he lowered himself over the side into our dinghy and began to row under the sterns of the larger, grander yachts anchored in the Yacht Club basin where we were only weekend guests. All had passengers sitting on the afterdecks, presumably as stunned as we. Larry had now cast himself as Cassandra crossed with Henry V. He stood up, a bit wobbly, in his little cockleshell and shouted up, "You're all finished! Done! Drink up! You've had it! *This is the end!*"

He then sat down and rowed over to the next yacht at anchor and repeated his proclamation. This clarion call from the future giant of the theater was repeated several times.

At the time Larry had a small line of mustache and closely resembled (at a quick glance) the older, very correct Ronnie Colman, whose own sailboat was peacefully anchored a bit farther out. In an hour or two a small motor launch came out from the clubhouse to the Colman yacht. After a few minutes this same boat came over to us. Our skipper was handed the following note, which he passed to me and I then read aloud. Addressed to the "owner," it read: "The commodore's office has received numerous reports within the last hour that Mr. Ronald Colman has been rowing around several members' anchored yachts calling out loud and abusive language. The commodore insists that an immediate apology be forthcoming, followed by a formal letter of explanation to this office at the earliest convenience." After an abashed guffaw at this release from the general tension, we weighed anchor and quietly slipped out of the harbor. It was some time before Ronnie found out who his "double" was.

On December 9, my thirtieth birthday, my cousin Flobelle and her husband, Shirl Burden, threw a big birthday bash for me and Shirl—it was his birthday as well. Pete and Sylvia came to this party at the Burdens' large house in Beverly Hills.

We all determined in advance to forget every serious concern and be thoroughly cheerful for the evening. Everyone succeeded in giving amusing and festive toasts. When my turn came, I impulsively broke my lifelong habit of manly undemonstrativeness toward my father. This time, after a few light quips, I directed a brief but affectionate toast "to Dad." Everyone appeared to be rather touched, and he most of all. I was happy I had done so then and even happier I had said all I had, because two nights later he died.

The day after the party he suffered what he thought was a bout of indigestion that a hurriedly summoned doctor diagnosed as a strained heart. The word went out: "Senior has had a serious heart attack." The restrictions imposed by the doctor depressed him terribly: "Stay in bed for some weeks."

He had often been warned that his excessive exercising, golfing, swimming, business board meetings—*and* staying up late to please Sylvia—would take its toll. Though he never drank (a reflection of the excesses of his father, H. Charles), few things would be worse for him than his almost constant smoking—from waking to lights out at night.

The next night Dad had a word with my Uncle Bob and told him he dreaded the idea of being an invalid far more than death. Indeed, I remembered that six years earlier on his fiftieth birthday he had said he hoped "to die soon—violently, in an accident of some kind." He added that he had done just about everything he wanted to do in life at least twice, that now when he woke up in the morning he couldn't think of anything new to do. He was bored with life and prepared to die, but not to linger. I was shocked at the time, but I could certainly sympathize with his fearing a long illness.

The world's press carried the story of Pete's death on their front pages in huge black headlines—London's *Evening Standard* actually put out one of their big posters with just the solemn shock printed on it: DOUGLAS FAIRBANKS DEAD. Movie and Broadway theater lights dimmed for a few moments of tribute.

The funeral service was at the Forest Lawn Cemetery, and Mary Lee and I accompanied Sylvia. A huge crowd of the curious ogled and muttered. Charlie Chaplin came—a small stooping figure, alone.

My first Christmas with Mary Lee produced new emotions, interests, and concerns that tugged and pulled. First of all, my father's absence from our world emptied it more than I would have imagined. I must have loved Pete, but for few reasons that I could name. Yet now, even though I was at last "my own man," oddly freer, no longer a shadow, I missed knowing that he was alive—here, there, somewhere.

Outweighing not my grief but my sadness and regret for so many things was my undisguised pleasure at the positive fact of being joyfully and truly married in a most beautifully conventional way. What was more, I was going to be a father in about four months. As if to provide a setting for this kind of normality, we had bought a rambling Spanish mansion, set on the crest of a hill in Pacific Palisades, overlooking a small valley with a tiny river below. The Pacific Ocean was clearly in view five miles away, and as the property faced west and was perched above a canyon, we named it Westridge. We moved in in the spring of 1940.

Late in the day on April 7, Mary Lee calmly announced that she had every reason to believe the baby would arrive within the next twenty-four hours. When the predicted signs of a miracle were imminent, I bundled the glowing mistress of ceremonies into my ancient Cadillac and we whizzed toward downtown Los Angeles and the Good Samaritan Hospital—just a bit off the ground. Mary Lee was in labor for about twelve hours. Although I was given permission to witness the birth of our child, prepped, gowned and hooded from a bleacher seat in a theater operating room, I could not (mercifully, I suppose) really see anything. Near noon on April 8 I was at last given a close look at our fine, funny, wrinkled baby daughter and was told she weighed seven and a half pounds. The moment when the baby was put in Mary Lee's arms was a timeless exquisite interlude of sheer loving and grateful joy. We named her Daphne because Mary Lee loved daffodils and the mythical Daphne had been a romantic Greek goddess. She was soon to be nicknamed "Dabby."

Closer to home big impersonal events thundered, and the louder and fiercer these war sounds from Europe became, the angrier grew the debate in the United States. Polls showed that 80 percent of our population wanted the Allies to win. But 90 percent said America should stay out of any conflict. A shrill nationwide isolationist organization that called itself America First was formed. One felt they didn't care if both American coastlines were invaded as long as our great midwestern heartland remained inviolate.

To give voice to the growing sentiments of anti-isolationists, a group of liberal Republicans and conservative and middle-of-the-road Democrats formed the William Allen White Committee to Defend America by Aiding the Allies. White was a much-respected Kansas newspaper editor and interventionist. This mouthful of an organization was an openly political pressure group designed to negate the effects of the isolationist America First Committee. Bob Sherwood invited me to be the head of the White Committee's southern California branch and one of its national vice-presidents. I was only too pleased to accept the offer.

Little by little, public opinion moved to our side. FDR urged us to put even more public, media, and congressional pressure on him to "push" him into more support and aid to Britain—to become, in his famous phrase, "the arsenal of democracy." In this context I recalled a previous visit to the White House when I was among a small, informal group. President Roosevelt was expounding the techniques of political leadership. He said we must first build up huge public support for a particular bill or law that would push the leader, "because even a president of the United States can only go so far without the majority of the whole nation—not just his own party—supporting him. Now, go out and get the public to *push* me!"

The White Committee soon won tens of thousands of supporters, and the president agreed as much as he dared with most of our proposals. Quietly, unnoted by the press, I now traveled to Washington and met with FDR and Secretary of State Cordell Hull quite a few times. I made some nationwide broadcasts backing the White Committee and the urgent need to support Allied defenses.

It was undeniably enjoyable to be invited to the White House from time to time and to have at least limited access to the president on a personal and private level. FDR always seemed relaxed in spite of the constant pressures of his high office, finding many moments in the day to banter and discuss trivia. Frank Junior was the Roosevelt I knew best (an old friend from my Central Park boyhood), and he wangled invitations for me and for Mary Lee. We would be asked to come to our national "palace" for an occasional cocktail or—even more occasionally—to stay overnight. The First Lady was the most considerate of hostesses. Mrs. Roosevelt would usually come up to our room on the third floor, sit on the end of Mary Lee's bed, and chat with the two of us.

On rarer occasions we were asked to spend the weekend at Hyde Park with what seemed the special permission of the ever-present matriarchal Sara Delano (Mrs. James) Roosevelt, who presided over a room filled with family and such intimates as Harry Hopkins, Bob Sherwood, Averell Harriman, and Joe Lash. The president would dominate the room by habit and personality, quite apart from rank and title. Sometimes he would tease me about movies, politics, or public affairs. During some of these easy times, he would make suggestions as to what we on the White Committee might do to help his campaign to stimulate national sympathy for the Allied cause.

Occasionally I would be asked my opinion on something or other. Always self-conscious and anxious to appear better informed than I was, I sometimes detected a good-natured condescension, or patronization if you will, of a young public supporter.

The president's polio, which paralyzed him from the waist down, was never discussed. When he had to be lifted into or out of cars or into his wheelchair, one left the room or else carefully turned away. Everyone, including his family, stood whenever he was wheeled into a room. His mother was at pains to tell Mary Lee and me that she always did so, even when they were alone, because, she said, "He is the president of the United States, and the office itself deserves everyone's gesture of respect."

At other times, however, she would tease him in ways that neither Eleanor nor any of his other intimates would venture to try. For instance, she would playfully tilt his chair back, as if to upset it, until the president in a semiexaggerated panic would call out, "Mother! For God's sake, *stop* it!" Whereupon, with what she presumably thought was a reassuring smile, she would obey. Eleanor, at such times, would look fearful but helpless to impose herself on her mother-in-law's first-claim possession.

I wished to join the navy before the war actually began, when I thought we might eventually be involved. I was discouraged at first, however, because getting a naval reserve commission in those days normally meant one had to have a university degree, and of course I had no such thing. By any formal standards, my academic record was not only lopsided but virtually nonexistent. All my life I had loved the lore of the sea, adventure stories of the bounding main, and almost everything to do with ships. Finally Bob Montgomery and I arranged an interview with the commander of the 11th Naval District in San Diego. Bob already had a university degree and I was allowed at least to apply. As things turned out neither Bob nor I had the time off to go down to San Pedro for all the required drills and other training. Bob had to return to work at MGM, and my continuing activities in Hollywood on behalf of war charities and campaigning for the president's reelection had inspired so much public controversy that even after a lucky three-year roll of hit films, there was suddenly almost nothing on the horizon worth considering. I was becoming too controversial, and an unacknowledged boycott appeared to be in effect.

When Election Day 1940 was almost upon us, my heretofore docile bride began to rebel. She was not going to vote for FDR under any circumstances. She liked the president personally, had been thrilled to be his guest, and was "absolutely devoted" to Mrs. Roosevelt. However, she just could not bring herself to alter the conservative Republican influences of a lifetime. Furthermore, she was privately not so sure as I that the U.S. was potentially threatened by the spreading dictatorship virus. Regardless of my own beliefs, Mary Lee firmly decided she would vote for Wendell Willkie!

The evening before Election Day I had joined a nationwide network broadcast in support of FDR. I firmly believed in what I had to say and was very pleased to be asked to make a speech under such impressive auspices. All fired up, before we turned in that night, I convinced the poor trusting mother of our firstborn that her vote for Willkie and mine for Roosevelt would cancel each other out. Therefore we should agree to sleep late the next morning and not go to the trouble of voting at all.

Bless her sweet, sort of innocent heart, she agreed. But I, a sinister cad, got quietly out of bed early the next morning. I drove into the village of Pacific Palisades, a few miles away, voted for FDR as planned, and got back home and back into my pajamas before Mary Lee awoke. And what's more, I didn't tell her of my dirty trick until the next day! She was—understandably—livid. But the president's majority was enormous, and (I was sharply reminded) he had not needed my deceitful vote anyway.

Shortly thereafter we were invited to stay with President and Mrs. Roosevelt for a few days during the inauguration in January 1941 and to attend the small (by Washington standards) dinner at the White House that the president would give before the two or three big inaugural balls to be held that night. Bob Sherwood was to act as the official master of ceremonies and make the dedication speech to be broadcast at the start of the festivities at Constitution Hall. As things turned out, Sherwood was suddenly taken ill and the president asked me to take his place. It was a stupendous evening. I somehow managed to rise above my anxieties.

* * *

Time flew forward so rapidly in 1941 that the myriad events of the year must be drastically condensed here. My wish to be "of service in any capacity to the Administration" was relayed in a memo to FDR by Sumner Welles, the under secretary of state, who suggested I might be appointed to help combat the pro-Fascist trend in Latin America. The president scribbled "very good idea" on the memo, and soon I received an invitation to undertake a mission "at the end of April" in certain Latin American countries. This mission was ostensibly to investigate the effects of American motion pictures on Latin American public opinion. But the *real* objective was to get in touch with influential national groups who "are now believed to be veering toward Nazi ideology." I was to submit an analysis of their current and potential influence—in addition to proposals of what we could do about it. I was also to make public addresses to boost our own American cultural policy and our films sympathetic to the Allied cause. I was to meet and exchange views with painters, sculptors, writers and film people. When I spoke in public I was to emphasize (as subtly as possible) America's anti-Fascist, pro-Allied policy. I was to ascertain in whatever offhand manner I could, whether each country I visited would be sympathetic to us if we were attacked and/or actively involved in the war. And most important I was to find out if we would be welcome in that country if we needed to use its ports as possible emergency repair bases for our navy. It was a flattering and thrilling request and I accepted immediately.

I was more anxious than ever about the slowness with which the navy was considering my application for a commission, even though I had by now passed my exams and had a little training. It was then suggested, by an old retired admiral, that if Bob Montgomery and I applied, as a first step, for a commission in naval intelligence *only,* we wouldn't be required to finish the rest of our training until later. *Finally* on April 10, Secretary of the Navy Frank Knox signed my commission as a lieutenant (junior grade) in the U.S. Naval Reserve.

My mission undertaken for president and country lasted roughly two and a half months. The odyssey that took us to five Latin American countries had included countless interviews, meetings, broadcasts, several dozen speeches, and a fair helping of adventure. We arrived home safe and barely sound at the end of June. The president wrote me, "From every source I have heard nothing but praise and commendation." I was very pleased indeed and wondered, "What next?"

I did once think that part-time, behind-the-scenes assignments in foreign affairs would be a fascinating avocation, provided I was given a position of some responsibility and influence. But I did not have anything like the amount of money necessary to be an ambassador to one of the better posts, and I wouldn't want a lesser one. Even in those prewar days when ambassadors had more real political responsibility than they do now, I didn't try to be more than I was already. I had no illusions of being a modern Metternich, but I did frankly enjoy being a fly on the wall in the corridors of power.

A boost to my diluted energies awaited me that summer of 1941. I began filming of *The Corsican Brothers*. I was still anxious to resuscitate my neglected career and settled into working ten and sometimes twelve long, hot, wearying hours a day.

One morning Mother's old friend from her Algonquin days, the now powerful Hollywood gossip columnist Hedda Hopper, decided, after hearing one of my Aid the Allies broadcasts soon after my return from South America, to turn on me with a vengeance. She set down for her millions of readers of the prominently isolationist Chicago Tribune Syndicate her regret that I had been so conspicuously a fool in the alien world of foreign affairs. She wrote, "The great senior Fairbanks must be turning in his grave in shame as his son plays at sending our young American boys to war while he, being an overage father [I *was* at the time thirty-one] stays safely at home making movies," or (as another columnist put it) "gallivanting to Washington and fashionable New York, and taking a jaunt to South America at the public's expense, hoping to push us into other people's wars."

These and a few similar comments appeared just a few days after a special hand-delivered envelope came to me on the set. It was an official confidential letter from naval headquarters, notifying me that as soon as I could complete my current business and professional obligations, I was to report for active duty.

Our charmed life at Westridge made my going on active duty suddenly seem an impetuous bit of bravado. Who was I impressing? Was

I going to win the war single-handedly even though we weren't legally in it—and might never be?

Before leaving California for the duration, we decided that Mary Lee and Daphne would stay with me as much as possible, but if I was sent away, they would settle at Boxwood Farm. We were lucky to arrange a rental for Westridge right away. Even more luckily, we rented it to Barbara Hutton and her new husband, my movie sidekick and always friend, Cary Grant.

Early in October, with no public fanfare or formal farewells, Mary Lee, Dabby, and I headed east. I was ready to report to the Navy Department in Washington, willing to end the war. Sir Galahad had arrived. Hitler wouldn't sleep well now. My boss of the immediate moment turned out to be a snotty lieutenant commander from the Bureau of Naval Personnel who told me to forget about any publicity (which I had taken considerable trouble to avoid so far). He said that Lieutenant Robert Montgomery had been too much in the press to please the navy ever since he was sent to our Intelligence Section in London; they wouldn't make that mistake again. "So, Fairbanks, the brass has decided the quickest way for you to be a seagoing deck officer is to go to sea and learn on the job. We're sending you to a supply ship sailing from Boston." I think he was surprised that I was so obviously pleased with the prospect.

The next day we were delighted to be asked by Mrs. Roosevelt's office to spend the night at the White House before leaving Washington. The presence of Bob Sherwood, and even the ghoulish Harry Hopkins, made for a fascinating informal evening. Just before the president went upstairs to his papers and bed, he wished me well and expressed the hope that I would soon be promoted to "Captain of the Head." I was too new and nervous to get the point of his joke about the shipboard slang for toilet, but I faked an embarrassed laugh. Mrs. R. escorted us to our bedroom and sat herself on one of our beds to put us both at ease. She was trying to assuage what she correctly guessed was Mary Lee's concern about my going to sea—that I was "so insufficiently trained."

This prompted Mary Lee to refer to Mrs. R.'s four sons (all in one or another of the armed services by now) and one daughter. Mary Lee, who earlier had glibly said she'd like "lots of children," then began to talk about "favorite children." She asked our hostess if she'd ever had a favorite child—and added (very tactlessly, I thought) that if so, "which one would it be?"

Mrs. R. thought a moment and then, with her sweet and very buck-toothed smile, answered, "Oh, I suppose the one who's most in trouble at the time."

With Mary Lee still in tow, and Daphne safe in Mary Lee's mother's arms in Virginia, I arrived in Boston, donned my uniform with its one-and-a-half stripes, and reported for duty. My orders were to report the very next morning aboard an old navy supply ship on its way to Newfoundland, for training as a "deck officer under instruction." Mary Lee and I tried not to be dramatic or sloppy about my last night ashore and stiff-upper-lipped it all evening.

The next morning, in gray damp and cold, we trotted down to the Navy Yard's dockside with all my gear. Mary Lee had given me a present of a ceremonial sword with my name etched on it. She waved as I clambered, with half a dozen others, aboard a launch and hove out to our anchored ship.

As we left, I glanced shoreward to see Mary Lee still waving. I dared not really wave back—I just lifted a gloved hand as if to adjust my cap. It was only now beginning to sink in that all this was real. The attention of family and friends, indeed all ordinary activities were fading behind the gray mist of the sea. I looked at the shore one last time and tried to smile as for a camera. My face wouldn't move. As the ship weighed anchor, I could still see the tiny figure of Mary Lee waving on the quayside. I damn near blubbered. What *the hell* had I got myself into?

"Our Story Continues . . ."

Chapter 1

Mary Lee's tiny figure, waving bravely from the dock of the Charlestown Navy Yard in Boston, became progressively smaller as the old ship pulled out to sea. I stood at the rail trying hard to prevent the tears starting in my eyes from rolling down my cheeks.

"Mr. Fairbanks, sir!"

I turned and a chief petty officer saluted. I returned it. "Yes?" I said.

"You're to report to the executive officer with your orders. Please follow me, sir."

After I had checked in and had been sniffed over by the ship's captain, a lieutenant in the Supply Corps showed me over the unpretentious tub, which looked just like what it was—a supply ship that had seen better days.

I was, he said, to bunk way forward, in the bow of the ship—"the sharp end." The young officer didn't exactly apologize, but rather explained that normally I would share a junior officers' cabin with regular bunks, except that the ship's company was already overmanned with not just its own officers but also more, like me, in transit—on the way to the Royal Canadian Navy Base at St. John's, Newfoundland, to transfer to other ships or bases in the north. As I was the last to arrive, that was "all the space available!"

I made my way forward to see my bunk. It was in the petty officers' quarters, and was not the hammock I expected but a small, grubby cot right smack in the bow.

I later learned that they all had assumed in advance that I was in some specialist branch, but just wasn't wearing the distinguishing marks on my sleeve. They then concluded I was with Naval Intelligence. I tried to persuade them that I was nothing more than a partly trained line officer, a lieutenant (j.g.) slated for God only knew what seagoing duties and hoping to learn in time to perform them. Though I was officially in training as a deck officer under instruction, I was actually not much more than a passenger. Since it was apparent that no one believed me, I made no more effort to win their support.

Soon after we were standing well out to sea from Boston's Charlestown Navy Yard, I was told I could begin sharing watch-keeping duties on the bridge that night—on the "dog-watch, from eight bells to four bells" (midnight to 4:00 A.M.). I'd be told my duties by a regular officer when the time came.

By then it was absolutely pitch dark on deck—no lights except some bits of hooded dark blue here and there were allowed to show. I groped and stumbled my way to the bridge, where I muttered something to the watch officer on duty.

"Okay," he grumped. "Stand over there and just look and listen. There's not much to do except get acquainted with the routine." The ship was rolling very slowly and rather inhospitably in the water, making about eight knots.

When the end to my four chilly hours of doing nothing came, I could still see nothing on the bridge but the hint of dark figures and just the faint glow of the big compass and some electronic gadgets. When properly relieved, I went below as directed, had a brief awkward word with a couple of new, much younger faces in the wardroom, and stumbled my way forward. I fell into my cramped bunk, a bit chilly, and dropped off into a *sort* of sleep.

I was up in another four hours, reporting to the wardroom for breakfast. I was told to join the skipper on the bridge where, in his own gruff time, he told me what to look out for, where to find whatever, and to ask the chief petty officers about anything I needed to know. I was well aware that the ship's officers had decided in advance that Lieutenant (j.g.) Douglas Fairbanks, Jr., was a freak, and that it was quite in order either to stare, try to bait me on one subject or another, or ask silly questions about movies.

One long day followed another in that October 1941. At last we passed close to the colorful Canadian seaport town of St. John's, Newfoundland, and then into Argentia, in the same province. We tooted our way in, giving all sorts of routine flag and light signals. The Canadians responded in kind. All around us were U.S., British, Canadian, and Free French warships, either riding at anchor or tied up alongside one of the docks. This was my first time in a working naval port, actually and legally in the war zone. We of the U.S. Navy were still the only technically nonbelligerent force present.

I was given back my orders, duly signed by the skipper, told to collect my gear, go ashore, find out where my next assigned ship, the USS *Ludlow*, was, and report aboard her. As I was leaving, one of the ship's officers shook my hand and said, "You're a better sport than we thought you'd be! The skipper was waiting to see if you'd complain about anything. We had lots of good space for you to bunk in midships, but he thought you'd be one of those rich, spoiled movie stars and make a fuss. We did a few other things to get your goat, but you didn't notice—or if you did, you didn't seem to mind! Good for you!"

It had been nearly three days since I'd left Boston, and Mary Lee. I tried to phone but of course I couldn't. I could, though, send an innocuous telegram assuring her of my continued well-being. After I'd done so I thought ruefully of the gold cigarette case she had given me in April for our second anniversary. It was in the form of an envelope on the front of which were engraved all the addresses where I'd lived, mostly in London, from 1933 until the present. Each address had a line drawn through it, to forward it to the next address. The last address, not crossed out, was "Westridge," Pacific Palisades, California, U.S.A.—where we had lived until several weeks ago. The return address, on the back of the envelope, was Mary Lee's Boxwood Farm, Hot Springs, Virginia. Inside was the message, "Finally, I've caught up with you, my love. Mary Lee, 1941."

My next problem was to find that middle-aged destroyer, the *Ludlow*. I was told at the harbormaster's office that it was out to sea on a brief gunnery practice sweep and was not due back until later in the evening. So, what to do? A young Canadian officer, standing nearby, recognized me and, reminding me that the U.S. Navy was dry but that Canadian, British, and other Commonwealth ships were most conspicuously *not,* asked with a good-humored wink if I would like to come along to the officers' club and then to the wardroom of one of their large patrol craft. I accepted gratefully and, taking my gear with me, went along.

By the middle of that afternoon I was, thanks to Canadian hospitality, well and truly sloshed. I asked if I might lie down somewhere. The young patrol-boat skipper, a cheery young full lieutenant, offered me his cabin. I gratefully lay down on his bunk to close my eyes for only a few minutes.

When I woke up—in a couple of hours—we were well out to sea. I frantically reminded the young skipper that I had to report to the *Ludlow* "right this bloody minute"—it had been due in port the hour before. The skipper apologized, explained weakly that they had tried in vain to wake me, and as they had been ordered out to sea for *two days* there was nothing to be done.

I was frantic—naturally. In the end, though, they laughingly said the *Ludlow* had been delayed by about three hours and they were only having a short routine inspection swing around the outer harbor and would be turning about at any moment. I had been "shanghaied"— and had had flashes of wide-awake nightmares that my first real sea duty was to begin disastrously. But all was well and I laughed—a bit too heartily, a bit too nervously.

What's more, I arrived at the bottom of the *Ludlow*'s gangway in perfect time. While waiting I saw a group of maybe six American sailors coming from another direction, marching under the orders of the navy's Shore Police. A whispered query to a fellow standing nearby as to why this gang seemed to be under arrest elicited the perfectly matter-of-fact answer that they had all been found "victims of a chief petty officer bugger," and were on their way to testify at the CPO's court-martial.

Clearly those old sailing-ship stories had modern echoes! In the days of sail, sodomy could be punished, in the most extreme cases by death (". . . to be hung from the yardarm"), *unless* the ship had been at sea for ninety days without touching port—in which case nothing happened.

* * *

There continued to be quite a few serious U-boat attacks on Allied convoys in the North Atlantic. Several Allied merchant ships and a couple of escorting American destroyers had been either sunk or damaged. Although still not legally a belligerent, we reserved our historic right to maintain "freedom of the seas"—at least within what FDR had decided was our own security area, the so-called neutrality zone. Therefore when any of our conspicuously identified ships was attacked, we were properly angry, though we had unquestionably been tempting trouble. We had built up an image of ourselves as invincible. Presumably these attacks on *our* ships, in *our* neutral zone, only confirmed that Hitler was mad—as had been said all along.

I had often been frightened by the mere possibility of something happening, but I always managed to disguise it by bluffing. Now the familiar fear of what could happen kept me exercising my kind of self-control: telling myself it wasn't actually happening.

The sea was only mildly choppy, but our skinny old "tin can" rolled and pitched, our bow rose up, twisted as if trying to escape the ocean that wouldn't let her go, and then splashed back into the cold white ruffle tops. When not on watch, I tried to get brought up-to-date by one of our CPOs on such things as navigation and gunnery.

I have always loved the sea—or at least the idea of it—and I grew up believing myself impervious to seasickness. The indignity of *mal de mer* was an experience others had known but not I—never, that is, until I served on the long steel sliver of the destroyer USS *Ludlow* in the irritable North Atlantic.

I was impatient with the need for the convoy, of which we were a part of twenty or so heavily laden merchant ships, to mosey along, necessitating our sheepdogging them at from six to nine knots—the speed of the slowest old tub in the group. Had the seas been only slightly choppy, I wouldn't have minded—but they swirled, swamped, and pushed us this way and that, over and back, up and down, until often the ship was in a trough that seemed yards below the crests of irregular waves, only to rise up as if on hindquarters to what felt like a vertical position, hold for a moment, and crash down in the next oncoming wave.

The alarms of submarine contacts with lurking U-boats sounded on our ASDIC antisubmarine detector, or sonar, which whirred, droned, and "pinged" night and day, day and night, tightening such novice nerves as mine. Discomfort, apprehension, and an awareness of my own inadequate training combined to render me so nauseous as to make the thought of anything except swallowing and breathing deeply impossible. Reminding myself that Lord Nelson was often seasick was of no use. To hell with Nelson! I dared not talk as I was certain that just the very act of saying a word would bring up all the day's and the night's dinner. I could neither move nor complain. If Hitler had ordered me to surrender my wife and baby daughter—and my coun-try—I believe I would have dumbly nodded acquiescence.

Despite orders for all hands to stay off the slippery wet decks unless ordered otherwise, I didn't give a good goddamn! I had to get some-where and let go. For the moment I felt a little better, but that dreadful nausea kept coming back until there was no more left to throw up. When I could, once or twice, make it to my bunk below, I just flopped miserably down and corked off into a weary, sick, dopey half sleep.

In fact I was scared of the unknown, scared because I didn't really know enough about my job yet, and scared of the war.

Fortunately the ship was well heated inside, because outside it was cold and raw. We wondered why the British insisted that their de-stroyers have open bridges. They claimed it was to give wider and freer views. We thought they just wanted to prove how tough they were. Anyway, when I wasn't seasick, I was just as glad to be a bit warmed when I took my turn with other junior officers on watch. I would try to break the nervous monotony of seeing nothing on night watch by silently having my own stay-awake game. This consisted of mouthing the lyrics to as many popular songs as I could remember without stopping. They were songs by Berlin, Porter, Gershwin, and Rodgers—and those made popular by Bing Crosby, Fred Waring, or Ukulele Ike. If I missed a line or a beat, I "penalized" myself by having to start all over.

Often the steady whining, the not really loud but still ear-scratching electronic monotony of the echo-sounding device, the ASDIC, in the near darkness of the communications room just off the bridge made me feel strangely jumpy. The fear-implemented irritation of its recurring PING made my flesh bump all over again whenever I heard it later, on other ships. There was an order for nearly absolute eerie silence on the bridge at night. (Sound travels surprisingly far over water—as I was to learn very well as a beach jumper the following year.)

I don't remember now exactly how long I was on the *Ludlow*—not more than a few weeks, I think. Destroyer sailors loved the intimacy of their small, fast ships. I understood at once how easy it was to feel the whole ship's company as a seagoing family. But I was much too unsure of myself and particularly anxious that my unease not be obvious. I would have been happier on a bigger ship where it would have been easier to get lost in the crowd. Nevertheless I got along very well with the skipper and with the other officers and men. This group didn't try to make life tougher than need be for me. In fact, they all did their best to give me an advanced crash course in how to be more than a semiqualified deck officer.

Not many reservists had yet been called to duty in that autumn of 1941. Although some of the Annapolis-graduate regulars ("the trade school boys"—or, because they wore Naval Academy class rings, "ringworms") were patient and helpful to newly arrived reservists, many in fact were impatient and behaved arrogantly, acting as if the newcomers were in the navy's way—necessary perhaps, but only for time-consuming chores that they disliked doing themselves. Seats at table for meals in the wardroom were assigned not just by rank, but by *date* of rank. It was a rare reservist, in those early days anyway, who was treated as anything more than a necessary evil—a filler-up of gaps, but really just a callow kid who could never qualify for really responsible jobs.

Most of us soon learned that the new boy, the otherwise untried reservist, could usually be spotted ashore by the "gold" chin strap above the shiny visor of his officer's cap, the gold buttons on his jacket, and the gold braid indicating rank on his sleeves. If they still looked shiny, he wasn't seagoing. As a result, all of us who were new to sea duty wasted no time in dragging our chin straps, extra sleeve stripes, shoulder-board braid and buttons (in a bag) over the side of the ship while under way. In time, the gold became a salty yellow-green, and we gained naval stature.

To anyone as uncertain as I was about everything—including what my exact duties were—being at sea was at once exciting and boring. The slim ship now undulated more slowly, erotically, in the gray November sea. The daylight duty hours were not at all bad. I used them for my own kind of crash course in what was expected of very junior (in both rank and experience, if not in age) reserve deck officers. At night the absolute silence—repeat, *"absolute silence!"*—on the pitch-black bridge and deck was broken only by the periodic ping as the thin green beam circled the ASDIC's big black clocklike face. The dark, still silhouette of the skipper in front of, beside, or behind me gave a spooky impression. I pitied anyone luckless enough to be ordered in terse, rough whispers to perform some duty, to go aft to do something back on the cold wave-washed deck; he would have to hold on to anything handy for increasingly dear life each time the bow rose, twisted, and smashed down into the next oncoming trough.

Friendly CPOs were really more helpful than the younger regular officers and were my saviors—*and* protectors. I was catching on, faster than I expected, to more than the rudiments of radio and visual communications. As for gunnery, I at least learned what things *were,* and I could just about get by in navigation, provided I was not in too responsible a position.

The first time our ASDIC's rhythm suddenly switched to a rapid (it seemed louder) PING-PING-PING-PING . . . everyone knew what it meant. Wits automatically sharpened. The senior officer on deck—the ship's captain or the exec—called out, *"All hands to battle stations!"* Suddenly bells clanged hysterically, and over the ship's loud-speakers was heard the brief "bos'n's pipe"—a sort of two-note whistle—followed at split seconds with *"Now hear this! All hands! Take your battle stations! Take your battle stations! All hands to battle stations!"* The graveyard silence of a moment ago was now broken by a bedlam of competing noises, voices, and rushing, clambering feet. Everyone was jamming on old World War I tin helmets, putting on life vests, and now and then giving odd indiscernible shouts—just shouts!

The blue-jacketed radioman first class, manning the ASDIC, called out the bearing of the contact he'd made. The skipper took command of the bridge, told the helmsman to turn a certain number of degrees one way or the other, and ordered the first lieutenant to ring up

"Flank speed!" to the engine room. The engineer below took hold as the wheel was turned sharply way over, and the ship twisted so much on her side as she wheeled about that for an instant it seemed that she would turn over. But she righted herself. The communications officer on deck was ordered to inform the other tin cans of our contact.

And then, just as suddenly, a near absolute silence descended as every man on the ship was now at his battle station—every man, that is, except me! I hadn't been given one yet. I didn't know what in Christ's name I was to do beyond staying on the bridge and keeping a sharp lookout. So I just stayed put, trying to behave as if I knew. I kept my binoculars up, looking out at all the odd white splashing in the black nothing of the North Atlantic night.

The contact on the ASDIC seemed to go away and then just as suddenly to return. It would *ping* out again, louder now and repeatedly, signaling its renewed contact, as if saying, *"Here it is! Here it is!"* The skipper ordered the gunnery officer to stand by and be prepared to launch depth charges. A louder, more insistent contact pinging came out of the radio shack behind the bridge and the order to drop a charge, preset to go off at a prescribed depth, was given. A big barrellike object was launched off the fantail, and a moment or two later, in just enough time for us to get the hell out of the way, a huge muffled roar belched up from the black water astern, followed by a sudden, high geyser rising from the sea, now even further astern. The pinging stopped. We'd made a *kill*! Maybe. It started again—and again we rolled in a circle in the dark, trying to center in on our target. Another depth charge astern rocked and shivered our ship, now well away from the explosion itself. The rest of the convoy and its escorts, having received our warning, had begun, according to standard operating procedure, to follow its commodore's lead, zigging and zagging at uneven times and speeds. (The maximum rate was still limited to the speed of the slowest ship in the group.) Then all was quiet for some while and we only hoped we'd made a hit. We couldn't prove it, but our ship's log entered details of the action and registered our "expectation" that the silence afterward meant that we had scored a kill.

After widespread searching, we caught up with the convoy shortly after daybreak and resumed our picket position on the starboard side of the group. Visual blinker signals were exchanged and we all proceeded inexorably. No one really slept for another day or so. As much as I feared and despised the Nazis, I couldn't help feeling a sting of sorrow, even a kind of guilt, at having been an accessory in the smothering death of young fellows at the bottom of the sea.

Some days later, during the daylight hours, while we were still pushing slowly this way then that in a gathering fog, another one of our destroyers chased a contact on the port side. Then suddenly it became our turn again to suspect a lurking sub in the vicinity. The sea had smoothed its ruffles somewhat, and we swept out in huge circles at flank (highest) speed, trying to pinpoint our target. We went so far in our ever-widening search that we found ourselves out of sight of the convoy. It didn't particularly disturb us at first, but after a while we had indications of possibly serious engine trouble. We slid along at reduced speed until eventually our engines stopped altogether.

It became as quiet as a watery graveyard all around us, and some gruesome types said they expected it might even be ready for us at any moment. The chief engineer reported no luck in repairing our serious engine breakdown as we just drifted, in a thickening fog. We were many miles away from our convoy group and strictly forbidden to break radio silence for any reason—not even to tell of our distress. For several interminable days we were unable to take our bearings, either by sun or stars. The sea became glassy calm and only the softest of breezes pushed us we knew not where.

Eventually, when the fog lifted enough for us to "shoot the sun" (I was catching up on my navigation quickly), we discovered we had drifted over the neutrality zone line and were now in the *official* war zone. That realization made our anxiety and fatigue even closer to untenable. If a U-boat or one of the wandering, marauding German cruisers, "pocket battleships," or armed "G-boats" had happened to be in the area—unreported by the British Admiralty or U.S. Navy Intelligence (which turned out to be not so far-fetched)—we would have been dead ducks. And furthermore, we would get no support from Washington, as we were indeed well into the area of "legal combat." Although I never confirmed it, the ship's scuttlebutt was that our logbook was rewritten to show we had not wandered so very far off course.

Our engineer officer finally got *one* engine going and, without any more excitement, we found our solitary way up to Iceland. We glided proudly past lines of Allied ships at anchor—all of whom signaled a "welcome back." I doubt if we ever admitted how very off course we had been.

The first time I saw the coastline of Iceland, I was on the *Ludlow* bridge, as were other off-duty newcomers to this part of the world. Our skipper was also looking at the bleak, treeless stretch of land, with groups of small houses on the seafront—but through binoculars. We were going fairly slowly, quite close to the shore. After a bit, he spoke. "Well, I can understand why we are here in Iceland, and I can understand why the British are in Iceland, but I'll be goddamned if I understand why the Icelanders are in Iceland!"

It is doubtful if any of our crew thought differently. It seemed drab and colorless. The people, once we got ashore and saw them at closer quarters, were understandably glum and resentful of the fate that obliged them to pretend to welcome thousands of Allied soldiers, sailors, and airmen. It wasn't that they preferred the Germans; they just wanted to be left alone. Who could blame them?

The troops did find one redeeming feature in this very ancient and highly schooled civilization: they bred the prettiest girls the boys had seen in one place for a long time. The interservice rivalry for the attention of these really good-looking Nordic women inspired more barroom brawls than any other single cause.

Having been reminded so often to make myself as inconspicuous as possible, I tried to avoid recognition by pulling my cap way down, my raincoat collar up, and inspecting the town of Reykjavík with a couple of younger shipmates as "cover." We did stop for a drink at the newly organized Allied Officers' Club. There were a couple of American and British civilians there. One, a particularly nice guy, turned out to be war correspondent Drew Middleton. Even though we later became good friends and kept in touch long after the Big Row was over, he inadvertently got me into my first trouble with the navy.

He was writing a piece on the Allied occupation of Iceland—the soldiers, airmen, and sailors of two nations who so suddenly swamped the bewildered peaceful Icelanders. Describing the local scene, he wrote that "among those seen walking the Reykjavík waterfront was movie star Doug Fairbanks, Jr., now on active duty in the U.S. Navy's Reserve. . . ."

I didn't even know about the story. He hadn't asked me *anything*.

Someone else had given him my name. In any case, when I was next at home and at the Navy Department, two senior officers, one from the Office of Naval Intelligence and the other from Navy Public Relations, gave me a very rough dressing down—accusing me of courting publicity and of breaking both security and naval tradition. I vehemently and honestly denied everything, but it did no good. Only after many more months and a reasonably clean record of keeping out of sight of the press was I more or less forgiven.

Once I had reported aboard the USS *Mississippi,* our biggest battleship in the area and the flagship of our Task Force 99, I found myself assigned again simply as a watch officer—"under instruction" for gunnery, communications, and whatever other odds and ends they thought of. The *Mississippi* was a fine ship, loaded down with all the appropriate armaments, depth charges, antiaircraft ordnance, and eight twelve-inch guns. After a couple of maneuvers and signal practice exercises with units of the British Home Fleet, to which we and the smaller ships of the U.S. Task Force 99 were attached, we returned to Reykjavík.

On the first Saturday morning in port, we had a routine captain's inspection of the entire ship. I was surprised to find that in a war zone, under at least semibelligerent status, these formal inspections were still carried out. The ship's band was broken out and played stirring music on the forward deck. *All* officers strapped on ceremonial sword belts, and with bugles and drums executing "ruffles and flourishes" and swords held in gray-gloved hands, we were inspected, as indeed were all our ships in those early Saturdays.

Then toward the end of November, when winter had begun to dig its cold toes into this antique Viking-settled island, we were ordered home to Norfolk, Virginia. The ship was to undergo some new fitting out, and the ship's company, many of whom had been away for months, was due some home leave. Escorted by our own destroyer screen, we weighed anchor, exchanged dipped flags, fired gun salutes, and slowly slipped out to sea.

Within a day or two we found ourselves in the midst of a great North Atlantic storm. Hull down, we slowed speed in order to cope with a gigantic sea and force 9, almost 10, winds (that is, gusts of something in the neighborhood of about fifty miles an hour). How the little "greyhounds," the destroyers that screened us, managed, I was too green to know, but sometimes, looking at them from inside our covered bridge, they seemed to be overwhelmed by the ruthlessness of the ocean's bitter cold and merciless waves, which looked like ever advancing ranks of white horse cavalry charges.

This time, for a change, I had a small but decent cabin that I shared with two other j.g.'s. None of us ever seemed to be off duty or sleeping at the same time. In any case, the seas became so high and mighty that sleep was impossible. By the second day of the storm, the water had sloshed through cracks and flooded the wardroom and Officers' Country ankle-deep. Iron ladderways were twisted as if they had been made of rope; lifeboats were ripped from their stanchions and all manner of equipment, however well secured, was broken off, made useless, or lost over the side.

The storm lasted, I suppose, for two or three days. The only thing we considered lucky was that we hadn't been on one of the proud little tin cans. Still, perhaps because they were so pliable, they appeared to have suffered less damage than we. We even had a few bluejackets injured and in sickbay under the medical officer's orders. When relative calm finally returned, we found that our former executive officer, Commander Jerauld Wright, was now commanding the ship. Our captain had evidently become incapacitated and, unable to face the fury of the elements, gave way to his next-in-command.

Wright was a monosyllabic character, tall, good-looking, and grave, except on rare and welcome occasions when he smiled. That was like the sudden uncovering of a bright lamp in the dark. Only later did I learn that he was very deaf. Somehow this slipped past the physical examiners (probably because he was brilliant at his job and the service didn't want to retire him). In subsequent years after some daring exploits, he rose to be commander-in-chief, U.S. Atlantic Fleet, and then a four-star admiral who was C. in C., U.S. and NATO Naval Forces, Europe—and, best of all, a good friend of mine. But in those days he scared the hell out of me.

A day after the storm, one of our junior communications officers became ill. Since I'd developed at least a tapping acquaintance with the mechanics of the secret coding machines, I was ordered to add to my duties the job of assistant communications officer (one of three aboard).

The process of decoding was easy enough. The decoder was a large sort of typewriter which, according to the setting for a particular hour of the day, would translate the meaningless letters of a radio message into clear understandable ones. Mostly the messages were for other ships or other forces. Occasionally there would be a message for the whole Atlantic Fleet and sometimes one just for our task force. Very often there were Navy Department messages addressed to ALNAV— navy talk meaning all the navy, everyone; all fleets, all ships and shore stations everywhere. Usually these were routine and hardly noticed. I tended to give them a quick look, and if they didn't seem too important, I'd tear off the ticker tape (on which the messages came out of the machine) and throw it away among the others in the wastebasket by my side. These messages would later be taken out and destroyed.

On one particular day I threw away a lot. Nothing much was going on of interest to us either as a ship or task force. During the late morning one ALNAV came through that like so many others meant absolutely nothing to my amateur-navy eyes. All it said was "AIR RAID ON PEARL HARBOR. THIS IS NOT A DRILL." That was all. It made no sense to me whatever. I tore the tape off and threw it in the basket and continued to type away.

After about ten minutes I began to wonder: What was that strange ALNAV? What could it mean? I dug around in the basket for a few minutes until I located it, and then, resecuring the steel door of the communications room behind me, made my way to the bridge to Commander Wright. I saluted respectfully, saying, "Sorry to bother you, sir, but this message came through. I don't understand it. I've brought it up to see if it is important or not."

Commander Wright read it and in a flash lost his famous composure. "*Is it important?* Why, you damn fool, it means *our* war has started! The Japs have attacked our biggest base! Quick, signal the task force and blow whistles—*do anything!*" We did. And the "cans" answered back, with their rising steam whistles, *"Woop! WHOOP! WHOOP!"*

Germany followed suit almost immediately and officially declared war against the United States. President Roosevelt rapidly convened a session of Congress, which authorized a formal declaration of war against the Empire of Japan and the German Reich. The kid gloves were off. We were in it now with both feet—and both hands—across two great oceans.

That December 7 Mary Lee, at Boxwood Farm in Virginia, just happened to turn on the radio. There was a cessation of all regular programs as she heard the announcements of our being now fully in the war—in both the Pacific and Europe. She rushed downstairs, shaking with fright and worry. The first person she saw was the sweet black woman who had long and devotedly worked for Mary Lee in Virginia. Mary Lee later told how she tearfully called out, "Oh, Nellie, what shall I do? *What shall I do? Where's Douglas?*"

Old Nellie calmly put an arm around her. "Don't fuss, Miss Mary Lee. You jes' put yourself in the hands of the Lord—an' He'll take care of everything. You'll *all* be all right. You see!"

Mary Lee took the advice in her own quite private way. And it was good advice, because I came home and went back out quite a few times over the next four years and a bit—and I am still here to write about it.

We all had our own worries, prayers, and pain. In fact, we had years of worry, months of hell, moments of terror, and minutes of heaven. And we were luckier than most.

Chapter 2

Some six months before Pearl Harbor, in the summer of 1941, I was beginning work in California on a motion picture adaptation of a short story by Alexandre Dumas, "The Corsican Brothers." Eddie Small was the producer and the charming Gregory Ratoff directed. It had been about a year since I had made any films at all, and I was much concerned that a great deal would be riding on this one. I had very high hopes for this movie and was probably more sensitive to its shortcomings than I should have been.

Small, though personally agreeable, had previously made inexpensive, inelegant films that fit his name and physique. He was not ready to risk an expensive, high-quality film. Consequently the cast, though good enough, did not have the reputation I would have preferred. The story cried out to be done in color, but Small insisted that even though I was to have a reduced salary (presumably to be added to later by a share in the profits), he just couldn't afford it. He said the picture's budget had already exceeded his original estimate, and we had hardly started! My early enthusiasm began to deflate.

The script was nevertheless intriguing: A pair of Siamese twins are born in Corsica, surgically separated at birth, and brought up in different places. The effect on each is that when, for instance, one is hurt, his pain is shared by his twin brother—half a world away. If one of the brothers is in love, the other shares his joys, even though they are apart. At one moment, when one brother actually sees the lovely object of his brother's love, he too falls in love with her! All rather silly as set down here, but fascinating fun as a short story and, in a way, even better as a movie. The plot oozed with villains, knaves, and scoundrels, violent swordfights, stunts, and derring-do action in which virtue is, of course, triumphant. This was the first real swashbuckling hero part I had ever played (in *The Prisoner of Zenda* I was the villain, and in the rowdy *Gunga Din* there were two heroes). But it had been a dozen years or so since my father retired, and movies had traded in their glorious silence and mime for sound and speech. So as a whole new generation was out there, I decided I'd ignore the old-timers sniffing, "He's not nearly as good as his old man was," and do all the stunts and action *my* way!

The wonderful part of the villain was given to an excellent Russian actor, Akim Tamiroff, but he was woefully miscast. He was physically too short and fat. He was supposed to be an agile swordsman capable of giving me, as the hero, the fight of my life. But Grisha (as Ratoff was called) made an unholy fuss of the matter in favor of his compatriot and friend, and since no one *I* recommended was available (at least for the price Small was prepared to pay), my views were overruled. I next made a big point of wanting an important name for our leading lady. Again Small insisted that no such actress was willing to play the part of the frightened, innocent beauty who, with blind faith in her White Knight, waits till the last moment to be rescued from the villain's clutches. We chose the very attractive but not yet well known Ruth Warrick for the part. The rest of the cast was excellent—H. B. Warner (a former star), John Emery, J. Carrol Naish, and Henry Wilcoxon. As I was to play twins, we needed a most ingenious cinematographer and special effects department. We *did* get both of those, at least!

I began to let my hair grow for the picture and set about training for such action sequences (having to play exceedingly athletic twins) that the film would require of me. In the mornings Grisha, the scriptwriter George Bruce, and I would meet, either at the studio or at my house, and would discuss scenes.

We engaged the best of the fencing coaches out there, Ralph Faulkner for sabers and Fred Cavens for foils and épées. I had known them for some time; they had advised on some of my father's old pictures. Over a period of weeks, with the help of our cameraman and art director, we devised a detailed routine of all the fights and action that the evolving script demanded—complicated, of course, by the needs of a dual role. I was out of shape, but my legs, painfully stiff for the first few days, eventually limbered up, and my tennis court frequently served as rehearsal space for the fights. Later we would go through all the action in the studio, in mock-ups of the sets we would be working in later. Because the only other face-to-face adversaries I was to fight with were Tamiroff and John Emery, and since neither of them were experienced fencers, I worked out with their doubles. (Many of the uninitiated confuse the job of double and stand-in. A double is disguised as one of the characters and is hidden behind bits of set. At a distance or with his back to the camera, he executes the player's supposed action undetected by the audience. A stand-in is the poor soul who just stands and stands, in the hot lights where the actor will eventually be, while the cameraman spends a very long time getting the lighting and the angles set exactly.)

We did several days of tests, concentrating for the most part on how best to do all the trick shots required for showing the twin Corsican brothers not only talking to each other, but one hitting the other, one carrying the other, and one walking *in front* of the other!

In the end the tricks we used in those pre-TV days were really quite marvelous. I characterized the twins so that despite their identical nature I could establish convincingly different mannerisms and personalities for each. We spent much time rehearsing the separate characters *and* the trick shots well in advance of actual production.

Some of the twin scenes widely written up at the time were done by the old and more obvious double-exposure system; that is, one side of the camera's lens is blanked out and the other side photographs normally. The dialogue of one brother is first recorded correctly, but the replies by his twin are spoken by an unseen actor offstage. Afterward, the film is rewound, the cover put on the opposite side of the lens, and the scene is repeated with the other brother now responding in his own voice on the recording made earlier.

Another method was to have a scene completely played through by one brother who spoke—presumably to his twin but actually to no one.

This would then be developed and projected onto a large screen behind the foreground action. The so-far unseen brother would then walk in front of, and sometimes cross over, the original scene being "back-projected."

When one scene required me, as one brother, to slap myself, as the other brother, it was a split-screen affair again. But this time it was an optical illusion. My hand that swept across and hit my brother (me) actually went out of the scene for a fraction of a second, too quick for the eye to catch. The illusion was helped by putting in the sound of the slap, so that even the most experienced camera tricksters were sometimes deceived.

Finally the mystery of how I could possibly carry myself in my own arms is explained by my having a plaster life mask made of my face. This was transferred onto thin rubber and fitted onto the face of a double. I thus picked up the double, with the mask of my face fixed to his, and carried him in my arms.

During fights, doubles were switched so quickly that one didn't realize it. Thus the mysteries, much easier to execute nowadays on video, are explained.

My long hours on the set were interrupted when I was called to active duty. I was given time to complete the movie and take care of other obligations. However far away the war then seemed geographically, black headlines never let us forget the thunderclouds that now permanently enveloped Britain, Europe and Russia.

I was too preoccupied to get to know Ruth Warrick very well. She worked expertly with the usual vapid material that leading ladies in romantic action pictures are given. H. B. Warner and J. Carrol Naish gave the best performances. Akim Tamiroff, the miscast villain, was menacing and properly hammy. Our swordfight at the end of the picture would have been ludicrous had we not used an agile and experienced double for him in all but the very quick, close shots.

When it was time to shoot our big climactic fight, I came down with flu and a temperature of 103.5 degrees. I was "up to here" in aspirin and sweating like a New Orleans stevedore in August. The fight, which had been well rehearsed for many weeks, took us through and around every corner of several palatial rooms. We had decided in advance that we would make one master shot, using three or four

cameras shooting from different angles at the same time, and that we would therefore, if possible, go through the entire routine in one go, or maybe two at most.

On the day for the shooting I was too ill and weak to try and duplicate the action and the spirit of the fight at different times for the benefit of all the desired angles. The close-ups and medium shots could be done another day, when it was hoped I would feel stronger. The entire routine of the fight was said at the time to be the longest sustained swordfight or duel ever filmed, and I had no doubt of it.

When Akim's double, our coach, our first choreographer, and I finally finished our routine, it was timed at a bit over three and a half minutes. It felt like over an hour! When Ratoff finally yelled "Cut!" the entire crew on the set—some twenty men and women, plus a few more from the outer office who had come down to watch—broke into spontaneous applause! I know that I managed, through my sweat and gasping for breath, a smile of sorts, and then I sank, dripping and absolutely done in, into one of those canvas chairs that are a symbol of movie sets. I spent the next day in bed on doctor's orders. Fortunately for the budget, it was a weekend—one I still remember vividly.

At this point we were anxious to get everything tidied up. I no longer even took the trouble to fuss over details anymore with Eddie Small. I no longer questioned the editing, the dubbing, or even discussed the excellent musical score by Dimitri Tiomkin. So impatient was I to get my disappointment with the movie out of my mind and report for active duty that, even lacking my customary acquisitiveness, I gave up my former determination to claim a percentage of the picture. I was convinced there would be few profits anyway.

I had no thought of *The Corsican Brothers* in the middle of December 1941. The poor banged-up "Old Miss" limped, like the old lady she was, back into the Norfolk Navy Yard to get ready for a complete face-lift and overhaul. Official visitors maintained they would have bet—from our quite heavy storm damage—that we'd seen enemy action. Although the country had not yet recovered from the shock of Pearl Harbor, the navy did its best to bring us all up to the properly belligerent mood suitable for a two-ocean war. So we half expected the

almost overdone enthusiasm with which we were welcomed home. Whistles from anchored ships and shore establishments tooted their pride and determination.

It was obvious that our ship would need months of work before she was again fit to sail out to the Pacific and join the few remnants of our battered, decimated Pacific Fleet.

As soon as we tied up, I (along with hundreds of others) requested permission to leave the ship in order to telephone home. When I managed it, Mary Lee shrieked with surprise and delight. But since I couldn't tell her *where* I was—except to give reassurances that I was well and safe—it was all very frustrating. She would, she said, check with a friend in Washington for advice. Meanwhile I would try to phone again the next day.

That night, our first one home since war had been declared, the ship's company was ordered to stay aboard. No one was allowed ashore, except for "humanitarian" reasons. The big battle wagon's seagoing clergyman, who always doubled as recreation and entertainments officer (a title that one might misconstrue just once), announced that there would be a special film shown on the afterdeck that evening. *"Everyone,"* he announced, "is expected to be present." I was one of the junior officers whose turn it was to have "the duty"—meaning we had either to do something routine but specific or stick around to perform whatever jobs needed to be done. Thus I would at least be spared having to see some dreary movie that was probably ages old.

However, there was so much kindly pressure from the admiral's flag lieutenant in the Navy Yard—and also even from Commander Jerry Wright—for me to be present on the afterdeck, that I went along, dragging my feet just a bit.

When all was dark and the film began, I felt a huge gulp rising from deep in my innards to my soundless throat. There on the big specially rigged screen, the titles announced *me* in *The Corsican Brothers*! Apparently the admiral's staff and ship's officers had known all along and were determined not to tell me. I cringed with embarrassment, particularly as every time I appeared on screen, all the assembled bluejackets roared and applauded. When I got into one of the film's many fights or did some leaping about, they sent up a cheer—not unmixed with sounds of ribald disrespect. This would be followed by shouts of "Go get 'em, Doug!" "Atta boy, loo-tenant!" "Yoo-hoo, Duggie!" and so on. But the worst was when the love scenes began. The wolf whistles, catcalls, and shouted recommendations as to what I should do next ("Hey, that's the pretzel position!") held me in rigid dumbness with, I was told, a stupid, self-conscious grin on my face.

Some weeks after that embarrassing big surprise I learned that the film was doing absolutely smash business all over the country—indeed everywhere, even abroad. The trade papers reported that it was racking up one of the biggest box-office grosses not only of the season, but of any picture of which I was the principal star (*Gunga Din* was a three-star affair). But by this time (of course, damn it all) it was much too late for me to so much as discuss a percentage deal. Residual payments, nowadays automatic, were unknown in those days. There was a compensation of sorts in realizing that it had been a long time since I had had a success of any kind all to myself.

I wasn't exactly aching to stay aboard "the Miss," waiting until she had been patched up to be sent lumbering through the Panama Canal to help remuscle our broken Pacific Fleet. I'd be of better use back in California doing another film than twiddling my thumbs here in Norfolk. I had little spare money and was even obliged to write our old friend Dickie (Lady Morvyth) Benson and warn her that in a few months I would no longer be able to support the "Douglas Voluntary Hospitals" (which I'd helped establish for volunteers to help the RAF in the British countryside in 1939), although I would go on and send what I could when I could. Fortunately they didn't have to close down, because the Order of St. John and the British Red Cross picked up most of the slack. My last checks for charities had gone to the American Red Cross, Russian War Relief, the U.S. Navy Relief Fund, and to an especially appealing one from England: Noël Coward, as head of the British Actors' Orphanage, had brought over all the little "residents" as refugees from the bombing and had asked the American acting profession to help in guaranteeing the children's welfare "for the duration." Mary Lee and I took on the guarantee of two of them.

I didn't have to stew about my future for long. Within a few days of docking, I received new orders to report to the Navy Department in Washington where, presumably because I had been serving under

the questionable colors of assistant gunnery officer, I was assigned to
the chief of the Bureau of Ordnance! It was as unfortunate a bit of
casting as having Lillian Gish play Attila the Hun.

I consoled myself with my luck in getting home so comparatively
soon, once more to be with Mary Lee and baby Daphne. I had the
smug conviction that my superiors would soon recognize how un-
promising was my career in naval artillery and the mathematical
science of ballistics.

I was right. I did not remain long in that section—just long enough,
however, to make what proved to be one of the most helpful and
enjoyable friendships of those years in the person of my temporary
boss, Reserve Captain Lewis Strauss (pronounced "Straws"). In private life he was a distinguished Wall Street banker-partner in Kuhn,
Loeb, Inc. In time, he moved up to rear admiral and eventually
became head of the mysterious Atomic Energy Commission.

Lewis, then and ever after on my side, had me temporarily transferred to an unsatisfying post with the public relations director. However, the job did include a better than average look-in on the Office
of Naval Intelligence. This was fun. It provided me with a quick lesson
in how intelligence was acquired, analyzed, and otherwise dealt with.
The chief (CNO) was Captain Alan Kirk, USN, a bright and usually
genial man who, with his attractive wife, was (like my *Mississippi* exec,
Jerauld Wright) one of the few career officers prominent in Washington social life.

Kirk welcomed me in two different ways. In the Navy Department
he was particularly brusque, as if he wanted to show that he was not
only unimpressed but also rather irritated to have a movie celebrity
pretending to be a naval officer in his department. Away from headquarters and after hours, on the still busy cocktail and dinner-party
rounds of the capital, he was warm, friendly, and almost boastful of
my presence in his group.

We hadn't been many weeks in Washington, where we had been
as publicly unobtrusive as we knew how, when a couple of newspaper
items told of my being "on duty" in the city. My presence in the
capital was also noted by some now forgotten congressman who was
himself clearly trying to get press attention for being alert to depart-
mental abuses. He had so little to do, since he was only passively

interested in the war's progress, that he made a phone call to the secretary of the navy asking whether my being stationed in Washington was a sign of "favoritism to a celebrity" or whether I had been given one of those famous "ninety-day wonder" post–Pearl Harbor commissions in order to push recruiting.

The appropriate naval authority subsequently provided assurance that I had been commissioned seven months before the war began and had indeed already been in action. Nevertheless Captain Kirk subsequently called me into his office and gave me a fierce bawling out for maintaining a press agent while in the navy during wartime!

It took considerable control on my part to politely convince Kirk that I had made strenuous efforts to be as nearly anonymous as I could and that I would far prefer to be at sea and in action (that last was a barefaced lie, but I made myself believe it for the time being). I then added, with as much arrogance swathed in transparent formal respect as I could manage, that if I wanted publicity I would have stayed with my profession, made a lot of money, and remained at home with my family—or I would have volunteered for a branch of military service that was not so persnickety. Apparently this correctly delivered reply convinced Kirk of my good intentions and innocence. However, he closed the interview by telling me that my presence at headquarters—indeed, ashore at all—was an embarrassment to the service and I would be transferred back to sea duty right away.

Well, it was and it wasn't "back to sea" exactly. The main thrust of their plan appeared to be to get me the hell out of Washington as soon as possible. That part was a success.

It was mid-winter 1942, and Daphne, who was now nearly two and in the habit of pointing to any man dressed in dark blue, including policemen, and calling out, "Dat's Daddy!" was hurriedly dispatched with nurse back to the farm in Virginia. Mary Lee and I bundled ourselves off to New York as soon as possible and settled (if that's the word) in an uptown hotel.

I was in no position to quibble, but it was clear that my new job was not precisely an exciting assignment. I was to be the executive officer of an aged minesweeper, the USS *Goldcrest,* based on Staten Island, a short ferryboat ride from lower Manhattan. The advantage to the job was that it would count as sea duty while I remained with Mary Lee.

On the other hand, the principal drawbacks to the assignment were several. First of all, minesweeping requires a specialized knowledge of electronics and of the very complicated techniques and mechanisms designed to locate enemy mines laid at various depths beneath the sea so that they may be exploded or otherwise neutralized. It meant having a fair idea of where enemy submarines lurking off our coasts might have positioned a wide variety of types of mines. It meant quick briefing and decoding of messages from Naval and Coast Guard Intelligence about the latest movements of mine-laying enemy U-boats. It required an officer with wide experience in pilotage and at least a working knowledge of navigation; of the rules and regulations of (in this case) New York Harbor and its approaches from the sea; of trick tides; of the machinery and quirks of a small ship with a small, tough, semidisciplined crew who often knew as much as or more than their officers; and finally of how to administer the ship as the captain's number one. In my case, I was again less than useless on every count. I suspected rightly that I was once more "on trial."

When I actually reported, I found the crew that slept aboard (that luxury was optional) the grubby, weather-worn old tub still recovering from a rough day before and a subsequent drunken evening. The skipper, whose rank was lieutenant-commander and who had formerly been a merchant marine officer, was still asleep below when I came aboard. I was greeted by a bewildered and messy young ensign, acting as the ship's officer of the deck, who told me in a frightened whisper that I'd have to wait until the skipper woke up, but in the meantime he would accept my orders and sign me in.

Of course it didn't take long for this ship's company to realize how unequipped I was for any minesweeping duty whatsoever. In fact, far from trying to disguise it, I decided to frankly admit my nearly total ignorance and place my reliance on their hoped-for goodwill.

The skipper, when he finally surfaced, still disheveled and woozy, was at first suspicious (this was to be expected), and tried for a time to be tough and rough. Finally, however, he got so interested in remembering who was who in movies and asking what it was like when such and such happened, that after a drink or two (ashore, of course) we warmed to each other.

For the next month or so, I got up from my warm hotel bed at about four every morning, donned my woolly long johns and my winter-weight uniform, took a subway down to Battery Park where the ferryboats nudged in and out and, landing on Staten Island, reported aboard my old minesweeper between 5:30 and 6:00 A.M. I seem to remember that particular winter as one of pervasive damp and biting cold, defying heavy sweaters and overcoats, gloves, socks, and quarts of hot coffee.

This job developed an additional quite unforeseen responsibility. The skipper, a warm-hearted roughneck, was rarely in good health. In fact, nearly every day (we set out from dockside at 6:30 and returned to our berth only after dark) found him ill with some pain or problem that required him to retire to his bunk. This meant that inside of a few days I had to learn enough to know what must be done, to use the right words of command at the right time, and lean on the experienced advice of the younger first lieutenant. It was miserable, unexciting, and utterly dreary out-and-back and out-and-back-again duty. Sleeping a little at "home" in a nice hotel helped only insofar as it was better and warmer than it would have been aboard the grubby old ship. And, of course, Mary Lee was patiently waiting, waving good-bye and greeting me every day.

My skipper was really a warm-hearted soul, so excessively grateful for my covering up his incapacities, keeping his ship in shape, and with the goodwill of our crew carrying out our daily cold, boring missions that he sent the next high-up command a fitness report that gave me the top mark (4.0) in every one of the fourteen items listed! As no one, not even the immortal Nelson, could deserve such high marks, the navy rightly surmised that something was amiss. I was suddenly detached and ordered back to Washington, where I was reassigned to the staff of Commander Task Force 99.

The new job was on board the big, new, beautiful battleship the USS *Washington,* whose commander was Rear Admiral Robert (Ike) Giffen. The rest of the task force was comprised of a large (for those days) aircraft carrier, the USS *Wasp;* a couple of light cruisers, the USS *Wichita* and USS *Tuscaloosa;* a good-sized gaggle of destroyers, supply, hospital, repair, and other support ships. The whole kit and caboodle was attached to the British Home Fleet, an even larger assortment of ships commanded by British Rear Admiral Jack Tovey. Both forces used Reykjavík, Iceland, as well as Scapa Flow, Scotland, as bases. Their chief mission was to keep watch and be prepared to challenge German naval units moving in Norwegian waters and on the approaches to and from the Baltic Sea out to the Atlantic. This seemed to promise something more in line with my hopes—even if I had no idea yet what my duties would be.

Sometime in March 1942—about a month before our third wedding anniversary—I was trying my best to get both Mary Lee and myself adjusted to my imminent departure when Mary Lee said, rather offhandedly I thought, "Oh, I've been to the doctor again this morning and . . ."

"Whaddayamean—the *doctor*?"

"Well, I've had several checkups and now it's confirmed. . . ."

"What is?"

"We're going to have another baby—end of November!"

I was stunned and, rare for me, speechless. Not *sound*less, but I uttered nothing recognizable as language. I managed a sudden, loving, and probably teary embrace.

Foo (my old nickname for Mary Lee) then said, "This time it'll be a boy! I'll bet!"

In a throaty but high-pitched voice, I replied, "Who cares?" Why had I been so damned noble about sorting out the world's ills and getting into anonymously active trouble? But, oh, this *was* a lovely bit of news! I'd just encourage my luck to stay with me a while—a long while—longer.

I took off for Montreal, there to board one of several of our big bombers being delivered to the RAF and RCAF in Britain. With a number of hours to kill until early evening when we were to fly to Scotland, I wandered about this attractive city and then decided to go into one of the better hotels. It was snowy cold outside, and a Turkish bath and a professional massage seemed a good idea. When I got down to their health club, I saw no one about. But following signs to the lockers, steam room, and showers, I signed the register, undressed, and went into a large, empty, steamy room. After groping about, I sat down on one of the several stone slabs.

I relaxed quickly into a hot foggy euphoria. Some minutes went by before my sweaty reverie was interrupted by the materialization of a huge hulk coming through the glass door. The steam was hissing and burbling noisily, but it only blurred the gruff, high-pitched, Slavic-accented voice. *"You Miest-err Fer-bianks?"*

"Yes," I said, sitting up.

"Lie down!" was the command. Assuming that I was now to get a relaxing massage, I obliged, putting one of the smaller towels modestly over my lower middle. The big chunk took hold of a leg and began not so much a massage, but a hard rubdown. *"Begin here on front*—finish udder side."

"Okay! Fine! Okay!" I looked up at the golem giving my upper thigh a workout, and I was now close enough to recognize that it—she—was a woman! I couldn't recall that I had ever had a woman massage me before—not this kind anyway. Even despite her uncongenial looks and superior muscles, I was terribly embarrassed. All my cloudy dreaming changed to awkward discomfort. I decided the best thing was to pretend I didn't care. But when her strong hands were kneading my leg muscles and bumping (only slightly) such natural obstacles of mine that are independently sensitive, it became only too obvious that I had to call it quits and leave with as much poise as I could manage in my sweaty naked state. The bewildered masseuse let me go with no more than a grumble. I showered quickly, dressed, and left a liberal tip, still buttoning as I slipped out. It wasn't so much prudishness on my part, but the unexpectedness of it all. The she-monster was not one I thought I could be at ease with before departing for war.

To my mild surprise I got to the correct RCAF airport and the correct embarkation point in good time. I was taken in hand by a cheery young Canadian flight lieutenant. I noticed at once that he was particularly solicitous—almost to the point of seeming sorry for me. The reason soon became apparent. These aircraft had been stripped of every passenger comfort except for one washroom forward. The seats were all metal and faced each other like benches, the length of the plane. Each seat had a depression, making a primitive bucket seat. The only way to make the slightest improvement was to put extra coats and sweaters on them as cushions. Seatbelts were, of course, fitted throughout. However, the main problem with this particular flight was that it had been fully assigned to senior Canadian, American, and British officers, and there was no seat for me. Nevertheless I *had* to get aboard somehow; my orders said so. But how?

My new friend couldn't spare any time to worry because the same situation took place several times a week. The proven solution was that the odd man out, the most junior in rank of all aboard, was obliged to lie down on his back, full length, below in the belly of the plane—the bomb bay—strapped tightly into it. The RCAF was very generous with two or three blankets to put under you to cover the ridges of cold metal. If you could accept this seat assignment in jut-jawed silence, there were two special warnings to bear in mind. The first was to wear as many undershirts and sweaters as you could beneath your heaviest greatcoat or duffel coat, and the second was to put on two or three pairs of heavy gloves. The reason for all this was that these aircraft were not only stripped of all trimmings in order to minimize weight (and therefore fuel consumption), but they had no provisions whatever for heat.

The bomb bays were isolated from the rest of the passengers above and didn't have even the meager advantage of body heat from the other passengers. I was warned it would be bitterly cold with the only semblance of heat coming through from the engines far off on either side. "And don't," I was ordered, *"for any reason* whatever, take off your gloves! One Yank came through three weeks ago, took off one glove, and four of his fingers got so frostbitten that they were amputated on his arrival in Iceland." I needed no convincing after that.

I dutifully put on two or three sweaters, a heavy uniform jacket, two heavy-duty raincoats over a duffel coat—one borrowed from the copilot—and waddled onto the plane and into its belly where they laid the bombs when in battle. It was sort of like a cradle. Down I lay, most obediently, having got rather too hot on land and finding further movement increasingly difficult. I was strapped tightly down so I wouldn't bounce around on the metal (however well-padded) if the flight got rough. Seldom have I felt more subordinate, before or since, than I did in that zero-degree night in that goddamn bomber on the RCAF airfield in Montreal as I watched all the bloody brass, also wrapped up, get aboard and strap themselves into their padded bucket seats.

After a long time just getting the four propellers to turn over and warmed up enough to move, we taxied out, bouncing heavily and noisily for, I thought, far too long. Finally, after what felt like miles still earthbound, we lifted off the ground and into the very cold North Atlantic night air.

The young flight lieutenant had given me some sort of sleeping pill and a swig of brandy. The combination helped to lull me into a semistupor for I never knew how long. The trip was to take about fourteen to sixteen hours without a stop. Some of the smaller short-range aircraft would land in Newfoundland and again in Greenland or Iceland before arriving in Scotland. But not us! No sir! We were going the whole damned way! We had a fine tail wind and hoped to make it in one jump.

After a dopey doze, I began to realize that the brandy and cups of coffee had now made their way through my system and were insistent on leaving me in the usual manner. But there was just no way. I dared not unhook myself, and I was even more frightened to take off my two pairs of gloves to rearrange matters somehow. The cold, even beneath two wool mufflers around my face and goggles over my eyes, was all I had been warned it would be. In addition, I began to develop a panicky idea that one of the crew might accidentally pull or push whatever released the bombs, the bay would creak open, and I would drop out into the winter Atlantic thousands of feet below. Of course no one would notice I'd gone until they counted noses after landing. This new scare made the need to rid myself of excess fluids more painfully urgent by the minute. I reckoned by a glimpse of a watch strapped outside my glove that we still had several hours to go. I wondered if there would be any possibility of landing in Iceland to refuel—perhaps to avoid arriving in Scotland in the midst of an air raid over Glasgow? I thought this not worth counting on. I was so damned sure—oh, Christ! I was *goddamn* sure I couldn't hold . . . oh, hell! There was just nothing I could do. I could only try my best to minimize the leakage—to control matters just enough to avoid popping like a balloon.

And thank God, the decision to do what I did may not have been covered in Regulations, but it did help just a bit. Furthermore it did something else I had not thought of—it was slightly warming. So agreeable was that nearly desperate experience with incontinence that

I was very nearly tempted to go on. And then, finally, a bit ahead of time, I felt us descending. My ears popped painfully but in all other ways I was relieved the trip was ending.

Though all my muscles were stiff from frigid inactivity, I managed one last brace for a bouncy landing. But oh, the joy, the relief of that dreadful experience finally coming to an end! I was now in the active front line of the European war. I was at Prestwick Airport near badly wounded Glasgow in Scotland.

The local U.S. naval liaison officer in the area hadn't the least idea of the whereabouts of Task Force 99 and still less of flagship USS *Washington*. But a question addressed by scrambler telephone to the London headquarters of all U.S. naval forces in European and North Atlantic waters asking what to do with me was soon answered with orders for me to proceed to London to await the "return to its base of Task Force 99."

When I got there, by a grubby but fine wartime train, I was stirred by nostalgia. London naval headquarters was located in the very same building as my old penthouse flat where Marlene Dietrich and I had had our fine romance in 1936. Of course, by this time our family solicitor, F. M. Guedalla, had arranged to keep it rented to different people. In London I reported to Admiral "Betty" Stark, our senior naval commander in Europe. This fine officer had not made the right decision before Pearl Harbor, and instead of staying in the top navy job there, he was sent to the shorter-range, but presently more active, European war.

Upon checking in, I was told my ship was out with the task force on what was called the White Patrol, a periodic foray off Norway and Iceland, on the lookout for German U-boats and the great modern German battleships, the *Bismarck* and the *Tirpitz*.

It was exciting to be in wartime London, and I took the opportunity to ring up as many old friends as I could. Larry Olivier and Vivien Leigh asked me for a Sunday lunch. They were living in a cold, messy little place in Sussex, from which each weekday morning Sub-Lieutenant Olivier, RNVR, hopped on his motorbike and rattled over to the nearby Royal Naval Air Station where he was a flying instructor for the Fleet Air Arm. We had a fine, giggly two-hour meal. I found my old friend from Hollywood Irving Asher still producing quota films, films made in Britain expressly to balance the preponderance of films made in America, for Warner Brothers at their already partly blitzed studio at Shepperton. I tried to see darling, blessedly voluminous Winifred Ashton (the writer Clemence Dane) almost immediately. Strictly by accident, I even bumped into some ex-girlfriends in my quick rounds of old familiar haunts that had not yet been destroyed or damaged. Bob Montgomery had been transferred to some duty back in Washington. Just by chance Dickie (Lord Louis) and Edwina Mountbatten were briefly in the country, so I did manage to whisk down to Broadlands for a meal on one of my few free days. What warm, loving joys they both were, then as always. I was full of questions about Dickie's Combined Operations Command. He was in charge of all amphibious training and development for what would be the eventual invasion of Hitler's "Fortress Europe." In none too subtle a fashion, I expressed my hope that one day I might be ordered to serve with the few other Yanks on his staff. I drove over to see the Bensons (Con and his wife, Dickie) nearby and visited one of "my" hospitals. No one knew I was their benefactor; they merely took me as a visiting celebrity in uniform. I rang the Kents, Princess Marina and Prince George (once I was able to persuade the royal telephone protectors that I was a personal friend and not a newspaperman or spy), but had no time to say more than hello.

On my last free day, I had lunch with Noël Coward. He had included me at the last moment in a group meeting at the Ivy. Long a famous luncheon rendezvous for theatrical folk, it was packed as usual with recognizable theater people, most of them men and women in uniform, many of whom greeted me with extra warmth because I was a Yank colleague, also in uniform. I hadn't seen them for several years, yet I was welcomed back with special warmth. I was awfully pleased to see Ivor Novello, who had been sent briefly to jail for disobeying the limits on fuel for his car.

Being back in such a clublike atmosphere was great fun at first. But halfway through this stimulating get-together, air raid sirens began to wail. No one in the entire restaurant paid any attention. The old waiters continued to serve calmly, and all the smart patrons went right on eating and chattering. All, that is, except one of our party, the highly gifted and amusing ballet star Robert (Bobby) Helpmann. As the sirens became louder and more persistent, I could hear for the first time the *thud-thud-thud* of antiaircraft guns fewer and fewer miles away. Bobby began to slip, ever so slowly, under the dining table. Of course if we'd been hit, the table wouldn't have protected a flea, but Bobby insisted—very comically, I admit—that it was psychological security.

I have no doubt that I, too, would gladly have become a human tortoise. But the example of everyone else paying next to no attention prevented me from making an exception of myself. Thank God it was an uneventful introduction to a real air raid.

I got through to David Niven on the phone. He was about to leave on a training expedition, but we promised each other we'd have a night out if and when I got back again. And so, happy to have had a glimpse of a few old pals in knocked-about but prideful London, I flew to Scapa Flow in a U.S. Navy plane, chugged out in a gig past several warships riding at anchor, and finally reported for duty aboard the USS *Washington*.

The first gray, misty sight of all those ships of two mighty navies lying there in that huge, landlocked sea shelter of Scapa Flow, in far northern Scotland, was breathtaking. In a setting of much drama in both world wars rode about every type of warship and naval auxiliary. Barges, gigs, whaleboats, and other small craft left tiny, short-lived wakes behind them as they crisscrossed on their several errands from ship to ship or shore and back. There were crude, widely dispersed buildings ashore that served as command and communications headquarters. The first successful radar was used by the British here just before we got into the war. There were barracks, recreation halls, and some sparse open playing fields. The base looked to be what, in fact, nothing in war *could* be—invincible.

Ike Giffen, the commander of Task Force 99, was a round, jolly, pink-faced rear admiral. He realized soon enough that I was no budding Nelson, let alone John Paul Jones, but this was a time when the navy was beginning to swarm with young reservists, many with even less practical experience than I. Consideration was given to dumping me onto the ship's captain and his own roster of officers, but there were not enough billets for anyone of my low rank and high age bracket. Thus taking into account the jobs I had briefly held, I was rather casually assigned to Giffen's "flag" or admiral's staff, in the job of assistant staff gunnery and communications officer. This meant I was accountable in "the execution of assigned duties" only to the admiral commanding U.S. Task Force 99, and not to the ship's captain or his subordinates.

To thus ease into a big-time task force was a fortunate break for me, and I did it with as much modesty as I could muster. There was the usual curiosity about me and surprise that I took the sharp commands and silly bait of calculated rudeness without visible objections. My take-it-and-keep-quiet attitude soon paid off in the early companionship of two men who became my champions from those days to these. One was a somewhat younger but very considerably more experienced lieutenant (j.g.) than I, called Chad (for Chadbourne) Knowlton. His strong Down East Yankee accent augmented his unfailing humor and ingenuous enthusiasm for all things nautical. The other was the young commander of the sizable marine detachment aboard our ship, a regular career officer, Captain (recently promoted from second lieutenant) Don Hittle, USMC. These two guided, advised, and warned me through my first stumbling weeks in the seagoing big league.

We first weighed anchor and took our position at sea for exercises and maneuvers with the Royal Navy's Home Fleet, largely in order to bring our flag signal codes more in line with each other. The occasional mix-up resulting from signal misunderstandings once caused parts of the British force to cross one way when the U.S. group thought they were to go another. The result was the war's favorite word for confusion: SNAFU (for "Situation Normal—All Fucked Up!"). Admiral Giffen ordered his then flag lieutenant, my predecessor, to hoist a signal to British Admiral Jack Tovey's flagship, comprising two pennants only—the "church pennant" and the "interrogative pennant"—which, when properly decoded, would say: *"Jesus Christ! What next?"*

My assigned battle station for my first exercise in the war zone was in number one gun turret, one of five great twelve-inch steel homes for three sixteen-inch guns apiece. I was there, theoretically at least, for instructions—and I *hated* it. I felt unpleasant twinges of claustrophobia. I had too little to do, didn't really understand much of that, and didn't like the idea of being locked into the turret if the ship got hit and was sinking. So very sheepishly I made an apologetic plea for any job at all but above deck, in the open—please!

The admiral told me since his flag lieutenant and aide had been transferred, he wanted me to try my hand at that. It promised to be an easy, fancy-Dan job. While at sea, I would be responsible to the admiral and his staff for the old man's signals, messages, and general communications. When in port I would be his social aide, checking visits and visitors, guiding other officers and commanders around, supervising gun salutes, and overseeing all other traditional courtesies from ship to ship. The admiral's senior aide was Chief of Staff Captain John Hall, a slow-talking, solemn, but gently humorous white-haired southerner. A fine senior officer, he was soon to be promoted to rear admiral. Next in the staff line was his flag secretary and aide, another but younger Annapolis graduate whose job was to supervise and help execute all the admiral's orders, plans, and operations. Then came me, flag lieutenant and aide. Aides had to drape their left shoulders with golden (looking) ropes that signified their responsibilities. When in more formal rig or full dress, we wore much fancier loops over the same left shoulder. For the first few days thus decked out, I thought I was pretty hot stuff until I realized the regulars paid less than no attention to anyone with such a junior and relatively unimportant staff job as flag lieutenant.

With the help of Hittle and Knowlton, I became accustomed to the new routine, made more and easier acquaintances, and was sometimes able to accompany my friends ashore to play touch football, soccer, or softball on one of the many playing fields on the treeless, bleak land. Sometimes we'd swap invitations with our opposite numbers on the British ships. We'd load their officers down with the fresh fruit and meat they couldn't get in exchange for their whiskey, gins, and wines that we, being dry, were not allowed.

To help kill such idle time as I occasionally had, I decided to do two things. I enrolled in a navy correspondence course in international law, and I also began to brush up my marksmanship by taking a refresher course in rifle and pistol shooting. After a few weeks of practice at a special range with some of our seagoing marine detachment, I took the official navy and marine shooting examinations. I was neither surprised nor disappointed when I failed my rifle marksmanship test (I was, in fact, better than I expected to be). What *did* surprise me and the marines was that I passed the arduous expert pistol shot test. This is not an honor that wins more than a superior sniff from the armed forces of other nations, but in our services it carries minor kudos. It means you are above average in the trained practical use of firearms and therefore more qualified than most to take care of yourself in close combat.

When at length I was formally presented with the bronze medal for pistol marksmanship and *instructed* to wear the dark blue ribbon with the two light green stripes on my uniform, I was outwardly self-mocking but privately very pleased. It made me feel I was getting beyond the oddball stage and becoming a real working naval officer. In fact, now that I had one American medal, I could wear the light blue ribbon and rosette of my Officer of the Order of the Southern Cross of Brazil decoration, awarded for diplomatic services on my trip to Latin America for FDR a year earlier. This caused a measure of real curiosity that I took pains to pass off airily.

Even Ike Giffen took notice and was warmer and jollier to me than usual. He went so far as to confide that he had some "exciting" plans in store for me—some "special duty" that he was sure I'd enjoy. I sensed by the way he spoke that I would not like it at all!

Chapter 3

ONE SATURDAY, shortly after inspection, I was following Admiral Giffen to his quarters above the bridge. We passed a very young sailor—no doubt a teenager just out of boot camp. He was sitting cross-legged on the deck, a cigarette dangling from his mouth and his round white cap plunked on the back of his head. As the admiral came by, he barely looked up, just going on with his polishing. The admiral stopped, looked at him disapprovingly, and barked, "Young man! How long have you been in the navy?"

The juvenile bluejacket, still with the butt dangling, still sitting cross-legged, answered, "Oh, let's see. About three months, I guess! How about you?"

The admiral, unprepared for such a question, barked back, *"Thirty-four years!"*

The boy shrugged and said, "It sure is hell, ain't it?"—and went back to his job.

Admiral Ike, bless him, did his poor best to stifle a guffaw and strode on, leaving it to me to instruct the boy in the proper military manner of answering an officer—particularly the big high-brass boss.

"Fairbanks!"

"Yes, sir!"

"I'll tell you what I've got in mind for you. The *Wasp,* a carrier here with our task force, has been delivering Spitfires and Hurricanes for the RAF down in Malta, in company with the British carrier HMS *Eagle*. They're having a helluva time there but are still holding off the bastards in spite of losses. So we're sending the *Wasp* down again to help those poor kids. My chief of staff, Captain Hall, is going down this time as my representative. I'm delegating my authority to him because I can't leave these waters now. I want you to go with him. You are to be his aide and responsible for checking on communications and gunnery operations. I know you don't know a helluva lot about either, but Captain Hall will give you your cues!" Giffen belly-laughed at his clever use of a theatrical term and went on. "Then the most important part—for you—is that I want you to write up the whole operation—every detail—in the form of a combined log report and history for the navy's official records—and mine too. I'll instruct the *Wasp*'s commander, Captain Jack Reeves, to assign you a battle station and a duty in the event of an attack or an action of any kind. That's all. Dismissed!"

My heartbeats were in a dead-heat race with the pounding in my brain as I tried to digest the full import of this. I did manage to get out a proper, "Aye, aye, sir, thank you, sir," and turn formally about face. I was leaving his quarters when he called me back.

"Oh, say, Fairbanks! One more thing—but keep it under your hat. If you come back safe—as I hope you will—and do well, I may send you on another job like this. I know you like lots of action, and perhaps I'll send you on one of the Russian convoys. You'll enjoy that!"

My mind went blank for a second before I could get out another "Aye, aye, sir" and leave in an orderly fashion. I had no idea of how to behave in the face of such a future. Me? *Like lots of action?* Who ever said that? Giffen had seen too many old movies—and, dammit all, had taken them seriously! I was glad that I'd joined up early and had luck so far in getting assignments that did not expose my insufficient training (some drill sessions and navigation and gunnery courses in California, where I'd passed the navy regulations exam by correspondence course). But I was not yet, even after my *Ludlow* and *Mississippi* adventures, mentally geared for real naval battle or "shooting to kill on purpose," as my marine chum Don Hittle called it.

Captain John Hall, my prospective boss and traveling partner, later warned me that the whole plan was still under the official canopy of "top secret," and I was not to mention it in *any way* to *anybody*. "No, sir. Of course not, sir! Aye, aye, sir!" I said nervously and went out on deck for some cold, foggy air.

One of the routine duties of an officer on board ship was taking turns censoring the men's outgoing mail. For unarguable reasons, no one was permitted to write about where they were, what they had been doing, or what they were probably going to do. Nor could there be hints of any kind—about prevailing weather conditions, for example—that could possibly be of interest to an enemy. Just before I left on this first of my "loan-out" expeditions, it was my turn to be one of the ship's mail censors.

It should be kept in mind that the time was late April 1942 and the draft board at home was, in its haste to build an enormous military force, beginning to scrape the bottom of the manpower barrel for recruits. Youngsters from factories and mines, from the backwoods and hills of Kentucky, West Virginia, and the Carolinas would claim to be nineteen when they were only sixteen or so. Those who joined the navy would be sent off to boot camp for a very few weeks of the basics of shipboard training and sent out to shore bases or to sea, aboard any kind of ship that was short of bodies. A surprising number of these kids were barely this side of illiteracy.

I surmised it was one of these beardless, pimple-faced kids whose letter was in the pile I had to go through and stamp "Approved" (or not, as the case might be). The scrap of lined paper on which he wrote appeared to have come from a notebook. The writing—if the tortured, barely legible scrawl could be so dignified—had been done with what must have been the stub of an old broken pencil. I also imagined his tongue tightly clenched between determined young teeth. His letter was addressed to his mother, somewhere back in the Appalachian Mountains. I was sure she looked like one of Al Capp's "Li'l Abner" comic-strip characters and had an illegal still where she turned out real old "firewater." I clearly remember it was a short missive, but to the point. It read: "Deer Mom—if only you knew where we was and what we was agoin' to do, you'd shit yerself—Love, Jake."

I knew just how he felt.

*   *   *

This gnat's-eye view of the Second World War makes no pretension to be a history per se. However, it was important for me then to refresh my knowledge of Malta as Britain's ancient island fortress, bang in the middle of the Mediterranean, which, along with Gibraltar at its western gateway, was a vital guardian of the sea lanes that were the shortest route to the Suez Canal and the Middle East. Staunch little Malta had often blocked German and Italian reinforcements on the way to North Africa. The Axis powers brought down upon Malta the wrath of Wotan, Thor, and Mars for good measure. It was a relentless effort.

During the first half of 1942, less than one third of all Allied cargo ships with food and supplies destined for Malta got through—and about one third of them were sunk in air raids while they were unloading in the harbor. Stevedores were reduced to ten ounces of bread a day. They had what fish they caught, but there was no meat, and no one had more than one square meal a day. Servicemen grew spindly crops wherever they could, in backyards or playgrounds. Somehow there were over two hundred thousand meals to be served to the shipyard and airfield workers daily. Everyone was to starve equally.

Malta-based British submarines suffered 50-percent losses in successfully helping to drive most of the Axis shipping from these waters. The RAF also suffered great losses. At one point in the spring of 1942, there were only five fighter planes left on the island's three airfields. Then the Royal Navy managed to muscle through a large convoy that was unsuccessfully challenged by the Nazi Luftwaffe and the Italian navy. As the dockyards were crippled, the Royal Navy's warships were obliged to make their main bases in Egypt and Gibraltar. The only ships that could now be spared from the Home Fleet in the North Atlantic or from the Indian Ocean and the Far East were two very aged, woefully out-of-date aircraft carriers, HMS *Argus* (soon to be sent elsewhere—and sunk) and *Eagle*. They reinforced the depleted air force on Malta just enough to bring down more than three dozen Luftwaffe attackers!

A request was now made at the highest level for the United States to lend a hand if possible. The sudden demands of our own almost mortally wounded Pacific Fleet at Pearl Harbor had obliged us to send as many ships as we could spare halfway around the world. But we did keep one carrier in Task Force 99, the USS *Wasp*. She and HMS *Eagle* were needed for a hazardous rescue trip with RAF reinforcements. Rommel had pushed the British back almost to Alexandria, the whole of North Africa had been strengthened with Germans, and the Allies desperately feared that it might fall within months or even weeks. Thus Churchill requested that we loan the *Wasp* for "just one more convoy" of RAF reinforcements in company with the *Eagle*. At the same time their own merchant and naval ships would bluster through with more supplies for both Malta and the Eighth Army in Egypt.

The evening before we were to leave Scapa Flow, I tagged dutifully in Captain Hall's wake as we came aboard the USS *Wasp*. I had never before been on an aircraft carrier. Although by today's standards it was only of moderate size or smaller, in the spring of 1942 it was very big indeed. The spaciousness of everything on this floating landing field and artillery platform was staggering. The men could play two touch football games end to end, each of regulation hundred-yard length, on the hangar deck. Impressive too were the very latest in precision instruments for communications, gunnery, and navigation, and the comfortable living appointments for officers and crew.

Nevertheless I was soon made aware that despite the proficiency of the ship's company, it was not a "happy ship." Even after accepting grumbling and bellyaching as time-honored naval customs, on the *Wasp* there was a special nervyness that even Captain Hall remarked upon. Was it the result of strain? Hard work? Anxiety? He couldn't tell right away.

According to my log report/journal, we were under way the next morning by 0900 and, hugging the west coast of Scotland, proceeded slowly down toward the estuary of the River Clyde. En route, Captain Jack Reeves, the *Wasp*'s commander, ordered radar-controlled gunnery practice against destroyer-towed targets. Later a group of planes practiced flight-deck takeoffs, and after some exercises at twenty thousand feet, landed perilously back on board. Then another group went through the same routine. I could not help but think these fliers must have been hard up for excitement to choose that job.

The next day, within minutes of our being wharfed alongside the giant King George V dock in Glasgow, the business of inspecting and loading RAF Spitfire aircraft aboard began, lowering them by elevators to be stored on the hangar deck.

Captain Reeves, via Captain Hall, asked me if I would think up some sort of entertainment to amuse the thousands of sailors and airmen who would be forbidden to go ashore again after the first two or three days in Glasgow. I had not so much as a flicker of an idea, as I didn't think I knew any entertainers in Scotland. Then suddenly I recalled *Rulers of the Sea,* the movie I'd made in mid-1939 when Mary Lee and I were getting married in California. Much of the film's setting had been a mock-up of the mid-Victorian shipyards in Greenock, a Clydeside ship-building suburb downstream from Glasgow where the first transatlantic steamship was built. One of the costars, along with Maggie Lockwood, was the great Scottish music hall entertainer Will Fyffe. But how to find him now? I hadn't a clue!

Once ashore, I made for the Central Hotel—a large grubby-looking place outside, but *inside!* (I had last stayed there when touring in *The Winding Journey* with Gertrude Lawrence in the early thirties.) The railway company that owned this hotel had kept it marvelously comfortable in dark, overstuffed Victorian luxury. I was recognized immediately—which was helpful—and was made heartily welcome in warm, plaintive Glaswegian accents.

I quickly enlisted the happy help of the old hall porter and telephone switchboard operator. "Where and how," I asked, "can I reach Will Fyffe?"

"Well, he doesn't live in Glasgow," they told me, but they would try to track him down.

How they did it, I never knew. Will's astonishment at hearing my voice an hour or so later was understandable. "Will," I said, "I want you to do me a great favor—and regulations forbid me to tell you *what* over the phone."

"Anything for you, laddy boy!" answered the roly-poly Scot. "Just name it."

"Can you come to Glasgow as soon as you can and stay one night at the Central? *Please!"*

"I'll get me bag and take the next train!"

Three or four hours later, in he rolled, preceded by his red-veined bulbous nose. After a warm embrace I explained about the ship I was on and why we were here. I then told him we had no movable piano or stage or anything—but a very great number of American sailors and marines and RAF airmen were stuck on the ship with no more leaves or liberty allowed. It wasn't necessary to explain their need to forget the strains they lived under, or that Will was just the guy to help out.

With nary a question more, he turned his bag over to the hall porter, grabbed my arm, and said, "Let's go, Duggie boy!"

I suppose well over two thousand men were assembled that evening on the hangar deck. Although only a very few of the Americans had ever heard of Will, I, as a sort of master of ceremonies, explained over a loudspeaker as much as I could about him and told them that with no accompaniment, he was at a big disadvantage. Thereupon old Will waddled on, took my microphone, and began telling Scottish stories, singing a great number of old and new songs (with no backup music), and kept the boys laughing, singing, and cheering for two or three hours!

After hearty thanks from all the senior officers, I was allowed ashore again in order to escort him back to the hotel. We had a couple of very stiff neat tumblers of the "wine of the country" (Will always called whiskey by its original Scottish name of *usquebaugh*) and parted. I never saw him again. He died later during the war, up in his Highland home. But what a dear memory he left to all the "bra young Yankee laddies!"

The following notes and comments have been excerpted from both my journal and my special report for Admiral Giffen, courtesy of the U.S. Naval Historical Records Section:

May 2, 1942.
    This was an active day. The early morning hummed with the exciting ship noises that go with preparations for getting underway. More incredibly young RAF boys came aboard. They appeared to feel strange in their new surroundings, not quite knowing what to do or where to go. It was difficult to get around the hangar deck by now as it was crammed with our own Grumman fighters and all the Spitfires. Every available space on the large ship was taken up.
    As the morning progressed the tempo quickened. Communications

officers checked over last-minute reports and decoded Navy
Department messages from Washington. Instructions were issued to
each division of the ship. Bluejackets and Marines scurried on the
double from place to place. Extra equipment reached the gangplank
at the last minute. Finally, with the arrival of the harbor pilot,
everything was squared away and we shoved off.

The land looked very inviting as it passed by us. The sun was
warm and bright, the fields a rich springtime green, and except for
the dockyards cradling warlike hulks and the occasional rows of
debris that had been people's houses before the blitz, the scene was
peaceful. We were all acutely aware of our situation and wondered
wistfully how long it would be before we would see green fields
again.

Later we dropped anchor and I was sent ashore with the navigator
and the communications officer to a British Naval Headquarters
building called Bagatello. There we were ushered into a private office
where every detail of our operation—now given the code name "Bowery"—was discussed thoroughly. The British carrier HMS *Eagle* would
wait for us at Gibraltar and then join us at a specially appointed
"fly-off" position. She was to launch her nearly twenty RAF aircraft
at the same time that we would launch our approximately fifty planes.

Our orders now were to pass out through the boom in the entrance
to the Clyde the next morning (May 3) at 0500. Passing down by the
east coast of Ireland, we would proceed out to sea, making a good 16.5
knots until we reached the first point assigned at 1800 on the evening
of May 6.

We would then be joined by an escort consisting of the battle
cruiser HMS *Renown,* the antiaircraft cruiser HMS *Charybdis,* and four
more escorting Royal Navy destroyers. These would be in addition to
four U.S. Navy destroyers. In the event of hostile aircraft over the
British Isles while we were still in adjacent waters, we would be
protected by fighter planes up to forty miles out to sea.

At last we finished our conference. The British officers on the staff
thanked us, wished us luck, and said that if we got away with it, this
operation might very well help turn the trick in the Battle of Malta. . . .
We were gratified this evening to see some of the new "floater

nets" the British use on their carriers brought aboard. They are designed for those who may be in the water without a belt or lifeboat and keep a great number afloat until they can be picked up. Many of the aircraft innovations, such as the slanted deck and other aids to launching and landing, were passed on to us by the British; some were said to have been invented by Mountbatten.

This was the eve of another great adventure, for me at any rate. For most others, it was routine. But for good or bad, Operation Bowery was under way.

I felt very old compared to these easygoing kids getting ready to have another go at the enemy. I was thirty-two, but the RAF pilots' ages ranged from eighteen to twenty-two—and yet they were in so many ways, suddenly and understandably, much older.

Most of them, when they heard the likes of me was aboard, began to stare, some with pleasure and some as if I were a mannequin, dressed up in uniform for fun or a recruiting film. Captain Reeves most emphatically did not approve of my autographing things for the airmen, but we managed to sneak a few, here and there. As a matter of fact, the captain apparently felt that I had been altogether too conspicuous aboard, and though I had been stiffly thanked for getting Will Fyffe to perform, he now decided to ridicule me in his sharp voice. It reminded me of the irritating, high-pitched voice of the violent-tempered director of my early Hollywood days, Herbert Brenon. Once I was given a dressing down because I had let a bit of white handkerchief peek out of my breast pocket. Of course it was a minor bit of irregular dandyism that I noticed some of our senior officers— and almost *all* Allied officers—indulged in. I was loudly rebuked for not knowing the uniform regulations strictly forbid such eccentricities—particularly by junior officers. I blushed and stumbled over apologies and admissions of ignorance. Needless to say, I tucked the hanky deep inside the pocket and took care not to let any senior brass-hat martinet catch me being irregular again.

This firsthand experience with Black Jack was, I was told, very mild—for him! Only the day before he had flown into a honking rage, all wings flapping, because he had not heard some poor bluejacket at the other end of the ship's phone to the engine room call him "Sir" when replying to him. Two regular officers on the bridge at the time assured the shrill skipper that *they* had heard the boy's respectful "Sir," but Captain Reeves apparently grew angrier at these incipient rebels. He then, so the tale was told, ordered the nameless bluejacket to the brig in solitary confinement and limited him to bread and water for three days on the charge of "insubordination." Nevertheless, in spite of these excessive displays of terrible temper, he was a fine, courageous, and knowledgeable big-ship captain.

But Captain Hall's original feeling that the ship was an unhappy one was being rapidly confirmed. If Captain Reeves was not exactly a prototype of Captain Bligh of the *Bounty,* he at least reminded many of his own subordinates of that notorious figure. Reeves was not called Black Jack for nothing.

There followed days of steady but nervy going. The ship's air officer, a Commander Kernodle, had a heavy face that disguised an easy amiability. He barely tolerated my early tactlessness in making fun of his name, but as soon as I learned my place, we got on very well.

I discovered that the senior medical officer aboard was a reservist with the rank of captain who had been a psychiatrist in civilian life. No harm in that, except that on our fourth day at sea, one of our bluejackets came down with appendicitis. There were four or five other medical officers of lesser rank aboard, and two were surgeons; therefore one of them prepared for an emergency operation. However, the senior medical officer insisted that his captain's four-stripe rank entitled him to decide on all medical and surgical matters aboard. Even though he hadn't touched a scalpel since his medical school days, he decided it was not, after all, a very complicated operation, so he would perform it himself. The young surgeons were horrified but powerless to alter the navy's regulations governing such matters. The senior medical brass hat went ahead. Happily, all turned out well, but I, the nautical neophyte, planned to "protest" in the body of my report and journal. Unfortunately, I was subsequently ordered to delete any serious criticisms of anything from my report—though I could make "unofficial" comments privately. "Do your job and don't reform the navy! It's been doing okay for a long time without your help." I had no argument to that.

I could, however, record one breach of proper behavior that delighted all except Captain Black Jack. Four of our group of destroyer screen were British. One of these was being commanded by a young lieutenant whose very first seagoing command it was. During our voyage it was laid down in the plans that at certain times a signal would be given from the *Wasp*'s bridge, or later from the flagship, *Renown,* ordering the group to "zig" a certain number of degrees to port or starboard, at such and such a speed. Then, after a prescribed time, we would be ordered to "zag" in another direction, and so on. At this particular time, Captain Reeves ordered the group to prepare to follow a new course and speed immediately on seeing our flag signal. At the signal we and most of the screen turned one way, but this poor benighted British destroyer and its virgin skipper did just the opposite! The result was that he barely avoided being ripped by our enormous sharp bow, moving at a fast pace. On the bridge, Captain Reeves was fit to be tied. He raged and shouted his deprecatory views of Royal Navy training, especially that of destroyer (tin can) commanders. He immediately ordered his signalman on the bridge to flash a light signal to the errant limey. "WHAT ARE YOUR INTENTIONS NOW?"

A few seconds later we received a flashed reply: "BUY MYSELF A BLACK BOWLER HAT AND A FARM!" Everyone laughed, except of course our skipper, who ordered a formal protest and an entry in the logbook.

My notes compared plane launchings to small birds being shoved from their nests and trying their wings. The landings were dangerous and required split-second decisions and great expertise. These were further dramatized by all the colors worn designating different job functions. The aircraft landings and the main arresting cables stretched across the flight deck made me think of so many gigantic bees, with stingers extended, being caught in a weird spider's web.

In another day or so, the once calm sea kicked up a gigantic row. The long, skinny tin cans were rolling and plunging and taking it "green" over their bows. Still, it was not considered rough enough to alter ship's routines. Almost nothing was left unrehearsed. A deciphered Admiralty signal from London advised us that at least three enemy submarines were known to be in our area. We had a "plot board" with an ever-increasing number of different-colored pins indicating the latest sightings of enemy ships. We therefore altered course and speed a few extra times; the rolling sea and strong winds made any visual sightings unlikely.

I was no more immune to fear than anyone else—maybe less so because of my active imagination. There is in warfare the ever-present risk of a contagion of nerves. I wasn't really frightened yet, but I was certainly aware of what could happen. I was damned glad I was not one of the fliers—particularly one of those boys who had never flown from or even been on an aircraft carrier before. I found I was rather embarrassed, even when quite alone, in my stumbling experiments with prayer, or doing things I wouldn't admit to afterward, like taking my little wallet of pictures of Mary Lee and Daphne out of my room and putting them securely in an inside pocket. The sea may by then have calmed a bit, but we had not.

We received new orders that altered our times for entering and leaving the Straits of Gibraltar, the new times and positions when we would be joined by the flagship HMS *Renown* and the old Royal Navy aircraft carrier HMS *Eagle*. New courses and times for fly-off positions were outlined as well. Then, when all assignments for Operation Bowery were completed, we were told how and when to get the hell out of the way.

The enemy carried out meteorological surveys twice daily from Sardinia and North Africa, and there were now estimated to be roughly eight hundred German and Italian aircraft based on Sicily, concentrating on nearly constant bombing of Malta. These attacks were augmented by naval raiders and very fast Italian motor torpedo boats (similar to our PTs).

We began to feel as if we were an "air force supply ship"—a seagoing delivery wagon—and some expressed the view that the risks to be taken with such a fine ship were greater than the reasons for our being there.

On the evening of May 6 we received a communiqué that our forces had surrendered to the Japanese at Corregidor in the Philippines. However much this defeat had been expected, it nevertheless made for deeply sobering news. MacArthur, it appeared, had been caught unprepared despite repeated warnings after Pearl Harbor, but he, his family, and his staff had escaped in a squadron of PT boats, heading for Australia. This blow forced us to put aside our own trepidation as we thought of the fate of thousands of our comrades on the other side of the globe at that very moment.

As we drew nearer to Gibraltar, our senior tin-can escort, HMS *Westcott,* advised us that the increasingly heavy seas made the going ever more difficult as they were being engulfed with every new plunge. We too in our huge ship rolled and pitched, though more slowly and evenly. Everything—aircraft and anything else movable on or belowdecks—had to be battened down. Nothing manmade was usable—only the men themselves. Ourselves.

Surprisingly, I wasn't in the least seasick. In spite of wearing foul-weather gear, I was sopping wet but feeling rather elated. I suppose I just wasn't frightened enough then. The lookouts reported sighting land off to our port side, and I realized we were getting nearer to the legendary Rock of Gibraltar—that over there was Cape St. Vincent. And there was Cádiz! Disregarding the discomfort of our ploughing airport, I got a historic thrill out of the realization that here we were just off Trafalgar! Here was where the great, immortal Nelson defeated the Napoleonic and allied fleets in one of history's greatest and most decisive sea battles—and here the great admiral himself was killed by a French Marine sniper's bullet. As my few duties were completed for now, I restaged that great event in my imagination. My wet reverie was ended by the captain barking at me. *"For Christ's sake, Fairbanks, if you've got nothing to do, get the hell off the bridge and out of the way!"* I mustered a hoarse "Aye, aye, sir!" and slithered somewhere well out of sight.

Finally, as dusk lowered upon our section of Operation Bowery, we were ordered to maintain absolute radio silence unless there was an emergency. An RAF patrol bomber that had been scouting for us in big sweeps was now heading back to base and blinking a good luck signal. He flew over us, dipped his wings in salute, and continued on his way home.

Darkness hid us at last. The seas were still advancing like lines of white-plumed cavalry as we approached the Straits of Gibraltar, and on our starboard beam there were the fabled Pillars of Hercules on the Moroccan coast. We took our first fix from the navigational lights burning on the Spanish mainland. Soon we saw the lights of Tangier.

The damp, eerie night helped us sneak through the narrow straits

to the Mediterranean, the Phoenicians' "holy water." Didn't the phar-
aohs' galleys push through this same watery defile and circumnavigate
the barbarous, misty isles in the north? Here it was, the fabled sea of
pirates and conquerors, philosophers and martyrs for Christ and
Muhammad. And here we were, the newest threads in the vast pattern
of history's tapestry.

Once past Europa Point, shortly after midnight on May 8, we
resumed our normal speed of eighteen knots and recommenced our
zigzag patterns. The sea moderated by daylight (by then I'd had a
good solid two and a half hours of sleep) and we could see the
mountainous coast of Spain, almost twenty miles away through the
haze. The hardy old HMS *Eagle* had joined up with us before dawn
and had taken her position astern. When all was in order, a message
was blinkered over to us: "FROM HMS EAGLE TO USS WASP: THE AGING
LADY LOOKS WITH ENVIOUS EYES AT HER SMART YOUNGER COUSIN AND
SENDS HER GREETINGS AND BEST WISHES."

To which Captain Reeves promptly replied: "THANK YOU. THERE
SEEMS TO BE PLENTY OF LIFE IN THE OLD GIRL YET IF I MAY SAY SO."

Now all eight destroyers were in line, ahead of the antiaircraft
cruiser HMS *Charybdis*. Directly behind in single file came the flagship
HMS *Renown* (which would give all the fly-off orders), then us, and
then the *Eagle*.

I had done my stint in the communications room, my watch on the
bridge, and had no more to do in gunnery, so I preferred to be topside.
When pandemonium began, I wanted to be well in the clear. I worried
about being late and locked behind damage-control doors below,
trapped in the damned ship as she went down. I squeezed my way up
to my gun-control battle station, and with my old tin hat on (like
everyone else), waited.

Now for the moment there was tension, but my dog-watch time-
passing game of humming words to old songs with no stopping
wouldn't work in daytime when everyone could see. Although I now
worked on the navy's correspondence course in international law
whenever I could, this was not the time to find refuge in technical
international legal questions either. Later, when things quieted down,
I could read from one of the three big paperback books that I took
with me from my first sea duty onward: the Bible, *A Complete Shake-*

Just six months before Pearl Harbor, Douglas Fairbanks, Jr., played dueling, swashbuckling twins with Ruth Warrick in *The Corsican Brothers* (1941).

With Franklin Roosevelt, Jr. (left) at the Boston Navy Yard Naval Headquarters, Fairbanks is given his orders to go to sea in the spring of 1941.

As a lieutenant (junior grade), Fairbanks served aboard the battleship USS *Washington* and the cruiser, USS *Wichita*.

Sent on a special mission to Malta, Fairbanks saw action aboard the aircraft carrier USS *Wasp*.

With Commander Kernodle (middle) and an RN officer in the chartroom of the *Wasp*, Fairbanks charts the course on the way to Malta in May of 1942.

Slews of RAF planes were taken to Malta aboard the same *Wasp*.

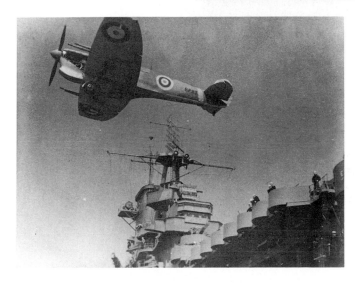

As sailors watch, an RAF fighter takes off from the USS *Wasp*.

On temporary leave, Fairbanks rejoices with his daughter Daphne.

Fairbanks relaxes with Jack Watson, his staff communications officer, during the Beach Jumper landings in the south of France, June 1944.

In his naval uniform, Fairbanks was still suave and debonair.

Fairbanks received a series of commendations for his efforts in the war. Here, he is receiving the Legion of Merit with bronze *V* (for valor) attachment.

Fairbanks stands with U.S. Ambassador to Italy James C. Dunn (right) after having received the Italian War Cross for Military Valor.

In a ceremony on April 12, 1945, French Vice Admiral Raymond Fenard presents Lt. Cmdr. Douglas E. Fairbanks, Jr., with the Legion d'Honneur and the Croix de Guerre with palm for his part in the amphibious assault on southern France.

Lord Halifax, the British ambassador in Washington (left), awards Fairbanks the Distinguished Service Cross.

Back in Beverly Hills after the war, Fairbanks kisses step-mother Mary Pickford.

When the hero returns at the war's end, Douglas and Mary Lee were the parents of two daughters—Daphne, born in 1940, and Victoria, born in 1943.

speare, and *A Complete Sherlock Holmes.* For now I couldn't concentrate enough even to frame a note in my head to Foo, but I found solace in planning one.

May 9, 1942.
. . . the ship began to bustle with lightless activity by 0430. In the wardroom below many "Good lucks" and "Happy landings" passed between our ship's young pilots and the RAF boys. We all felt a nervous exhilaration. So much would depend on how things went in the next few hours.

By 0530 the men were at flight quarters and gun stations—waiting. Up on the bridge, at air control, and topside, men moved about in the busy blackness, feeling their way by memory and instinct. Weather reports from Malta were confusing, doing nothing for the air officer's confidence. There was very little wind, and it was hot, muggy, and still. There was barely enough light to see our USN Grummans and the RAF Spitfires silhouetted ominously against the deep purple of earliest dawn. Their propellers were like swords set belligerently skyward at weird angles. As we came closer to takeoff time, every pilot was in his cockpit. The plan was that twelve U.S. Navy fighters would take off first and patrol the skies during the launching of the RAF Spitfires. Then a dozen or more Spits were to take off at intervals of twenty seconds. When the deck was clear of these, more Spits would be brought up, one at a time, via the after elevator. Then the last group would come up and be spotted for takeoff. There would be about fifty takeoffs in all.

It is harder for Spitfires to take off than naval planes as they are designed for longer runways. Also RAF pilots are not trained for carrier techniques, which are at best difficult and hazardous. To improve the headwinds for takeoff, both carriers increased speed.

At 0605 our radar picked up a plane some twenty-two miles away. We were too far from Gibraltar by now for it to be British, and we prayed that in the dark cloudy dawn he would pass us by. He did. Nevertheless we took no chances and the air officer ordered our Grummans to warm up their motors. The navigator took sights on the few stars that could still be found and announced that we were approaching our launching point. By a stroke of good luck our added speed was assisted by a slight twelve-knot natural breeze. At 0618 both carriers were ordered to keep heading directly into the wind.

At 0623 through the loudspeaker bull horns came the bos'n's pipe, followed by "Now hear this! Stand by to launch planes!" Shipboard crews unlashed the wing lines and pulled the wheel chucks from beneath our Navy Grummans. The red warning flag was flying from our Air Control Bridge. Exactly at 0630, with only a fair westerly wind whipping inconsistently over our bow, the white "GO" flag was substituted for the warning red and the order "LAUNCH PLANES" rang out. One at a time, a dozen of our protective Grummans roared deafeningly down the deck and were off and up with defiant majesty.

Then came the Spitfires' acting squadron leader, twenty-one-year-old Flight Lieutenant R. H. Sly of Sydney, Australia. His motor was revved up, and at 0636 he was flagged to take off. The smooth powerful hum of his Rolls-Royce engine took him down the flight deck and out to sea. Eleven of his air mates followed in rapid succession. We held our breaths with each launching. The slight wobbling of the planes as they left the runway confessed their inexperience. The *Eagle,* running along the prearranged course of three miles off our starboard quarter, began launching her aircraft at 0640. Our second group of Spits began their shaky ascent at about 0645.

One of this latter number apparently was not getting full power from his engine because when he started his run, it was obvious that he was not going to realize sufficient flying speed to lift off. The pilot seemed to know this too, because he appeared to change his mind two or three times on the way down the deck. First he applied his brakes and then released them again as if he still hoped to get up enough speed. As he passed the bridge, all hearts bumped. He didn't seem to be going more than thirty knots. He began to weave to the port side of the ship, unable to make up his mind. These brief moments presaged inevitable disaster in slow motion. Then the worst happened. Again he gave full throttle, but it was too late. He rolled right up to the end of the flight deck and dribbled off the bow and into the sea. As it fell, the plane turned over on its back, breaking off a wing. Our relentless ship rammed it squarely in the middle, driving its two halves and its pilot down beneath us.

There was a loud blast on the emergency signal from the bridge, and the ship swung first hard right and then hard left, hoping to clear the Spitfire. No use. After we passed over the spot where the plane had fallen in, we looked astern for some sign of something. But there

was nothing. Just the dark blue Mediterranean, irritated only by our
wake.

A destroyer, H.M.S. *Partridge,* immediately went to the spot in the
hope of rescuing the pilot. She circled around for some minutes but
reported only minor bits of wreckage coming to the surface. We
knew nothing beyond the RAF pilot's name and rank as his records
had gone on ahead to Malta by ship.

Now the command from the bridge was given: "Continue to
launch planes." Faces were sheet white, but the job continued without
respite. Flag hoists and blinker signals passed between ships while
they rejockeyed their positions into the wind. Soon the second twelve
of the first twenty-four planes were off and were getting into flying
formation before heading eastward for the hell of Malta.

Then the second half was signaled off. These last twenty-four got
off without incident—some, of course, showing more assurance in
their piloting than others. The officers on the bridge and the entire
ship's company topside had been shouting and cheering each plane as
it took off, much like football fans.

The last Spitfires had left both the *Eagle* and the *Wasp* by 0730.
Then we spotted two lone Spitfires still circling the ship. As the last
group headed off, one of these two stragglers fell in with it. He had
apparently lost his bearings and had waited to rejoin another
formation. The second Spitfire signaled that he had lost his spare fuel
tank and needed to land. We had been forewarned of the probability
of such an accident. Word was passed from the bridge to air control
and then through the bull horns to "Clear the flight
deck!—firefighters, get ready!—start pumps on fire hoses!—prepare for
a crash landing!"

A Spitfire, naturally a fast-landing aircraft, has no tail hook to catch the
cables on a carrier flight deck. Nor could one be fitted on as she is
simply not built for this special type of landing. Besides, a novice is
not expected to land properly, or even safely, on the deck of a carrier. For this particular pilot, the loss of his extra fuel tank made
it impossible for him to reach either Malta or Gibraltar, and the
African coast would have invited internment. He would therefore
either have to ditch his plane and bail out in his parachute, hoping
to get picked up out of the drink by a destroyer, or try to save his air-

craft by landing her intact. Pilot Officer Smith, RAF, chose the latter course.

(May 9, continued)

The medical corpsmen down in sick bay hurriedly prepared for whatever they could. Our navigator, himself a veteran pilot, said he preferred not to watch as the boy had only one chance in twenty of making it. The whole ship became utterly resigned to another awful accident.

In a few moments all was set as the landing signal officer stood at the end of the flight deck with his two little red and white flags. He signaled Smith to land. Smith came around, low and fast. The LSO waved his flags in an effort to make him go higher. The Spit was coming in so low, in fact no higher than the fantail, that it appeared he would crash into our stern. The nose of a Spitfire is long and high, and it was therefore impossible for the pilot to see the deck clearly from his angle. Closer and closer in split seconds he came, until at the last moment he caught sight of the flags, which by now were frantically signaling him to fly off–to keep going. Like a sudden roll of thunder, the Spit's engine answered the throttle as the pilot swerved his plane hard to the left. His wing nearly scraped the edge of the flight deck as he zoomed up and off. The LSO had to jump into his net off the deck's side to avoid being hit.

Smith circled again and again got into position to land. The initial relief was not enough for those on board to relax. No one could move. No one could talk. But this time the plane came in at a perfect height, though at about ninety knots, a bit fast. Finally he set his craft down. He was quite a way forward of the spot he should have used, but it was a perfect landing. His speed, however, was still so great that although he used his brakes immediately, they failed to do more than check him momentarily. He continued to roll on. He released and reapplied his brakes and slowed himself a little more. But still the plane moved inexorably to the end of the deck. About fifteen feet–no more–this side of eternity, Smith brought the plane to a stop.

There was a second's hush; then a great cheer went up from all hands. Men whistled, applauded, and shouted their delight at this great handling of a plane under impossible conditions. Young Smith (he is only twenty) was taken up to Captain Reeves right away. He seemed quite unshaken and only wanted to have an extra tank put on so that he could get off and rejoin his mates immediately. A message from the commodore on the *Renown* approved the spirit but disapproved the request. Smith was "to stay and live to fight another day." We are to fly him off for Gibraltar in the morning. Wherever he went on the ship the rest of the day he was applauded and congratulated—all of which only made him blush a deep scarlet. He confessed to being "a bit jittery," but he was in good spirits and well under control.

Our fighter planes returned a little before 0800. One Spitfire radioed back asking for an emergency homing signal as he was lost, but due to security precautions we could not do this over the air. We heard no more from him.

By now we had turned and were headed back for Gibraltar. The old *Eagle* summoned up some last reserve of hidden power and stayed puffing and panting along with us at twenty-two knots. Sometimes she would fall a bit behind, but she would make it up by cutting the corners of one zig and the next zag. "She's too proud to give in," said Commander Kernodle.

At about 2400 hours, we received our first word from Malta on the Spits—via the *Renown:* "FIRST THREE FLIGHTS LANDED AT 1010 WHILE BIG RAID WAS ON. EXPECT TO HEAR OF REMAINDER LATER." We did: "ALL GROUPS OF SPITFIRES HAVE NOW ARRIVED MALTA. THEY HAVE BEEN REFUELED AND WERE IN ACTION WITHIN THIRTY-FIVE MINUTES OF LANDING. FIRST CASUALTIES COUNT NOT YET POSSIBLE."

In respect to Operation Bowery—so far, so good.

Ship's routine returned to near normal. In the wardroom after the evening meal the USN landing signal officer made a short speech honoring Pilot Officer Smith, RAF. According to aircraft carrier tradition, the ship's band, led by two men with signaling flags, marched around the room. Smith was presented with a special cake, baked in his honor, and our air officer, Commander Kernodle, presented Smith with an honorary pair of U.S. Naval Wings for being "the first pilot within memory to successfully land a Spitfire on a carrier."

May 10, 1942.

A signal came through that six Swordfish planes from the Royal Navy's Fleet Air Arm would fly aboard from Gibraltar at 0815 this morning. They would take some guns and equipment for the

Spitfires, a few members of the ground crew, and mail. Smith and his Spitfire, with a new extra fuel tank attached, would take off with the Swordfishes for Gibraltar and go on to Malta later. (Smith was secretly glad of this. He did not want to go back home just yet because he had been warned of a possible court-martial for some low flying over a city and he hoped to stay away long enough for the misdeed to wear off.)

We passed the "Rock" at 0420. There was no moon at all. Just a star-speckled sky and a warm clear predawn. The African shore was lit up as before. The "Rock" was silhouetted by the lights of Algeciras and La Linia.

In the morning as soon as it was light enough for signals, the commanding admiral on H.M.S. *Renown* passed on all the news from Malta. Apparently an almost continuous air battle had been in progress since the first Spitfires arrived over the island. They had refueled and returned to battle many times during the day. In addition to the mishaps on the *Wasp,* there were a few other aircraft that never reached their destinations; one force-landed somewhere in North Africa where the pilot was interned; another plunked into the sea off Malta—presumably shot down en route—and one more was just unaccounted for. In the day's battle, thirty enemy planes were shot down or so damaged that they had to land and surrender, as against the shooting down of three Spitfires. Not a bad score—ten to one (official) for us. The RAF commander on Malta added to the message: *"We are most grateful to you all!"* We wondered which of our former shipmates were the unlucky ones—the cocky blond, curly-haired pilot or the rosy-cheeked fellow who admitted he was scared and didn't want to go.

The brightest event of all the next day was a message—again passed on by the *Renown*—from London. It read: "From the Prime Minister to the captain and ship's company of the U.S.S. *Wasp*: Many thanks to you all for the timely help. Who said a wasp couldn't sting twice? [signed] Winston Churchill."

In the late twilight on May 14 the Scottish shore hove into sight. We wove between large and small islands. Great tufts of clouds hung like loose white wigs on the friendly Highland hills. It was a most welcome green-gray sight. The men of our special sea detail were ordered to "drop the hook" at 0855, the morning of May 15. At Scapa Flow crazily painted naval ships of all kinds lugged barrage balloons waving high above to dissuade low-flying enemy attacks. Operation Bowery was completed. Captain Hall and I requested and received permission to leave the *Wasp* and rejoin the *Washington* in Reykjavík.

Within the next month or so the USS *Wasp* was detached from Task Force 99 and sent out to the Pacific to help flesh out our depleted power there. Air Officer Commander Kernodle was promoted and succeeded Captain "Black Jack" Reeves as skipper. Soon after her arrival the gallant *Wasp* was mortally wounded by a Japanese kamikaze and sank into the South Pacific. Captain Kernodle was picked up from the water and months later received the navy's highest combat award (after the Congressional Medal of Honor), the Navy Cross, for "conspicuous bravery under fire."

HMS *Eagle* was to make only one more trip to Malta. She got there in good order, but just as she launched her last plane she was attacked with torpedoes by enemy subs and bombed by enemy aircraft. The report stated that the old gal settled bravely but wearily down into the sea, her guns still firing on her killers. We knew she would never give in easily.

I had the beginnings of a bad cold when we dropped anchor back in Iceland and I was not happy to be sent ashore by the admiral to deliver and collect classified documents from our headquarters in Reykjavík. While there I saw a Navy Department bulletin announcing that ensigns, lieutenants (junior grade), and full lieutenants with certain registered numbers were to be automatically promoted to the next highest rank. To my happy surprise I found I was soon to be a full lieutenant, the equivalent of a captain in the marines or army. Despite the fact that it reminded me of Wellington's feeling about the Order of the Garter—"there's no damn merit about it"—I was almost childishly gratified. I now ranked the same as Bob Montgomery, who I'd heard had got a rare spot promotion to go with his headquarters job.

Another morale booster was the announcement that in a month or two the issuance of what was called the American Defense, or Pre–Pearl Harbor Active Duty Medal, would be given to those who were on active duty prior to our formal entry into the wars against Japan, Germany, and Italy. For those of us who had seen service in the embattled but unofficial war in the North Atlantic during this period, a small bronze *A* attached to the ribbon was also authorized.

This news helped me to forget my cold, and my usually enchained

emotions broke loose as I picked up the huge bundle of letters awaiting me. Best of all were the accumulated daily reports from Foo about
herself and Daphne, both well and as content as they could be in that
Hot Springs mountain air at Boxwood Farm. Mary Lee reported she
was now getting "way out to here," and loving that another baby was
on the way. She reported meeting old Mrs. Cornelius Vanderbilt (an
eccentric grande dame dowager if ever there was one) one day at the
elegant resort hotel the Homestead, a mile or so from the farm. The
old lady had noticed Mary Lee's increasingly conspicuous bulge. She
smiled knowingly and, clucking her sympathy, asked how and where
her husband was and how long he had been away. Foo, meaning to
boast of my prewar service, replied proudly, "Oh, he went to sea over
a year ago—months before Pearl Harbor!" The old lady's jaw slacked
and she mumbled haughtily, "You poor dear . . ." and bustled off
before Mary Lee caught on and could correct her misimpression!

A note from Larry O. reported that he'd heard Bob Montgomery
had been promoted and was returning stateside. He echoed my earlier
confidential complaint that Bob had got inexplicably pompous and
indescribably stuffy. He wondered if his headquarters job had gone to
his head. The mail from California contained news that old "Coop"
(Gary Cooper) had found an elephant painted pink in his dressing
room . . . Freddy March and Bob Taylor were joined by Bill Saroyan
in some sort of deviltry . . . Duke Wayne was about to start a new war
picture, and Errol Flynn was still daring the devil all over the place.
I was pleased they were all well but a bit jealous that they were getting
the pick of all the fat parts in the new pictures. I consoled myself with
the thought that even if I wasn't leading the U.S. fleet to glorious
victory or smashing Jerry all by myself, I was at least where I had
finagled my way on my own and doing what I'd planned to do.

Back on the USS *Washington,* I dove into paperwork—the admiral's
personal and official business, my report-cum-journal for the admiral,
my (so-called) correspondence course in international law—and returned to my other regular staff duties aboard ship. I also wrote a
not-too-subtle letter to Dickie Mountbatten, reminding him, as best I
could within the limits of censorship, where I was ("ask the staff in
Grosvenor Square and I'm sure they could find me"). I went on to say
in a transparently casual manner that I had heard he had a few

American officers attached to his Combined Operations Command and perhaps one day it might be my good luck to be transferred and join them. I reasoned that at worst he wouldn't ask for me; or, if he did, Admiral Stark in London or Admiral Giffen in Scapa Flow would refuse to let me go.

From my journal-diary, June 7, 1942, Scapa Flow:
   Although for obvious security reasons nothing had been announced beforehand, the King [George VI] flew up to Scapa Flow this morning to visit and inspect the principal units of his Home Fleet and our U.S.S. *Washington,* the flagship of U.S. Task Force 99.
   He was received with as much traditional naval ceremony as wartime conditions in a vulnerable base allowed—twenty-one guns fired salutes from each of the capital ships, appropriate signal flags were flown, and sailors lined the rails. When the time came for him to come aboard the *Washington,* he was piped on by a chorus of bos'n's mates, greeted by a U.S. Marine Guard of Honor and the ship's band playing "Ruffles and Flourishes," followed by both "The Star-Spangled Banner" and "God Save the King." At the same time the Royal Standard was broken out, and the White Ensign of the Royal Navy was hoisted beside the Stars and Stripes. It was an impressive moment. The day was bitter drizzly, but H.M. (as the British nicknamed His Majesty) went on a long tour of the ship without an overcoat. We, therefore, dispensed with ours.
   I was lined up with Admiral Giffen's other staff officers, last according to my still lowly official rank. As the King came down the line, he suddenly recognized me, stopped, and smilingly held out his hand, saying, "Well, what are *you* doing up here? I've not seen you since we played golf at Sunningdale about five years ago!" As the ship's photographer snapped this encounter, I stammered a reply, and after his parting "Good Luck," he went on along with the admiral.

The special royal greeting was a nice surprise gesture, but I did get a lot of teasing about it afterward.
   That night I was sent to the British flagship HMS *Duke of York* with photos of the king's visit to ask one of his aides-de-camp if he would sign one for Admiral Giffen. While waiting in the wardroom, I was invited by one of the ship's officers to have a drink. I accepted like a

shot and told the story of the time I'd accompanied John Barrymore to a luncheon in his honor given by the Women's Press Club of New York. He had arrived solemn and formal, though not just a little sloshed. After he was presented to everyone, a room full of worshipful women fell silent. Then up spoke the nervous, kittenish club president, bubbling heavy charm and saying, "Now, Mr. Barrymore, could we perhaps interest you in a drink?" Barrymore, in his best stentorian voice replied, "Madam, wouldn't I be a fine horse's ass if you couldn't?"

This yarn earned me two more drinks, a dinner in the officers' mess, and a trip ashore later to a dance in a ramshackle building. There about forty RN and USN junior officers vied with each other to partner the less than one dozen Red Cross and naval nurses from the nearby hospital. On this rare and special evening, officers could bring guests (including nurses and Wrens) aboard their ships for very brief and closely restricted tours of certain parts of the *upper decks only*. Under the sharp-eyed scrutiny of officers of the deck and/or marine guards, a hurriedly escorted guest would be taken once around and then off to shore again.

On this night I must have downed one too many pink gins from the *Duke of York*'s wardroom because I joyfully and most irresponsibly invited the best-looking nurse I saw to come aboard the *Washington*. Out we went in one of the better barges. Once aboard, I tried to appear sober but jolly, properly officerlike, and energetic. I gave her a quick tour, fore and aft, and then, impulsively showing off, I suggested she might like to see what a big ship's captain's quarters looked like—or, even better, an admiral's. I knew damned well that all the interiors, belowdecks, the bridges, and all the living quarters were strictly out of bounds. Most particularly prohibited were the relatively large and comfortable cabins of the admiral and the captain—both of whom were, I knew, visiting one of the British ships for dinner. Certainly, however, the executive officer, second-in-command, two other staff officers, and some of the ship's officers remained aboard. Nevertheless I suddenly said I was going to show her how the big brass lived. Quickly I guided her topside, past a preoccupied marine guard, and ushered her into Ike Giffen's own sacrosanct quarters. I had not the faintest idea of why I took her inside or what I would do next. Conventional thoughts of either a seduction or even some hurried necking had not, curiously enough, entered my hazy mind. What my intentions *were* I never really knew—except that once again I was deriving a certain kick out of daring to do something absolutely forbidden, something for which I could be court-martialed and possibly dishonorably discharged.

The silly, wide-eyed girl never questioned anything. To add to the suspense, the marine guard who sauntered up and down couldn't have helped noticing or at least hearing us. When I suddenly came to, as it were, and concluded I was a damned fool, I grabbed the girl's hand, took a quick peek at the marine who was walking away from us, and quickly ducked out the nearest exit to the quarterdeck. I've no doubt that the marine saw me, but he must have been either an old fan, a good sport, or blindly trusting because he kept his back to us as we slipped out and away. In fact, I couldn't wait to leave the ship altogether and return to the dance. I had spoiled my own evening by this stupid exhibition—which proved nothing except that it was a hard way to sober up quickly.

Chapter 4

THE NEXT day Admiral Ike called me in and, after some bellowed praise for my "good work" on the *Wasp,* advised me of the details of my "reward": a chance to do a similar job. This time I would be on the USS *Wichita,* a heavy cruiser which, along with its sister cruiser, the *Tuscaloosa* (allies and foes alike were often confused by such old Indian names), and four or six destroyers would be part of the covering escort of the next big convoy going to Murmansk and Archangel, Russia.

At the time there seemed no alternative to helping the Russkies. We couldn't yet relieve the awful pressure on them with our armies. Allied air force bombings were of help but not enough. It was known that most of the senior naval and military planners were opposed to the convoys as risking too much for too little. The sailors dreaded it, calling it "hell below zero" in the wild, frigid winter of those latitudes. The halfway point was called "suicide junction." Even the calmer summer seemed deadly. The famous midnight sun of that time of year was no guarantor of calm seas or clear skies—only that the enemy was out in greater force. One is reluctantly obliged to record that Churchill, who, with President Roosevelt, insisted on the convoys as politically necessary in order to help sustain the Soviets, was not at all popular with the Royal Navy of 1942.

Admiral Ike continued his briefing, giving more details: the Russkies had been pushed back about eight hundred miles from their border with Finland and most of their towns in that area had been flattened. He quoted secret intelligence reports—civilian and military losses were estimated in the millions. It was in our own interest, as well as theirs, to keep the Soviets in the war, to keep them fighting and help them hold on to Moscow and Leningrad.

In obedience to Admiral Giffen's orders, I collected what little personal gear I thought I would need and proceeded to report aboard the *Wichita* for what was ambiguously called "temporary additional duty." The skipper, Captain Hill, and Executive Commander Orem were calmly reassuring. In accepting a maverick like me they were neither patronizing, offhand, nor tough. They welcomed me as they would anyone on assignment and relaxedly absorbed me (however temporarily) into the ship's company.

Only the senior officers really knew that we were to be part of the protective force for the next big convoy to Murmansk and Archangel, code-named "P.Q.17" on the outgoing trip and "Q.P.13" home-bound. Of course only an idiot could be unaware that something out of the ordinary was brewing. Allied sinkings by the enemy had been on the increase on the arctic routes taken by the Lend-Lease equipment convoys over the top of Norway to the USSR.

There was, of course, some reassurance to be gained from the still secret knowledge that convoy P.Q.17 would be the largest of any so far, comprising thirty-five merchant ships altogether, the majority American. They carried three quarters of a billion dollars' worth of tanks, planes, guns, food, and supplies. In addition there were to be three rescue ships and a couple of oil tankers sailing in the convoy. Because it was so big, an even greater number of Allied warships, forty-seven vessels, were assigned to protect it. The "close covering escort" of twenty-one destroyers and two submarines was all British. A heavier supporting cover force of four powerful cruisers would sail farther out on each flank. Two were British and two were American (of which my ship, the *Wichita,* was one), and three more small destroyers would "hide" in reserve. Added to these was a distant covering force of nineteen ships, including one British battleship, HMS *Duke of York;* one American battleship, the USS *Washington;* and one British aircraft carrier, HMS *Victorious.* The rest were cruisers, destroyers, and support ships. These were to come out of Iceland and patrol our rear off Norway, hoping to lure the German super-warship *Tirpitz,* and any other enemy vessels, into a trap.

Before we left, anxieties and scare stories about earlier convoys brought on a plague of troubles. First there was an event of great rarity in modern days—a mutiny! It began when an unconfirmed rumor went around that some merchant crews had been so mutinous that they had to be confined belowdecks. Rather than continue, other merchant shipmasters hauled down their national flags and ran up *"Surrender"* signals. Further reports told of a few ships deliberately run aground and abandoned. All this was in shameful contrast to the many more numerous reports of breathtaking heroism and gallantry by both Americans and Britons.

I heard that just before the *Washington* started out for Scapa Flow to join the other big ships, my marine pal Don Hittle got word that the crew on one of the merchant vessels had broken open cases of booze destined for our ambassador in Moscow and had not only got roaring drunk but had mutinied, herding the officers into a corner and taking over the ship. This time it was no rumor. Don and an armed squad of marines took a whaleboat over to the troubled ship and, with weapons drawn, boarded it and quelled the fuss in what our Virginia navigator called "jig time." Don and his lads returned to the *Washington* acting as if nothing had happened.

A few of the merchant ships carried dummy aircraft on their decks, hoping the ruse would alarm any German reconnaissance planes. All four cruisers carried two real scout planes designed to be launched by catapult and recovered from the sea by cranes. The weather was misty and muggy, obscuring the hills around us—a partial cloak against possible spy planes, for which we were thankful. The day before we set forth was a Sunday, and rarely were divine services so well attended. The young, popular R.C. priest had our bluejackets lined up all day, ostensibly for "Last Communion." But most of us knew that his sacramental wine bottles were filled with Scotch whisky—a gesture that won many converts to his conception of the true Christian spirit!

The merchantmen of the convoy slipped out of Hvalfjördur to form up slowly outside of Eidesfjord, where the escorting forces would take their protective positions the next day. As they passed us they looked like so many dirty ducks waddling out to sea. They were not given the salutes usually exchanged by naval ships, but I daresay all who watched the motley tubs offered some half-thought prayers.

The next morning the ships of the naval escort stood out and crept around to the top of Iceland, beyond the temperate influence of the Gulf Stream, where the sea and the misty air were appreciably chillier. Finally we reached Seydisfjordur, Iceland's third city (more like a one-street, no-horse town), with a large deep-water harbor. It was dramatically bleak, a suitable model for a picture by Gustav Doré. As we wound around the gap in the land and proceeded up the narrow channel to join the assembling flotilla, the spectacle about us was satanic.

In the evening the chief petty officers were given a briefing by our executive officer, Commander Orem. Diagrams and charts showed where we would all be stationed and what signals would be made. Otherwise all radios and radar would stay unused until or unless we were the first sighted.

One uniquely moving moment came when Captain Hill had done with his pep talk. He leaned on his table and smiled, his eyes glowing. "Do you realize," he said, "I've been in the navy since before many of you were born? All that time I've been studying, training, and waiting for this moment—and now it's come!" He sighed, wagged his head, waved, and added, "Good luck to you all!"

Just before midnight on June 30, all engines began to turn and anchors to be weighed. In about an hour we were taking our position in line astern of the *London* and *Norfolk,* with the *Tuscaloosa* astern of us.

Excerpts from my report beginning July 1 follow:

We had prayed that the low-hanging clouds, like the Lord God of Hosts, might "be with us yet." They were, and He was—so far.
There was only a moderate wind and white-capped sea on our port bow. Heaven's gray camouflage hung down to about three hundred feet above sea level. Visibility was fairly good on the surface, and our scouting planes, which have been flying in four-hour shifts, have had no trouble finding their way.
We are steaming at eighteen knots, zig-zagging according to plan.
A signal was received from the Senior British Naval Officer

(SBNO) stationed in North Russia . . . : "It appears that about one third of Murmansk has been burned down and other buildings gutted." He predicted that for the coming period of relatively fine weather, heavy, concentrated attacks on shipping in that area will be of increased ferocity. SBNO went on to advise that it was a "grave risk" for ships to come to Murmansk as the local defense was not adequate.

The signal also stated that the Germans will be tempted by the sighting of P.Q.17 *and* Q.P.13 (the returning convoy), now of thirty-five ships each (two of ours had already dropped out with engine trouble), to use combined naval and air forces against us.

Our primary object is to get the convoy through—to keep it moving—even if it is suffering damage. In addition to that main objective, there is another one. It is to provide an opportunity for the enemy's heavy ships to be brought into action by the big battle fleet "hiding" way back. This may lure the enemy farther from his bases and into our reinforced submarine zones. It is known that the enemy has also concentrated more U-boats in our proposed path, presumably with the same idea in mind as ours.

The destroyers have an extra set of orders. Their main objective is the complete destruction of such enemy units as may be encountered—*with the exception of any unit* that includes the *Tirpitz*. This they must shadow and try to lead to an interception point with the main battle fleet. In the words of the destroyer commodore, "The only ship which will not fight again is one which is sunk!" They are to defend the convoy and give each other mutual support. . . .

The weather began to blow up early this evening and the scouting plane was brought in, but now at midnight it is clearing and another aircraft will be catapulted off shortly. The ceiling has lifted and there are ominous, untimely breaks in the clouds. It is getting much colder as we are now well within the Arctic Circle and heading northeast.

Underway, July 2, 1942.

We are drawing nearer to the convoy we are expected to cover and protect. We are carrying out a normal sea routine, modified, of course, by our advanced condition of readiness.

At 0915 the returning convoy reports it is being shadowed by two aircraft, and at 1043 it passes us on our starboard beam, ten miles distant.

We are still going through what they call quilted weather—"it's all
in patches." For a while it will be quite clear on the surface with a
strong glare; then suddenly it will fog up so that the other ships in
our company are barely discernible. . . . Word is decoded from the
Admiralty that a German submarine sent in a first-sighting report on
"a convoy or important unit."

The convoy commander, Captain John E. Broome, on H.M.S.
River Afton spoke to all ships present by radio saying that at 1313
three torpedoes had been fired at the convoy. No hits.

From about 1500 to 1600 our radio was able to pick up an enemy
aircraft sending a homing signal—almost directly astern of us.

1638, and a group of flags are hoisted from H.M.S. *London*'s signal
bridge. They are orders to us all to assume "FIRST DEGREE OF
READINESS."

1646: *"Air defense—take battle stations!"* The bugler's blast sends
everyone running.

1655: The U.S.S. *Tuscaloosa* sounds a sudden emergency blast on
her foghorn and hauls off at flank speed to starboard. She later
flashes: "3 TORPEDOES FIRED AT US ON PORT SIDE." Some swear it is a
school of fish and others say there is nothing there at all. In any case
the whole force picks up its skirts and runs.

Fifteen minutes later: "RESUME FORMATION."

At 1712 we hear again from the convoy of merchant ships. "AIR
BOMBERS COMING IN TO ATTACK!" Then a report that two torpedoes
are heading for the convoy. We aren't yet close enough to see
anything, but we can hear the roar of engines and the firing of guns
over the radio. Reports of torpedoes and bombers are coming
through intermittently, but we have not heard of any hits yet. We all
wish we could go in and help out as we are so close, but our job is to
wait on the sidelines for enemy surface warships.

One Heinkel is down! It is 1740. Not sure if we did it or one of
the others in the escort. A U-boat has surfaced and is trying to pick
up possible survivors. All ships try to hit it from a distance but fail.
We think we hear of another plane down. The British chap
broadcasting developments sounds as collected as though he were
sitting by his fireplace at home, reminiscing about the whole episode.
Commander Orem remarks, "People like that can never be beaten,
so why don't the Heinies give up trying?"

In less than an hour the attack is over.

Underway, July 3, 1942.

The fog is still with us early this morning, but the sea is sleepy calm. By 0900 visibility lifts considerably and it is decided to launch the scouting planes later in the morning.

P.Q.17 Commander advises that they are being shadowed again, this time by two aircraft. We don't think that *we* have been spotted yet.

Senior British Naval Officer, North Russia, reports that the last raid on Murmansk has practically destroyed the entire city. It was still burning as the message was being sent. The sixtieth raid on shipping in the harbor caused frightful carnage.

During the night we were obliged, because of the fog, to go much farther north. That puts us roughly sixty miles S.W. of the tip of Spitzbergen. Ice patrols by our own planes keep us advised about icebergs.

A little after 1100, three life rafts, two on the port side and one on the starboard, are sighted, but our aircraft scout reported no one on them. In these waters they are floating tombstones. . . .

At 1700, P.Q.17 reports sighting what looks like two vessels, ten miles distant. A few minutes later it turns out that they are large icebergs.

At 1900 an Admiralty message, just broken down, confirms our previous report: the *Tirpitz,* the *Hipper,* and four large German destroyers have left Trondheim [a major Norwegian seaport].

2010: *Enemy aircraft sighted!* Several planes are circling low on the horizon. One young sailor gets his first look at them and shouts, "Hi-yo, Silver!" The planes have been identified as Blohm-Voss 138s. We still have two scout planes up patrolling.

2023: The two enemy planes are now circling around our port side, one ahead of the other. Now one of them is going around forward. The other is on our beam. We open fire.

2029: H.M.S. *London* opens fire with her eight-inch guns.

2049: Now H.M.S. *Norfolk* opens fire. We have been steaming on a parallel course to P.Q.17. At 2102 we are ordered to drop back and come up astern of the convoy.

2221: One of our aircraft sweeps low over an object and drops a depth charge. The *Wainwright* sends us a visual: "JUST PASSED SMALL WHALE—WITHOUT A TAIL."

2320: Visibility is worsening rapidly. The planes are having a

difficult time to keep from losing us and still scout far enough
around. The signal to recover aircraft is hoisted at 2330. Fliers now
cannot fly over fifty feet above sea level if they wish to see anything.

A message from the Admiralty states that although the *Tirpitz* and
Hipper are moving northward and are a threat to the convoy, there is
no *immediate* danger.

At 2350 the Admiralty advises that the shadowing German aircraft
are using a beacon procedure in conjunction with their U-boats, also
shadowing P.Q.17.

It is 0017 and we are in a fog bank again. We pick up a plane on
our radar two miles astern of us. Whenever the glaring haze lifts, we
are able to see several large icebergs. We are now between six
hundred and eight hundred miles from the North Pole.

The continual daylight makes it difficult to keep track of the days.
We pick up sleep in snatches, whenever and however we can.

Underway, July 4, 1942.

Our national anniversary is ushered in with no untoward incident.

At 0805 this morning the Royal Navy's Cruise Squadron-1 sent a
general signal to all U.S. Navy and merchant ships in the operation:
"ON THE OCCASION OF YOUR GREAT ANNIVERSARY IT SEEMS MOST
UNCIVIL TO MAKE YOU KEEP STATION AT ALL BUT EVEN TODAY
FREEDOM OF THE SEAS CAN BE READ TWO WAYS. IT IS A PRIVILEGE FOR
US ALL TO HAVE YOU WITH US AND I WISH YOU ALL THE BEST OF
HUNTING."

Captain Hill of the *Wichita* replied: "IT IS A GREAT HONOR TO BE
HERE WITH YOU TODAY IN FURTHERANCE OF THE IDEALS WHICH JULY
FOURTH HAS ALWAYS REPRESENTED TO US AND WE ARE PARTICULARLY
HAPPY TO BE A PORTION OF YOUR COMMAND. CELEBRATION ON THIS
HOLIDAY ALWAYS REQUIRES LARGE FIREWORKS DISPLAYS. I TRUST YOU
WILL NOT DISAPPOINT US."

A short while later the captain of H.M.S. *Norfolk* also sent us
felicitations: "MANY HAPPY RETURNS OF THE DAY TO THE ONLY
COUNTRY WITH A KNOWN BIRTHDAY!"

To this our captain answered: "THANK YOU. I THINK IT IS ONLY
FITTING THAT YOU SHOULD CELEBRATE MOTHER'S DAY!"

At 1430 several enemy planes are sighted—JU-88s! Then the radar
picks up some more on a different bearing. A little less than an hour
later, at 1523, the number of reports of planes coming in all around

convinces the captain we should man antiaircraft batteries. Ten minutes later we launch two of our scout planes, which, with the *Tuscaloosa*'s two, make four American naval aircraft in the air.

The clouds are still low, but now and then the sun breaks through.

Small black, brown, and gray bursts of smoke on our starboard hand are seen like sudden splatters of mud against the eggshell sky. Seconds later we hear the sound of gunfire. A new attack is on. The attacking planes look like small fast bugs skimming rapidly just above the waterline.

Strange little Arctic birds, flying or landing on our ships, looking half sea gull and half penguin, seem to know something is wrong. Their peaceful kingdom has been disturbed. Greater birds than they have ever had to contend with roar by and explosions shake their air. They flutter in groups, not knowing where to go.

Everyone feels we should do much more to assist. But our orders remain as before, stay apart until a surface attack is imminent and let the destroyers handle close-in defenses. Should one lucky German torpedo or bomb hit one of our cruisers, it would be worth ten merchant ships, loaded to the gunwales, to the enemy.

1647: The *Wainwright* fires, still steaming toward the lines of ships. Cruise Squadron-1 signals that we are to stay in the vicinity until the enemy surface craft situation is clarified, but certainly not longer than tomorrow noon.

Our two planes with Lieutenants Browning and Dillon return at approximately 1650. They bring back some exciting tales. They both sighted a variety of German aircraft. They had been flying in and out of cloud banks when they lost each other momentarily. Dillon came into the clear and found himself flying at right angles over a JU-88. His gunner opened fire. The bullets seemed to go right into Jerry's nose but had no effect except to make him mad. He turned and chased Dillon back into the sanctuary of a cloud. Asked if he had been frightened, he answered, "Guess I was, kind of."

1716: H.M.S. *London* fires. We follow suit. The convoy is well in sight again and there is a lot of smoke. The convoy's barrage balloons look like so many toys. Not at all warlike, they look festive and gay as they are tugged by their long cables.

One of the ships in the convoy, the *Christopher Newport,* has become the first holiday victim. At 1740 Cruise Squadron-1 advises that a lone plane slapped a torpedo into its side. How many survivors there are we do not yet know. There are now four fewer ships in the convoy than when we started.

1821: The antiaircraft batteries are manned once more. Reports of more enemy planes and U-boats are clogging the air. The radio room is bedlam. The bridge cannot keep up with the reports. New flag signals are hoisted before the orders for the previous ones can be executed. More enemy aircraft approach the convoy on its starboard side.

(Note: It is now nearly midnight the same night. It was impossible to record things as they happened. It was all too fast. We are still here. We have been in the front row of a big Fourth of July fireworks display. One of the stricken British merchantmen was hit. As its crew raced for lifeboats—no one could survive fifteen minutes in that water—they signaled: "WHO SAYS WE'RE NOT GOOD SPORTS—CELEBRATING YOUR HOLIDAY WITH FIREWORKS AS SUGGESTED." The old tub sank shortly thereafter.

Now we are in retreat. We have withdrawn our main forces with hardly any fighting. We seem to have been outmaneuvered. If that is so, it couldn't be helped. There was nothing we could do about it. Perhaps that condition will change shortly. *Many* things have changed since the last entry in these pages.)

1825: Firing continuing from all sides. Commander Broome reports twenty-five enemy aircraft attacking. Then more are reported by radio.

1829: A plane is falling in flames—it crashes near us! Great blinding flash of fire—seems hundreds of feet high—then black smoke. Big cheer from *Wichita* crew. We think we are responsible. Now the cry, "Go get the bastards!" More explosions and the sickening "whoosh" of the fire. Looks like a merchant ship is hit badly. Fat smoke curling skyward. Now another Nazi plane dives in flames.

1840: Looks like a tin can [destroyer] is afire. We are zigzagging up and down the length of the convoy. Now most of the action is abaft our starboard beam. Two more merchant ships hit! Smoke so thick—must be a tanker. Can't see *Wainwright* now.

Cruiser Squadron-1 reports German units still headed north along (Norwegian) coast with heavy aerial protection. The scene is confused. We on the *Wichita* are steaming by and attacking wolfpacks of U-boats when possible. They are on our trail, but we snake around them. Only occasional bursts are seen over the convoy. Some "shadowers" are still sighted, circling around and about.

1911: Suddenly–shockingly–from *"Admiralty to Cruise Squadron-1:* CRUISER FORCE MUST WITHDRAW TO WESTWARD AT HIGH SPEED!" The news comes with a stunning impact. Why? How? Is the whole German fleet out? If so, what of it? That's what we came here for, isn't it? No one expresses an opinion. There is hardly a comment. We are waiting until further word comes in. It does, twelve minutes later.

1923: *"From Admiralty to Escorts of P.Q.17:* BECAUSE OF THREATS FROM MAIN ENEMY SURFACE FORCES, CONVOY P.Q.17 IS TO DISPERSE AND PROCEED TO RUSSIAN PORTS."

On our shortwave radio we can hear the word passed to the convoy, using code names for the different ships. Each is given a specially designated route. The ships are spotted for miles. Some are still burning and smoldering from bomb hits while others are just getting up steam. Their smoke looks like huge black ostrich feathers growing out of tubs.

Visibility is increasing and the sun is beginning to shine brightly and innocently, just as if no one had told him of the carnage that took place while he was hiding. The sea is glassy calm and a deep full blue. We are all silent. We slice through the eerily placid water at a fast clip. The quiet seems more unreal than the war.

2037: We ask the engine room for revolutions to give us twenty-five knots. We hate leaving P.Q.17 behind. It looks so helpless now since the order to scatter came through. The ships are going around in circles, like so many frightened chicks. Some can hardly move at all. If only our men knew the details, they would not feel so bad about it. Morale throughout the ship is very low. The men feel ashamed and resentful.

2100: Six of the P.Q.17 Close Ocean Escort of destroyers now join us. The *Wainwright* comes ploughing over the water looking very smug and self-conscious, having done the most shooting. She is grown up now–can wear high heels and everything–a real veteran of the war.

The *London*'s scout plane, sent on ice patrol, failed to return. They have been trying to raise the pilot on the radio but he does not answer. The guess is that with compass out the poor devil went further and further and could not find his way back.

The *Wichita* log had nothing more worth noting on this bloody Fourth of July.

Underway, July 5, 1942—Hindsight Day.

Admiral Hamilton (CS-1) sent a signal late last night addressed: *"General:* I KNOW YOU WILL ALL BE FEELING AS DISTRESSED AS I AM AT HAVING TO LEAVE THAT FINE COLLECTION OF SHIPS TO FIND THEIR OWN WAY TO HARBOR. THE ENEMY, UNDER COVER OF HIS SHORE-BASED AIRCRAFT, HAS SUCCEEDED IN CONCENTRATING A VASTLY SUPERIOR FORCE IN THIS AREA. WE ARE THEREFORE ORDERED TO WITHDRAW. WE ARE ALL SORRY THAT THE GOOD WORK OF THE CLOSE ESCORT COULD NOT BE COMPLETED. I HOPE WE SHALL ALL HAVE A CHANCE OF SETTLING THIS SCORE WITH THEM SOON."

We hoped the same—fervently. Yesterday there had been a detached feeling about war and killing and destruction. It had been a spectacle—a free show with the favored underdog doing right well for himself. Come one . . . come all! See the Dance of Death! . . . See the airplanes shot down in flames! . . . See ships sink before your eyes . . . torpedo wakes passing around you . . . real shells in the air . . . real depth charges erupting into geysers . . . real blood in the water. All absolutely free . . . Come one . . . come all!

Today that has changed. The men are sober now and war is more personal. Personal honor is more real. We all feel we have run away. We cannot yet analyze the situation. Information is restricted. We are "high-tailing it" westward. We could have been of great help against the air and submarine attack. And what if there was a risk? What kind of high command have we that, with such a great force in operation, we cannot fight it out? Have the British become gun-shy? How can wars be won this way? Those are the angry questions heard throughout the ship.

Captain Hill, who was so sure this was to be "the big moment," is silent. He sits in his chair on the bridge staring blankly out at the bright and now so peaceful sea. The sight of the proud little convoy bothers our collective conscience. The little, messy ships had looked like a procession of pilgrims on a solemn holy mission when we first saw them strung out on the slate-gray water; then they were like so many confused and smoking specks seeking the palladium of the open sea.

Then more news came through and the situation came into slightly sharper focus. It told of the sightings of the big German ships, the *Tirpitz* and the *Hipper,* with eight escorting destroyers, speeding along the Norwegian coast at twenty-two knots, and supported by a veritable armada of shore-based aircraft—the dreaded Luftwaffe. Never at any time had we intended to engage the huge unit in which the *Tirpitz* operated. Rather we were told to get the hell out of the way and lure them in the direction of our large Anglo-American battle fleet. But with their preponderant air escort, we could not even hope to deal with the situation. It was becoming clearer now why we had to withdraw.

Midnight—eight bells. Hindsight Day is over. Like the day after any holiday, the hangover has been the worst part of it.

Underway, July 7.

On our return, we sighted the main battle fleet at 0818, ten miles away. It was very hazy, but the silhouettes of the ships stood out in ironically brave relief. Here were thirty-three important warships in formation. Seven were American, the best of their class. It looked almost like a peacetime regatta.

More conscience-pricking reports came in from poor scattered P.Q.17. Its tattered remnants were still under attack.

Hvalfjördur, Iceland, July 8, 1942.

We proceeded without incident up Hvalfjördur harbor and anchored. The men are amused at early German claims, first of sinking "an American and a British cruiser" and then later of sinking the entire force—convoy and escorts.

How else could we have acted? No one could be sure. How could we have possibly suspected that only a few days from the beginning of the venture our convoy would be attacked by a total of 264 enemy aircraft coming in waves over a period of several days and lightened nights, with constant wolfpacks of U-boats. The superiority of our adversary, plus errors of judgment, resulted in P.Q.17 suffering one of the most devastating and pusillanimous Allied defeats on record. Two thirds of a huge convoy, supposedly guarded by a massive task force, went to a frigid grave after only token resistance.

P.Q.17 was feared in advance by some merchant shippers as likely to be as painful as Pearl Harbor. It turned out to be at least more shameful. Churchill himself later called it "one of the most melancholy naval episodes in the whole history of the war." Luckily, I was not in one of the merchant ships or the very close-covering destroyers. I was, so to speak, in the balcony—not right on stage, but still close enough to see almost too much, though not one of the prime targets. The worst part was the inability of any of us to be of real help. How did it happen?

Before the start of P.Q.17 there had been thirty-five merchant ships assembled. Of this number, only eleven ever straggled into Russian ports. Surviving seamen were those who made it to lifeboats or rafts. The few lucky ones were only maimed by frostbite or capture. One hundred and fifty-three died.

The sunken cargoes included 430 tanks, 210 aircraft, and some 100,000 tons of miscellaneous war goods—enough to equip an army of 50,000.

One of the explanations was mistaken naval intelligence. It was shocking to find out that the big enemy ships—particularly the *Tirpitz*—had *no interest whatsoever in coming out to challenge the Allied defenders!* All they were doing was changing from one base to another farther up the Norwegian coast. The Admiralty and Allied Naval Intelligence had been completely fooled; we had completely misinterpreted the enemy's intentions. The big brass had jumped to dreadful conclusions for which no one who had been part of the operation would ever forgive them. The bottom line showed nothing less than the cowardly running away of units of the Allied navies in the face of an enemy whose major forces were not even planning to attack. Of the many books and articles on the subject, perhaps the best and most colorful was *The Close Covering Escort* by Captain Jack Broome, RN, who was commander of the destroyers.

By the twelfth of July, we were back in Hvalfjördur—too safe and sound for our collective consciences. On reporting back on the *Washington,* I learned that I had new orders to report for duty in London. A few days' leave in harbor was a pleasant enough thought, but to report for duty in London instead of remaining at sea with the fleet was worrying. The admiral assured me that I had performed all my duties "more than satisfactorily" and he would give me a fine fitness report. Furthermore he had no idea of how or why I was to be detached after less than three months with him.

I was given a fine farewell; the admiral presented me with a photo of himself, inscribing it "Well Done!" Most touching of all was a presentation from Don Hittle and a small honor guard of a few of his marines. It was a miniature replica of a lifebelt with the flags of the United States, the United Kingdom, the USSR, and Iceland painted around a message that read: "To Lieut. Douglas Fairbanks, USNR—A sailor almost good enough to be a Marine—from the U.S. Marine Detachment, U.S.S. *Washington* Flagship, Task Force 99. July 1942." Nothing before or since has given me quite the same quality of pleasure as that gesture.

Eventually I got a lift to Belfast in Northern Ireland. Because flights from Belfast to London were hazardous, I siphoned in a few stiff drinks and by a bit of blarney wangled a private room on the night boat to Liverpool. Before leaving I noted the terrible blitzing of poor Belfast—rows upon rows of houses were destroyed. Still, that cruel panorama was somewhat softened by the wonderfully reassuring sight of a solitary tree standing in the midst of the rubble.

Within hours of arriving in London and reporting to U.S. Naval Headquarters I learned why I was back. Dickie Mountbatten, bless him, had wasted no time in reacting to my written hints about joining other U.S. officers on his Combined Operations staff. The reason for a U.S. presence was to teach our people how the mixed amphibious command worked. Later the British would help us form a similar setup within our own military establishment. I reported to Dickie at Combined Operations Headquarters in Richmond Terrace, off Whitehall, the next day. He was marvelous to me. He was always to be rather like an older brother in my eyes. I was introduced to the heads of several departments. Colonel Robert Neville of the Royal Marines, now head of the Combined Operations Planning and shortly to succeed to Intelligence, was one of Dickie's oldest shipmates and prewar polo pals.

The first week or so I was bounced around from one part of this fascinating outfit to another. I soon met several other Americans, the most senior of whom was a regular navy captain, Elliot Strauss. They were attached as observers to such departments as plans, operations, air, communications, and research and development. The purpose of the organization was to develop amphibious war plans in every detail: weaponry, methods, types of ships and vehicles—everything that might be needed for a successful amphibious invasion of the Continent. Dickie, the chief of Combined Operations, was charged with training, developing, planning, and executing a number of small but daring raids in selected parts of Nazi-held Europe. This would at the same time be a means of experimenting with the newest amphibious craft, vehicles, and equipment and also a way of keeping the enemy worried and on the defensive. These operations (which were both large and small) were carried out by volunteers from every part of the armed forces, but mostly from the Royal Marines. All of them had to undergo very tough special training, mostly at secret bases in Scotland. They were called *commandos,* a name originally used by Afrikaners during the Boer War. By the time I joined headquarters (Dickie had taken over soon after visiting us with Edwina in California less than a year earlier), the organization had carried out several daring (and costly) raids on French, Norwegian, and other continental targets.

For a time I was assigned to study the effects of explosives and bombing with two scientists. One was Solly Zuckerman, a former anthropologist and Renaissance man, and the other was J. D. Bernal, an extreme left-winger, I was told. Even though I made quick friends with Zuckerman, nothing in my scattered education equipped me to understand one damned thing he and his associate were doing. I was then moved to intelligence and from there to special weapons and camouflage development, under a nice, though deceptively stuffy navy captain, Tom Hussey. This was a congenial start for me, and I applied myself enthusiastically to the mechanical development of all manner of devices and ways intended to trick the enemy.

To say London in wartime was unforgettable is to confirm a cliché. No one who was there and survived would wish to forget it. It had been well and truly bashed about and burned. Everything was dirtier than usual. Sandbags were piled up against monuments and buildings (even Buckingham Palace got a couple of direct hits, with the royal family in it). But it was the people of grubby proud London who were so inspiring. Indeed, the whole country and most of the large, crowded cities wore their scars like campaign medals. Towns as yet unscathed or only slightly bruised felt rather out of it—even apologetic. I was grateful to be there then. It brought to mind a paraphrase of the St. Crispin's Day speech from *Henry V*. I thought that those who were "now abed will think themselves accursed they were not here to fight with us" in this worldwide war. In my still incurably romantic mind, Britain in beleaguered wartime reminded me of Mary Lee, very small and indefatigable with her resources of courage, loyalty, and humor.

One of the first old friends that I tracked down was Irving Asher, who was now running MGM film interests in London. Part of his deal was a suite in Claridge's! This dear old pal invited me to share it with him whenever I could. The fun of his company and the still unbelievable luxury—even in wartime—of that world-famous caravansary (especially in comparison with the navy's officers' quarters) made my acceptance a certainty.

Claridge's was also the base for many temporarily exiled heads of state, such as the queen of the Netherlands and the kings of Norway and Greece. One night Irving threw a large cocktail party to which he invited many theatrical friends and friends-of-friends, as well as the expatriate American member of Parliament and London's social arbiter, Chips Channon. The hotel put on the best show of drinks and hors d'oeuvres it could arrange and King, its well-known headwaiter, was assigned to supervise.

I trickled in late, heartily greeting those I knew and nodding politely to those I wasn't sure about. Finding myself drinkless, I called out to my old lifesaver of a headwaiter, "Oh, King!"

At that, a familiar bald-headed gent in a khaki uniform turned to face me and politely said, "Yes?"

It was King George II of Greece.

Irving and I loved reminiscing about our bawdy prewar times together when we were filming *Man of the Moment* in Monte Carlo. Now we frequently took dinner at the most popular black-market bottle club in town, Les Ambassadeurs. It was small, just off Hanover Square, and run by a hulk of a man who claimed to have been the heavyweight boxing champ of the Polish army. He had changed his name to John Mills, but he had nothing else in common with my actor chum. He had been among a large group of Poles who managed to escape from both the Nazis and the Russians. Thousands of such refugees somehow got to Britain and were all naturalized at once by an emergency act of Parliament.

Big John administered his bistro with great efficiency and always had his very pretty girlfriend, Virginia, in tow. One night, John and Irving plotted a joke on me. They persuaded Virginia to flirt with me and come to my room after I'd gone bone-wearily back to Irving's suite, hoping to catch up on some long-lost sleep. I was just getting into bed in the small spare room when the door opened and in came Virginia. She smilingly displayed the extra door key Irving had given her. I sat up blearily, stammering inanely. The beauteous blonde confessed in a whisper that she had had "too much to drink," had long "fancied" me and, well—it was wartime. . . . She had slipped away from Big John unobserved and come to me with Irving's naughty help. Then she came over to my bed, sat down beside me, and began to slip off the shoulder straps of her gown. Exhausted and bewildered, I was groping for words when I heard the outer door bang open and Big John's heavily accented basso profundo asking for me. Suddenly he burst in and saw me sitting up in bed in my pajamas with his girl, one shoulder strap at half-mast, beside me. My shock and inability to be coherent probably lasted only a few seconds, though it seemed an hour. Then around the door popped Irving, and he, Big John, and Virginia all began to laugh like fools. I collapsed with relief, although I'd been had.

At last, joke over, I was left alone—exhausted from this first night out after some arduous physical training at the Royal Marine commando base in Inverary, Scotland. I had still not fully recovered from the accumulated fatigue of my Malta and Russian convoy adventures, and I soon fell into a deep sleep.

I later learned that in the early predawn hours I slept like Rip Van Winkle through an ear-piercing air raid, complete with alarm sirens and antiaircraft noise. Almost everyone in Claridge's—guests, exiled royals, government heads, and staff—made for the very large basement storage rooms. But not I. I was still sound asleep.

When the all-clear sounded, it was still dark. Two air-raid wardens took the end of the raid as an opportunity to meet in the mews three floors below our windows. Breathing freely again, these overage Home Guards began to compare notes and chat in clear cockney accents. Although I had slept through the warning alarms, the bombing that followed, *and* the all-clear sirens, the subdued chatter of the wardens below did penetrate my slumbers. I woke up with an angry start, very annoyed. I called out in the best music-hall English accent I could muster (in order not to be thought American), "Carn't you cheps be *quiet?* We're all traying to sleep!" Lots of others on the backside of the hotel heard it all and responded with hoots of laughter.

The job at Combined Ops went very well in this summer of 1942. Though Dickie himself was given to "loose talk," he trusted my discretion, and it was exciting to be so near the high inside. When I was moved into the study of camouflage (erroneously thought appropriate because of my knowledge of films, photography, trick shots, and sound effects), I was let in on a new and very secret tactical deception and diversion development.

This project had begun with the building of dummy tanks, armored cars, and wooden replicas of big guns, landing craft, and airplanes. All this evolved into an idea to deceive the enemy by projecting the prerecorded sounds of tanks and landing craft from a hidden distance—behind smoke screens. They were testing the sounds of a moving squadron of armored cars, together with soldiers' voices and related noises. These sounds were to be projected from within a forest or wooded area, for example, to give the enemy the impression of movement by an armored group.

The intention was for the enemy to adjust his local defenses to meet our nonexistent group. The idea, originated by Brigadier Dudley Clarke, had been tried out first in a small way in the North African desert and then enlarged against the Italians in Ethiopia from the sea toward the land. For amphibious purposes a motor torpedo boat projected the sound from behind real fog or a smoke screen.

From that small start, the Combined Ops camouflage section began further experiments on a larger scale for army use on land. Now they had returned to an amphibious concept, to which I was assigned, in addition to other ways and means of creating deceptions. However, this did not mean that I could entirely avoid the regular amphibious training for hit-and-run raids, the muscle-agonizing commando courses, and so on. But for most of this time I could make London my base.

One of Mary Lee's heartening, bubbling letters came within a week or so of my arrival. I'll never forget how moved I was by her poignant description of hearing on the radio that the Germans had attacked and sunk an entire convoy destined for Russia. She knew I had been in and out of Iceland and northern Scotland and knowing about the special mission with the *Wasp* to Malta, assumed I was on the Russian one as well. She had rung up all sorts of friends in the Navy Department in Washington, but of course none of them could—or indeed *would*—tell her anything either good or bad. When she was just about at her wits' end with worry, she received, out of the blue, a cable from Dickie. The cable read: "JUST HAD WORD OF A GREAT FRIEND OF YOURS WHO IS IN FINE FORM AND EXPECTING JOIN ME HERE IN FEW DAYS. LOVE. DICKIE." None of us could ever forget how he managed to spare a private thought about old friends in the midst of all the pressures of war.

David Niven soon found me. He complained that his job involved little but training until "invasion time"—whenever that would be. Meanwhile he had been promoted to major, had lots of time off, and was making the most of it. We had both been made honorary members of Buck's Club, small, attractive, and very exclusive. Buck was Major Buckmaster, a retired former Horse Guard captain who knew everybody. He had been an old friend of my father's (also an honorary member years ago) and a former husband of actress Gladys Cooper. Niv was also a member of Boodles, one of the three oldest and most elegant clubs in the world, after White's and Brooks. I confessed how jealous I was of all the great times he had been having, but now perhaps I could catch up.

The nearest we came to anything off the "proper" track was one night when, just for the hell of it, we decided to roam the West End in the blackout. It was a total blackout, except for an occasional illegal flashlight or cigarette lighter. We decided we would talk loudly in different accents—Niv in his idea of Australian and I in tough New York Brooklynese. It seems damned silly now, but we had a hilarious time that night, saying the most dreadful things where no one could *see* us. "Not loik this daown unda!" wailed Niv. "The bloody pommies live like bloody pigs . . . !"

I replied with "Goddamfuckinawful jernt, dis here is! Let's get de hell outa dis place, ferchrissakes!"

As we stumbled about, we were at length accosted by two ladies of the blackout, whom we gathered were partners, as they spoke more or less together. One was French, with a hoarse, throaty accent. The other spoke no-nonsense, adenoidal East End cockney. They asked if we'd "loik a bit o' fun an' gaymes, dearies?"

We said we were more or less lost, had nothing else to do, but we were not, unfortunately, "potential customers for at least two good reasons." The cockney gal replied, "Gorn! *Two?* Wot are they?"

I piped up, "Well, de foist reason is we don't have no dough . . ."

I was quickly interrupted with "Wa-al, you can tyke the other reason and stuff it up your arse!" They started to leave, but Niv stopped them by saying that though we were not customers in the accepted sense, we'd pay for a drink in their quarters—wherever that was.

They were so accustomed to their "beat," even in the blackout, that we reached the black-curtained entrance to their flat in no time. In the dark I took the arm of the jolly cockney gal and Niv latched on to the hoarse copy of Piaf—both of them still unseen. We were ushered in and blinked at the sudden shock of light. My limey friend was jolly enough all right, but as big as a house and very probably muscular beneath the loose black and bulging sweater she wore. Niv, true to his luck, had drawn a really cute though tough little Frenchy, which she advised us was in fact her London nickname.

Hardly had we entered when they again suggested how each could help us "have a good time." I fear I took the pompous lead in this, but Niv did quickly back me up in telling them that we were really not interested in "that *kind* of a good time." We just thought it would be fun to have a drink or two, exchange some stories, and then go back to St. James's Street. Meanwhile we would see to it that their "hospitality" would not go unappreciated. We both dropped a fiver into their

welfare fund, located in a small bowl on a table, and the girls were happy.

Just as we were gulping down our drinks, though, my big limey friend let out a happy scream and cried, "Blimey! Look 'oo we've got! Recognize 'em, Frenchy, do you?" Frenchy looked bewildered, but only for a moment as my own lady wrestler pointed to both of us in turn, shrieking out our names.

I have never before or since seen Niv at a loss. But we shared a silly embarrassed grin. When we acknowledged our identities, the limey put aside the bottle of woopsie wine and brought out a bottle of Scotch whiskey. We accepted it with a haste that in more sedate circles would be thought unseemly. We were beginning to feel more relaxed when we heard the steps of two people thumping heavily up the stairs outside. Niv and I shared a brief moment of panic lest we be "discovered" and provide a scandal-hungry press with a juicy disclosure. When the footsteps reached our landing, we heard the door next to ours open and someone enter. An elderly, military-type voice mumbled, "Thank you, young man!" Presumably the words accompanied a generous tip because it elicited a "Thank you, major!" in reply. Then the latter voice called out after a knock on our door, "Oh, Frenchy, that's the major again. It's Thursday, y'know!"

"Cheri—dahling! I'm *so* sorry!" said Frenchy to Niv, her *R*'s purring in her throat. "Zis ees my old major. 'E always sees me on Thursday. Forgeave me, dahling. I shan't be long!" She quickly slipped out of her dress, revealing a very sheer black-lace undergarment, exchanged her sensible shoes for a couple of extraordinarily high-heeled ones, and went into the other room through a connecting door.

While we chatted and drank, we had a grand sideshow as *entendeurs*. We heard the major's bronchial but polite military voice say, "Oh, hullo, my deah! Lookin' pretty as ever!" Then the old boy asked if she was ready—and she was. Whereupon we heard her little heels clicking on the wooden floor and, we supposed, on one or two small rugs on her way around the room. Then to our wondrous surprise we heard the cracking of a small buggy whip, followed by the major's voice, "That's the fine pony! Giddyap! Giddyap." *(Crack, crack!)* Round and round the ring we go." *(Crack! Crack!)*

Frenchy was then heard giving a series of weak, totally unconvincing "whinnies."

"Fahster! Fahster!" commanded the major. More and more quickly the little heels clicked as they pranced around and around the room, sharpened by the snap of the whip, which was certainly not hitting her—or anything else.

Eventually, as Frenchy's speed reached its outer limits, the whip ceased to crack, and we heard an animal-like moan from the major. Then a low "Thank you, m'dear! Thank you! That was splendid! Here you are! A little something as usual, eh?"

With that we heard the rustling of clothes, followed by some exchanged good nights, and the heavy thump of the major going downstairs. Almost at once Frenchy rejoined us, just as if she had only left the room to take a telephone call.

Our glasses were refilled and we spent a happy hour lying like hell to the girls' questions: What are movies like? Hollywood? Garbo? Cooper? And so on. We asked our own questions as well: How long at this job? Like it or hate it? (*Love it,* they said!)

At length we politely, almost gallantly, took our leave and with their expert directions staggered down blacked-out Piccadilly and into St. James's Street, where dimmed-out lights of taxis could be found and we bade each other a happy good night.

Since I was an American officer "under instruction," and destined for naval amphibious operations, apart from some hard physical preparation for the first week or two, I was not obliged to go through such rough training as the commandos from the Royal Marines and the army's infantry up in Inverary. Our particular quarters were at the supposedly haunted Achnocarry Castle, near the even more secret base for deception development at Ballantrae. It kept reminding me of the movie I'd long wanted, but failed to make from Robert Louis Stevenson's book *The Master of Ballantrae*. Flynn finally made it in 1953, damn it! Although the ideas for deception equipment and diversionary planning originated with the Eighth Army in Egypt and evolved further at Richmond Terrace Headquarters, it was at Ballantrae that most of the actual experiments with visual tactical ruses and

camouflage devices were carried out. Other wicked tricks, including all manner of booby traps (some designed inside most convincing horse and camel pats) were developed in an Egyptian base outside Cairo under the supervision of Major Jasper Maskelyne, in peacetime a prominent member of a famous family of professional magicians.

More sophisticated equipment and new tactics were evolving daily. Various special units, such as Britain's Long-Range Desert Group, the Special Boat Section, and the Special Air Section, performed fabulous feats of imaginative daring, often helped by deception devices and tactics. There were scientific experiments with ways to project sounds over considerable distances—say, of tanks or armored cars moving through forests or landing craft coming in to shore. Jamming or deceiving radar, constructing masses of dummy landing craft and tanks to be spotted from the air, and overloading and misdirecting radio chatter with false codes were other experiments carried out. The diversionary units, small as they were, had to become, in effect, military decoys.

Life at Ballantrae was a far cry, if not a loudspeaker shout, from Claridge's. Meals were mostly "bully beef" or salmon, gouged out of cans with filthy fingers; sprouts and bread were pulled apart with regulation commando daggers or pocket knives. At night cold winds blew through slits in the wooden houses and we slept on boards covered with thick khaki blankets. Yet I did enjoy it, really.

I was helped a great deal by the goodwill of other younger officers in training—particularly by a tall, seemingly frail sublieutenant known as Nimmo. We often walked several miles to the village pub for a few flagons of booze. One night he challenged me to a rough-and-tumble wrestling match. At first I declined. I protested that I was far heavier and no doubt a stronger and better-trained athlete than he. But he persisted, so I shrugged and agreed. Just outside our base, we doffed coats and in the moonlight on a muddy section of road, we set to. In far less time than I can write it down, he had bested me. I protested, good-humoredly, that I had lost my balance and had resisted being too rough. So he challenged me again. I accepted again. In another quick jiffy he had pressed my shoulders to the mud mat a second time. He had a mysterious reservoir of strength and I had no more excuses, so we brushed ourselves off and rollicked back to base.

* * *

It wasn't possible for me to know much in advance about Operation Jubilee, the code name for the raid on the French coastal town of Dieppe. I knew a big show of some kind was in the works and that the original plan to use large British army, navy, and marine units had been changed. A great number of valiant young volunteer Canadians was becoming so impatient for action that they grumbled noisily and politically. They had been sitting about, thousands of miles from home, highly overtrained and without a battle outlet to prove their mettle. They were fussing to go home unless there was some action. This restlessness translated itself into a high-echelon political decision that they be the major armed force in the big Dieppe raid and that a Canadian general be assigned as the overall land commander.

The first batch of American fighting men were in the U.K. by now, and a small new quasi-commando army unit, calling itself Rangers, had been assigned additional objectives as part of Operation Jubilee. Eventually I was allowed to know a little something of this impending dress rehearsal for an invasion.

Solly Zuckerman had worked out all the probable weather conditions and predicted there never would be a dependably suitable time. Gradually I got a hint of *what* was to happen, but not yet where or when. I occasionally saw high-level friends like Averell Harriman (in London on Lend-Lease matters), Churchill's sidekick Brendan Bracken, and various old colleagues. Somehow I led them to believe I knew more than I actually did. Indeed, Dickie himself let hints of the impending action slip out once in a while—as many high officers, equally slack in security matters, often did.

The upshot of all this was that I tried to maneuver myself into the operation in some way. A select few foreign correspondents got wind of something and bombarded Dickie's ex–Hollywood PR officer, Jock Lawrence, with requests for "passes" to be officially assigned to correspondents. Even I had a call from Quent Reynolds, a marvelous guy, a fine newscaster, and an ardent Irish Anglophile. He was not on the select list of war correspondents and wondered what I could do. I thought up a convincing reason for Quent to go along, but I couldn't get myself a job unless I went on the command ship to stand around

as another liaison for the press. I decided that was not my kind of job.
It would be embarrassing and would suggest a publicity connection,
an identification that I scrupulously ducked.

In the end I stayed with the "hocus-pocus" group from Ballantrae.
On August 19 we set out from some Channel port in one of several
small boats, all rigged out to experiment with our newest electronic
tricks. After we returned from our small operation, the Allied media
announced "a great raid on the heavily defended French port of
Dieppe, carried out according to Admiral Lord Louis Mountbatten's
Combined Operations plans, Canadians being the main assault
troops." The action was further trumpeted as a huge success with
heavy German losses. I was disappointed not to have been close to this
action, seeing nothing except our own experimental magic (the immediate effects of which in this instance we were never to know for sure).
Nevertheless I sent Dickie a personal telegram of jubilant congratulations.

Coming back to headquarters next day, I learned the *real* news:
Operation Jubilee had been a disaster on the whole. The main frontal
assault, decided upon in opposition to Dickie's pleas (in fact he was
opposed to Dieppe as a target from the first, but was overruled) was
little short of a tragedy. The Germans claimed 50 percent Allied losses
just on the beaches. Actually, the official tally sheet was even worse:
68 percent of the Canadians and 20 percent of the British commandos
were either killed or wounded; two thousand were taken prisoner,
and a thousand dead had to be left behind.

Finally the press was allowed to admit the "glorious failure," and
everyone involved tried to blame everyone else. One widely printed
news report was that "Doug Fairbanks Jr. had been seen—face blackened, commando-style—on the beaches. . . ." Mary Lee read this too
and once more was frantic with worry. I hadn't heard it myself and
was in any case forbidden, for the time being, to communicate with
anyone at home. But though suffering the undeserved blame for the
debacle, the anger of the Canadians and his own people (civilian and
military), Dickie managed once again to find the time to cable Mary
Lee that "a friend" was "fine and well."

* * *

Just before Operation Jubilee in early August the Combined Ops Headquarters secretaries got into a small tizzy one day when one of their number sent word to me that "H.R.H. the Duke of Kent (King George's younger brother, Prince George) would like you to ring him." I had been shy of ringing either him or his wife, Princess Marina, after my first arrival for fear of seeming pushy. Except for his appreciated, but declined invitation, just before I'd reported for active duty in 1941, to join him as honorary U.S. naval aide on his official Canadian inspection trip, we had not been in touch in ages. The mysterious ice that I imagined had formed between us so long ago happily appeared now to have melted. I rang up and we met for a drink in Buck's Club.

P.G. was now in RAF uniform with the honorary rank of air marshal, appropriate for the inspector general of the RAF, and as they put it, a "Prince of the Blood Royal." (He was the present queen's uncle.) After a couple of welcome pink gins, he confided that he was "aching to see some real action," but because of his position, custom demanded he be "overprotected." In his opinion members of the royal family should be more exposed to the risks of war. Did I have any ideas?

I arranged for the prince to lunch with General "Tooey" Spaatz, our American air force commander in Europe, at a tiny little Mayfair restaurant (Le Bon Viveur) near Shepherd's Market. In order to deflect curious eyes, I ate at a different table. Tooey proved sympathetic. He suggested—strictly off the record and tentatively—that the prince "inspect" the RAF bases in Iceland in his capacity as inspector general. Then, as a courtesy to the king's youngest brother, he would be invited to visit the American air base there. After that, Spaatz said he would propose that a member of the royal family be assigned as a liaison between the two air forces as "a fine Allied gesture." It seemed an excellent idea, and we agreed that no one would say anything more about it until it happened.

As we parted, P.G. proposed I come for a weekend with him and Princess Marina at Coppins; I don't remember clearly, but I doubt if I'd been there since the abdication crisis. As the proposed visit was some weeks away, I gratefully accepted. I was due back from a training trip then, which turned out to be the Dieppe raid, Operation Jubilee.

As it happened, I did get back on the Friday before the planned weekend and was given a leave until Monday. I checked in for the night with Irving, soon to join the U.S. Army's Signal Corps but still doing his last bit of wallowing in MGM's bounty at Claridge's.

Saturday morning, as I was packing a small case for at least one night, the morning papers, carefully folded, were delivered to Irving's suite by a bellman. There was an envelope for me on top. It was a handwritten letter from P.G. In it he apologized for putting me off but said my weekend visit would have to be postponed as he had to leave on a "special assignment" for the RAF. He indicated discreetly that my efforts on his behalf, along with the suggestions made by Tooey, might be bearing fruit since his plans and destination were in line with discussions we had had recently. This meant that he was on the way to his inspection trip in Iceland. He suggested that I ring Princess Marina and make another, later date.

I put the letter aside and unfolded the top morning paper to see what was new in the world. It showed a large, bleak, black headline: DUKE OF KENT KILLED. The report stated he had been en route to Iceland in line of duty with the RAF when his plane crashed into a mountain in Scotland. All others aboard the RAF plane were also killed instantly, including his aide-de-camp, Flight Lieutenant the Hon. Michael Strutt. Strutt was the husband of one of Mary Lee's closest friends, Arielle Frazier.

The funeral services were held in the beautiful medieval St. George's Chapel within the ancient walls of Windsor Castle, where so many other royals have been buried over the centuries. Although we were in the midst of a great war, a moving formal ceremony that had not changed since William the Conqueror took place. Mourners included most heads of state whose countries had been overrun by the Nazis: the Dutch, Norwegian, Danish, Greek, French, and Luxembourg, in addition to diplomatic representatives from the Commonwealth and the United States. P.G.'s own immediate family consisted of his mother and his wife; his elder brother, the king; the queen; his next older brother, the Duke of Gloucester; his sister, the princess royal; the Mountbattens; and the prince's old nurse. His once favorite brother, now the Duke of Windsor, chose not to attend.

I was given special permission by the navy to accept Princess Marina's invitation. Except for the foreign royal relations and diplomats, I think that I was the only "private" foreigner there, certainly I was the only nonofficial American.

First in the procession came the ashen-faced king, then the queen, holding Princess Marina's arm, and then his mother, the elderly Queen Mother, Mary. All the ladies were heavily veiled. There were also old and close family friends (I spotted Noël across the aisle), servants, and many other nonroyal, ordinary people from all walks of life—anachronistic bodies. In those drab, stark days of tightly rationed food, drink, fuel, and transport, of blitzes and blitzkrieg and concentration camps, the soldiers in tin hats, sailors and airmen in service dress, officers in various shades of khaki and civilians in heavy mourning did not seem out of place. The only color was provided by the white-plumed and scarlet-and-blue-coated "gentlemen-at-arms" who lined the way. RAF and Horse Guard trumpeters sounded taps and the Windsor Boys' Choir sang angelically. The ancient ceremony and pageantry inside seemed more appropriate to the gray reality of the world than the lovely summer's day outside.

Before I left on my next trip north, I paid a visit to my old Grosvenor Square penthouse, now being rented to the rich American divorcée, Mrs. "Pops" d'Erlanger, a once popular piano performer known as Edythe Baker, from Kansas City. Some years before she had been the special girlfriend of Prince George, a connection that went out the window when he married Princess Marina. The gossips said Edythe was given a healthy settlement to bow out of her royal relationship gracefully, though no one I knew could prove it. Nevertheless she continued to live a luxurious expatriate life in wartime London, while carrying a flaming grudge. The day I went to see her, she was entertaining a group of young fliers from different parts of the Commonwealth. She greeted me so warmly that I assumed she had gulped down one too many of her own cocktails, and then she resumed haranguing everyone about the fatuity of "fighting to save useless England." She said she wished "the whole island would sink" under the Nazi bombs, "taking Mayfair society with it." So vehement was she and so shocked and disillusioned did the impressionable young pilots seem that I left in barely controlled anger.

The next day I mentioned the incident to Robert Neville, Dickie's marine colonel chief-of-staff. A few days later, Scotland Yard called on her and "invited" her to leave the country for the United States. She was livid and, on learning I was responsible, never forgave me. I can't say I blame her for that, anyway.

One day soon after the funeral at Windsor, Dickie called me into his office. His ebullience seemed to have returned, although it was clear that he felt P.G.'s death and the tragic failure of the Dieppe operation keenly—*except* for the valuable lessons so expensively learned. He also knew he was the inspiration behind Combined Operations. He was still a handsome, dashing national hero, and was aware that he must maintain morale within his command by seeming to play the role.

He greeted me cheerily but soon came to the point. My "celebrity" status continued to be not just an embarrassment to the command, but also, he added considerately, it threatened security because so many people noticed my comings and goings, and wondered what I was up to. All this was not just in London, but even at the Scottish training and experimental bases. I was very upset to hear this, as I had been fascinated by my job (and the relatively relaxed life I was now leading).

Dickie continued. He was very anxious that the U.S. Navy and Army develop their own special tactical deception operations, using all the new equipment we had been developing. He wanted me to be the emissary for the idea. But first I had to learn all phases and tactics of amphibious raiding operations—which included real raids in the small landing craft and, later, the command of a flotilla of them at sea.

This proposal stunned me for a moment. I thought to myself (very quickly) that I had already had a fairly good share of active warfare at sea. My wits began to trip over themselves thinking of ways to "beg out" of this proposal without seeming frightened, though I knew I was. Dickie, under the illusion that I was only shy and would be just as exhilarated by being shot at as he, misunderstood my half smiles and muffled words of protest and barked out that he knew I *longed* for more action and the experience of "the real thing at close quarters."

Of course, I nodded agreement rather than disillusion him altogether, but I soon followed up with an idea that I thought would get me out of what promised to be an uncomfortable and dangerous job: as I was an *American* officer, Dickie's real operational bodies of British fighting men would not take kindly to my giving them orders. "What will I do if they ignore me or tell me to go to hell—which by law they could?"

The only reaction I got to this was Dickie, smiling confidently and proudly and, clapping me on the shoulder, saying, "Cross that bridge when you come to it!"

The next thing I knew I was doing just what he'd proposed. I began by reporting to Commander Derek Wyburd, Royal Navy, at another secret base called HMS (like a ship) *Tormentor*. It was a small amphibious naval base, with hurriedly assembled wooden huts for living quarters and a large variety of small amphibious landing craft, located near Warsash, not far from Southampton. I remembered the old pub nearby that I had once frequented with Gee Lawrence and the Bensons—the Crab and Lobster. I found it had been firebombed and destroyed only a few months ago.

This was a new kind of training. It entailed not just navigation and pilotage but learning to shoot with a tommy gun (when necessary); to stab and wrestle; and to command the maneuvering, beaching, landing, withdrawing, and defending of a flotilla of six to eight small landing craft called Higgins Boats. These were amphibious craft that carried one or two officers, six to eight sailors, and perhaps up to twenty troops. The latter were commandos, marines, or an equivalent number of regular infantry to be put ashore and recovered after a raid.

I was wonderfully helped from the first day by my newly assigned mentor, Lieutenant "Shocker" Byerly, a bright little chap who hopped through war like a bantam rooster. Few knew his correct name because he gloried in his nickname. He was under the British Navy's minimum height limit for young seagoing officers, but somehow he got in. Through his pointed beard and perky mustachios, I judged him to be only in his mid to late twenties, but he had quickly moved up to the rank of full lieutenant in the RN's Volunteer Reserve. What's more, some months earlier as commander of an amphibious flotilla, he had actually gone ashore as a key figure in the commando raid that blew up much of the important Nazi naval base at St. Nazaire on the French coast. He was thereupon awarded the Distinguished Service Cross.

Shocker, in his roisterous, blasphemous, but always puckish way, soon instructed me in how to command a flotilla of amphibious craft. He educated me to become a real naval commando and to do "anything the bloody brass hats might tell us to do!"

I was assigned a bunk in one of several areas sometimes referred to as rooms, divided by composition board in a tin hut. As in Scotland, the so-called beds were wooden planks supported by rusty springs set in a box frame. I remember no such luxuries as mattresses—they were for "softies." Comfort was rationed in the form of three or four thick, rough blankets as mattresses on the bunks, with two or three more to pull over us to help reduce the effects of chilly damp nights. We *did* get two pillows each. I remember they were pretty hard, as if stuffed with starched dishrags.

Our base, HMS *Tormentor,* was served and serviced by a couple of groups of WRENs. Some were dears and all were cheerful. They cooked, waited on table in the mess hall, kept things more or less tidy, ran errands, and (a luxury undreamed of in the U.S. military services) awakened the officers with a tray containing a pot of tea and a couple of biscuits. They woke us at bedside, as Shocker slyly advised, "each morning with the cock's crow!" But after that, the day was hard, cold and/or hot, and always a bit salty wet.

It was decided that the quickest way for me to learn my new job was just to *do* it. Actually I was ordered to accompany Shocker as a silent (frankly useless) assistant and watch how *he* did things. Everyone was expected to sleep in their boats, fully (and warmly) dressed. My corner in such quarters was no more damp or stinking than any other. Nevertheless I did sleep soundly—for a few hours anyway.

The first time out, ours was one of several flotillas of Higgins Boats and some larger landing craft; there were perhaps twenty-five or thirty boats altogether. We made our slow way across the Solent in the late twilight, from Warsash over to the Isle of Wight. About seven hundred Royal Marine commandos got aboard there in a mad, dark scramble. I was surprised to find their leader was a tough-looking guards captain, a fellow I'd known in peacetime as an aristocratic Mayfair playboy—Lord Ponsonby. No one told me where we were going or why, and I was too anxious to appear calm to ask.

It was quite dark by the time we were out in open sea. Two small escorting destroyers loomed up on either side and then fanned way out of sight. When daylight returned—too soon for my comfort, but appropriately for the time of year—I still had no idea where we were. There was no land in sight.

Alarms went out just before dawn that two German E-boats (enemy versions of fast torpedo boats) had picked us up on their radio waves and were coming in to attack. With no duties, no hiding place, and only a service pistol and a commando dagger for self-protection, I was surely one of the unhappiest aboard. All boats were signaled to throttle down engines, reduce speed, and "bloody well keep quiet!" We could see next to nothing, but after a while, Shocker's small radio told us that our destroyers had chased the E-boats away at high speed into a fog off the French coast.

On the second twilight of plunging around in the Channel, we heard that a few Luftwaffe planes were looking for us. Just in time—like an old Pearl White serial—two RAF fighters came roaring over and chased the Jerries away before they found us. The chase happened too far away for us to have heard anything at all. What's more, it wasn't until after we got back that I learned why I hadn't known our destination or mission; we had never had a *real* raid planned at all. It was always meant to be an extended exercise in the form of a feint to make the enemy nervous. We would repeat this a few times more until one night we would actually land—somewhere.

After another week of training back at our base, we were again at sea, but closer to shore this time. The weather was warm enough to go skinny-dipping off the sides of the boats before boarding our troops. Though the water was on the chilly side, I was pleasantly reminded of other days, other summers, and other—happier—places.

"Come on, chaps!" called out the ever-bubbling Shocker, his little pointed beard turning him into a jolly, mischievous Mephisto, still dripping. "Let's pick up the dear little pongos!" For over a year I'd been hearing the British navy refer to all soldiers as pongos. It seemed a cozy-sounding nickname for our foot-slogging comrades like our GIs and their Tommies. The soldiers themselves seemed to like the name. I asked Shocker where the word originated.

"Gaw bless ye, Duggie-boy! You're the first bloke who's ever asked me! I had to look the bloody word up meself. It's only found in those big-effing dictionaries." His uptwisted moustache twitched with wicked humor. "It says there something about it" (pause) "being really a specimen of Central African ape with light tan hair and remarkably low intelligence!" With that, his small frame shook with crackling laughter. We went ahead with the job of loading the pongos aboard after we all had a couple of stale sandwiches and *very* hot tea in large dirty cups, filled from the several dirty old buckets in which it had been brewed.

After a few more strenuous weeks of this, I got a weekend's leave and spent one night of it with the Mountbattens in the country at Broadlands. Both of them were wound up like springs in Swiss clocks—full of talk, nonstop questions with few openings for replies, easy laughter, gossip, and reading of priority mail. Edwina was now completely absorbed in heading up the women's end of the St. John Ambulance Corps. She worked in the worst parts of the bombed-out slums and with the aged and children in emergency hospitals. With all the distractions, they tried to be good hosts at the same time. Their two girls, Patricia and Pamela, had been sent to America for the duration.

Dickie boasted of his young nephew Prince Philip (then "of Greece"), who was now also in the navy and at sea in destroyers. He'd had splendid reports of him. Edwina asked about Mary Lee and when she was expecting. In replying with my own family news I stopped and pulled my words back sharply. I had been just on the point of recalling Mary Lee's pleasure at the time Bunny Phillips and Edwina visited Boxwood Farm. I suddenly realized that Bunny—a charming, handsome young guards officer who very much resembled a younger Dickie—was said by gossips of the day to be Edwina's current lover. We were so innocent of all this at the time that we very nearly dropped tons of ill-timed bricks. It was whispered that Dickie knew of Edwina's wandering but chose to be too absorbed in his duties to rock the domestic boat. I never knew for certain, at that time anyway. This and other similarly suspected attachments were usually assumed to exist, but for the most part were left undiscussed.

This Broadlands visit was especially memorable. Dickie asked if I'd like to walk with him along the small but lovely River Test, which rippled with trout and refracted sunlight on that fine summer evening. I accepted. Edwina decided to remain behind with the only other house guest that weekend, their strangely miscast but inseparable intimate, Peter Murphy. He was a large, devout Irish homosexual and communist sympathizer, and neither his carnal nor political preferences seemed to fit in this branch of the Mountbatten family. But both Mountbattens had been devoted to him for years.

As we went down the sloping lawn toward the river, Dickie put on a jaunty old Tyrolean hat with a small feather. As he did so, Edwina called out, "Oh, Dickie, for God's sake take off that dreadful hat! It makes you look so frightfully *German!*"

This clearly made Dickie quite tight-lipped with suppressed anger and embarrassed in my young hero-worshiping presence. However, he said nothing. I don't think Edwina's anti-German sentiments had anything to do with her Jewish blood, because neither she nor her sister Mary thought any more of it than did their titled father and German grandfather. I think it was due partly to the image of villainy that the Germans projected and a mildly mischievous sadism with which she sometimes enjoyed putting Dickie down. He was always so grand-looking and handsome, it must have been irresistible.

Edwina was very rich and beautiful, and had, until the shock of war, preferred a more fashionably trivial life. To Dickie most people (except his own personal heroes and friends) were components of squadrons, fleets, teams, masses of leaders and followers. To her, people were individuals, each unique.

Dickie and I just walked on silently for a spell. Then the easy pleasure of each other's company took over and he asked me about my relations with my late father. Pete's outsize public image and personal magnetism had made him one of Mountbatten's heroes. In reply, I talked of the complexities that had existed between us, our poverty of communication, the suspicions of rivalry, our ironic closeness in the month before his death in 1939, and of the mostly hero he had been to me. I didn't finish because Dickie apparently wanted to create an opening for himself so he could describe his well-known, far more intense hero worship of *his* father. He hinted that the cause of his driving ambition was his determination to avenge the injustice done to his great naval officer father, who, even after changing his name from Battenburg to Mountbatten and exchanging his German title for a lesser British one, had been relieved of his high post in

World War I merely because of the public's hysterical prejudice and suspicion of his German birth. And perhaps that, too, inspired Edwina to make her stinging remark.

On my way back to base (in the little beat-up car I borrowed from Shocker), I dropped in on Noël in Kent, where Larry and Viv were weekending. That was quite a change and more in my line. We laughed, gossiped, and scarcely mentioned the war until late that night, in the distance, we saw searchlights near the Kentish coast. Tracer bullets were chasing night bombers, and we heard the distant *whoomph* of bombs landing. The raid over, we returned to our jokes.

A few nights later our several flotillas crawled in formation around southern England, hugging the coast until just beyond Brighton we reached the small seaport of Newhaven. The sea was ugly and inhospitable. I threw up twice on the way, but no one seemed to notice (very polite of them, I thought).

It was the first time I was to see a large-scale camouflage of an important target. This had been used on various places near London and other big cities, hoping to dissuade enemy night bombers from hitting such prime targets as the classic Battersea power station, Parliament, and Westminster Hall. Here in Newhaven a masterly imitation of the River Ouse was created nearby that successfully persuaded the Luftwaffe to bomb it, hurting no one and nothing. Not far away the real river, a very small and narrow one, was covered over for quite a distance with netting, making it look for all the world like a continuation of the fields, farms, and hedges that did in fact lie on either side, just outside the town itself.

We hid our boats under the camouflaged netting, bow to stern, on each bank. Our living quarters were in the town hall. It was the night before we were due to load our craft with pongos and carry out a small, well-rehearsed nuisance or pajama raid (so called because of the late hour) on some of the gun emplacements on the enemy-occupied Channel Islands. That night I had "the duty," which meant I was the officer-in-charge of the base. All my shipmates went to the local village pub and got sloshed in preparation for the next night's predawn adventure.

I assumed that I was chosen because I was both a new boy with the outfit and a Yank. I "held the can" by sitting at a desk reading a paperback and trying to keep awake. I had one RN chief petty officer standing by to help me if needed.

It wasn't long before help *was* needed. The local shore Police made a noisy entrance dragging a poor young sailor, drunk as only the better sailors can get. As the record showed, he was not only drunk but two days over leave. I signaled my CPO to come over so I could whisper, "What'll I do, chief? I'm an American officer—I don't have any legal authority to do anything to him!"

The CPO grinned and in joyful sotto voce cockney replied, "Oh, it's orl-right, sah! Just read the bloody book o' rules at the poor bugger! 'Ee dunno wot 'is rights are anywise!"

So that's what I did. I checked the standard punishment for "poor buggers" (something like a couple of days in solitary with bread and water), the Shore Police saluted and dragged him off, and that was that. He might actually have been glad to be spared the next day's operation.

We started out very early at about 2:30 A.M. By now I had had plenty of practice and could command my miniature flotilla quite ably. I'd mastered all the newfangled signals and maneuvers. In any case Shocker had the lead flotilla and a twinkling eye on his protégé. As usual, I was scared but had nearly mastered the art of disguising it. Our briefing had taken place a few days earlier near Brighton in a deep underground shelter code-named Fort Southwick. The weather continued to be capricious. After several false starts, we turned back in the face of a force-8 gale. Though edgy about the whole thing, I was disappointed since I believed the operation was such a small one that once begun, it would soon be over. With luck we could have a decent chance of getting away, if not totally unscathed, then only a little scathed.

Finally, after long, soggy hours in the Channel, we made a useless dash (though our boats could only make about eight to ten knots per hour at best) to whatever island it was and immediately alerted the sleepy enemy guards. A few ill-aimed shots were exchanged, and back to sea we fled. In misty daylight at mid-Channel, we saw a yellow RAF inflatable rubber dinghy wobbling. As we drew nearer, we saw a man waving madly at us. We steered toward him and saw his wet, tattered RAF uniform. As we picked him up, I thought to myself what a bloody awful job he had. To be shot down (we presumed) to land mid-Channel, to shiver in the wet and cold, possibly wounded, to sit in a rubber dinghy and hope that *somebody* would come along and rescue you! It made me rethink our own, relatively cushy situation.

"Where you blokes from?" he asked as we dragged him into my leading boat. "What the hell are you doin' comin' over from the Froggy coast all gunned up like that?"

One of our commando lieutenants spoke up. "This is a Combined Ops thing—just back from a little demonstration show-off—a little better than a practice shoot-up—at one of the blinkin' islands, that's all!"

The airman's eyes widened and gave way to an admiring half smile. "Christ-a-mighty!" he said, in awed though shivering tones. "Commandos, eh? *Gawd!* I wouldn't have your bloody job for all the bloody tea in China! Thank Christ you're here."

Chapter 5

By MID-OCTOBER 1942 Rommel's German legions had recovered all that Mussolini's Italians had lost in North Africa. Rommel pushed the British back into Egypt, almost to Alexandria. But as the late Lord Harlech once said, "The British never know there is a wall until their backs are to it." On October 23, General Montgomery's Eighth Army Desert Rats opened up at El Alamein with a fury so fierce that once it started the Nazis' heretofore invincible Afrika Korps fell back. At 3:00 A.M. on the morning of November 8, 1942, the western coast of North Africa was invaded by hundreds of warships and transports—the first joint Anglo-American operation of the war. It was also the largest amphibious invasion in history, up to that time: five hundred ships carrying over a hundred thousand troops. Landings took place over a six-hundred-mile front from Casablanca to Algiers. This was a squeeze play on Rommel.

I had known something very big was planned, but I couldn't know what. All I did know was that its code name was Torch. Whatever its objective, I tried my best to be a part of it—to try our new gadgets on a large scale. I heard hints of a huge deception plan. A very limited list was "in the know." And I was certainly not on it.

Just before the North African invasion, in late October, I suddenly received orders to return home and "report to Vice Admiral H. Kent Hewitt, Commander, Amphibious Force, U.S. Atlantic Fleet Headquarters," in Norfolk, Virginia.

A whoop of joy rose in my throat. I would be getting back to Mary Lee in time for the new baby's arrival. I was keenly disappointed at not going along for Operation Torch, even though none of us yet knew what it was. But my regrets were definitely deluged by my flood of joy at going home.

Dickie had given Captain Huse, my immediate USN boss, a far better fitness report on my duties with him than I knew I deserved. But I was not one to quibble. After all, Admiral Giffen had also written up a fine report for me, even though some officers joked that navy propaganda would be helped were I to become some sort of casualty.

My trip home was, to my surprise, aboard the fairly new (1938–39) Cunarder, the RMS *Queen Elizabeth,* advertised before the war as the world's largest passenger ship. According to the ads, it carried 2,233 passengers. Now, converted to a troop ship, it carried (we were told) about 15,000 souls! I was luckier than most because I didn't have to sleep on deck, in a passageway or dining room. I was in a stateroom designed for two, though now, thanks to the installation of triple-deck bunks, ten to twelve could be squeezed in. Though noisy and smelly and, except for the quarters of the very senior officers aboard, over-crowded, the ship was as luxurious as anything I'd had at sea since I went to war.

I was especially surprised to find friends on the ship among such a mixed mob. Never in the world would I have expected Irving Asher, whom I thought had quit MGM and gone back for Army Signal Corps training weeks before. And Alex Korda, of all people! *And* Eddie Robinson, back from a U.S. propaganda tour. Jammed to the gunwales as we were, and chased by U-boats (vainly, thanks to God and our zigzagging thirty-something-knot speed), my only grouse was that a senior army colonel in the bunk below me suffered nightly, almost overwhelmingly, from wind.

My suspense in racing the stork was greater than any other con-cern, including our reported eluding of any number of U-boats. We now all knew that Operation Torch was the code name for our landings in North Africa, but even news reports of our initial success there took second place in my interest. I had a feeling I was needed at home and couldn't get there fast enough.

As soon as we docked in New York in mid-November and I could get off the mammoth liner and get to a telephone, I rang Mary Lee.

She cried out with incredulity when she realized I was actually in New York. I collected my footlocker and what little other personal gear I had and bumped off in a familiar New York taxi, then as now with grubby, uncomfortable seats and grumbling driver.

The rest must be imagined. Neither of us could recall anything beyond our mutual joy. I was at home in good time because the new baby didn't join our wounded world for another fortnight. This was fortuitous because *she* made her nine-pound debut on December 2—one more Sagittarian in the family.

Both Mary Lee and I felt deeply about the massive issues that were being fought over in this second world war in less than twenty-five years. We therefore linked prayers for victory with our new baby and named her Victoria. And because we liked the name Susan, we gave her that for a middle name.

After almost a month of compassionate leave, including the homecoming leave to which I was in any case entitled, I reported to Admiral Hewitt in Norfolk just before Christmas. Admiral Hewitt was a shy and soft-spoken brass hat. I was taken by his flag secretary, Lieutenant Julie Boit, to the Amphibious Force Headquarters in nearby Virginia Beach. All Hewitt's staff, including an ex-Bovée schoolmate, his flag lieutenant, Ben Griswold, made it quickly clear that the Old Man was very affectionately served.

I was to be temporarily assigned to a still vague job, somewhere between the War Plans Section and Intelligence. When settled in, I would outline my proposals for a unit trained in special commando-type raiding operations, employing new electronic devices as aids for tactical deceptions and diversions.

Then after a quick trip to Washington to touch a few bases, I went back to my flourishing family—including a cooing grandmother (my mother Beth) and step-grandfather Jack Whiting, now playing in *Beat the Band* at the Forty-sixth Street Theatre. Suddenly just after Christmas, I came down with a severe wartime flu called cat fever and was hustled off to a hospital. When I got out a few days later, more or less cured, it was New Year's Eve, and Mary Lee joined me at the huge old resort hotel the Chamberlain, at Old Point Comfort (what a misnomer—at least then) in Virginia.

I began my new job at Virginia Beach on a high note: Dickie's,

Admiral Giffen's, and Admiral Stark's reports on me encouraged Hewitt to listen sympathetically to my unconventional recommendations. But his support failed to persuade the Joint Chiefs of Staff in Washington, the army, or even the navy that deception operations were anything more than a waste of time and money; they thought the idea just another set of wasteful silly tricks. Only Hewitt approved developing special tactical diversions that employed complicated electronic deception equipment. On receiving the recommendation of Bob English of the War Plans Section, he was able to authorize me to recruit volunteers with advanced training in electronic, sonic, and visual sciences.

The welcome encouragement I got from Admiral Hewitt was hindered somewhat by my own overzealousness. Little things I did invited understandable criticism. First there was my preference for adapting the Combined Ops working uniform for wet-duty work. It consisted of a thick, warm, navy-blue version of the army's battle dress or Eisenhower jacket. I was thought to be overinfluenced by the limeys. Perhaps my critics were right. Yet in self-defense it should be mentioned that many other American officers who served in Britain had new uniforms made by British military tailors, had their brighter gold stripes sewn on their sleeves, sported a glimpse of a white handkerchief in their breast pockets, and wore softer tops to their caps. I was still conspicuous, but I had learned to be more careful.

However, some of my minor modifications in working rig made certain practical sense, and Hewitt approved several of them. Most other proposals were technical, such as coordinating special operations (diversions) with main assault plans, adapting night goggles for use with infrared light, writing an amphibious diversionary training manual, and using fluorescent smoke and projection for our operations.

I wore a commando dagger in my belt and was temporarily permitted to wear the small Combined Ops shoulder patch. It helped gain a certain grudging interest when word got around that I had seen action along the way. Hewitt and Plans boss Captain Bob English didn't seem to mind.

I was told to prepare a formal paper for the Joint Chiefs of Staff to serve as the basis for a directive for future deception and special-operations task groups. I was authorized to begin forming special small-boat flotillas with the scientists I would recruit on the order of our Combined Ops units at HMS *Tormentor*. Our now very secret base was near Virginia Beach at an island waterway called Camp Bradford, itself commanded by an ex–Naval Academy tough guy with a fierce disposition. I was accompanied on my recruiting junkets by another officer who was an electronics and science expert. We visited a few select universities to interview students with advanced technical qualifications and asked for volunteers for potentially hazardous duty, the details of which could not be divulged in advance. Some of these bright young men were shortly to be drafted anyway. That many declined such a scary invitation was less surprising than the number who jumped at it. In the end, these newly named Beach Jumpers (Special Operations Group) numbered roughly seventy young officers and about four hundred sailors—all volunteers!

Although my top-secret memos for tactical diversions, special training, and development were on the whole approved, I did not have sufficient rank to take over the project. Because the U.S. Navy was not so flexible as the other services and unable to give spot promotions (Admiral Hewitt's recommendation for my promotion to lieutenant commander was declined), a senior captain with a Naval Academy background was given the job of commanding these Beach Jumpers. As this new character appeared to be something of a nautical Jekyll and Hyde, I shall refer to him hereafter as Commander S. Nevertheless I was unofficially responsible to Hewitt's staff for "tactical developments" (a term that could mean anything) and was given an "open sesame" letter, a most impressive and provocative paraphrase of one Dickie had given me at Combined Operations Headquarters:

> To All Concerned: Lt. D. E. Fairbanks, Jr., U.S.N.R., is the special operations officer in the War Plans Section of my staff, in which capacity he is of course informed on all secret planning. He is in addition to his regular duties charged with arranging for the acquisition of special material and personnel and with the preparation of plans for the execution of special operations. It is particularly requested that those concerned will give him every possible assistance and appreciate that for security reasons he will not always be able to give full explanation of the duties he

is performing. Signed: H. S. Hewitt, Vice Admiral U.S.N., Commander Amphibious Forces, U.S. Atlantic Fleet.

When amphibious force training for the next invasion (Sicily, as it turned out) intensified, Mary Lee and Daphne (tiny Victoria was left in New York for the time being) and I moved into the navy's requisitioned Princess Anne Country Club at Virginia Beach. Every morning I got up at 1:30 or 2:00 A.M., gulped down some breakfast that Mary Lee had prepared, and was out in the chilling predawn struggling with electronic equipment, dummy weapons and boats, or just standing around on the beaches getting wet and hoping I gave the impression that I knew what I was doing.

When an occasional few days' leave was granted, Mary Lee and I would pop up to New York or drive to Boxwood Farm to make silly noises at the lovely, laughing Victoria and then drop down to Washington where I'd make a few courtesy calls—most important, on old Secretary of State Cordell Hull (though I once sneaked in for a quick chat with FDR). I was invariably surprised and flattered when Mr. Hull confided certain diplomatic objectives then under way—for example, the continuing bitter rivalry for Free French allegiance between de Gaulle and Giraud, and the delicate matter of encouraging the reestablishment of a constitutional monarchy and parliament in recaptured Greece. I was further encouraged to send Hull my own private views of events as I saw them, from time to time.

By the last of May, it seemed that everyone under Admiral Hewitt's command, except me, had been shipped to North Africa and transferred to the new U.S. Naval Headquarters just outside of Algiers where Hewitt's new title was "Commander, U.S. Naval Forces, North West African Waters." The U.S., British, and Free French high commands also made their headquarters near the city of Algiers.

I would be ordered to follow soon. As my old bête noir, Admiral Kirk (who had dumped me on the Staten Island minesweeper), was to take over Hewitt's command back in Norfolk, I was glad to be leaving. Yet I was anxious about my future in addition to separating from my shiny young family. I had more or less created the Beach Jumpers, but as a staff officer I had no operational duties with them. To add to my confusion, I had not been included in the first group to go to North

Africa with Hewitt. I'd had my wings clipped—not too surprising, as I had wangled, conned, and slid my way into official areas well beyond my real capabilities. And I knew it better than anyone. The official explanation, sensible and proper in retrospect, was that I just did not have the requisite rank to take over something of such importance.

By early June 1943, North Africa had been cleared of the enemy. Monty's Eighth Army had bested Rommel and the Anglo-U.S. invasions and conquests of the rest of North Africa had at last cleared the remainder, crumbs and all.

My orders, when they finally came, a month or so after the others had left, were to report to Admiral Hewitt's command in Algiers. I took off from New York in a Sikorsky seaplane (a jittery novelty for me) one morning at about ten with a final destination of Algiers. There were a number of stops. Botwood, Newfoundland (desolate but wildly beautiful), was first. Then after some eleven hours of flying time, we touched down in Foynes, Eire. All of us on the plane were in an American military service. But as Eire (the Republic of Ireland) was a neutral in the war, we were not permitted to admit what our jobs were nor to wear our uniforms—even in transit. We had been warned that if we (as uniformed belligerents) acknowledged our military status, we would either be returned to the United States or interned by the Irish for the duration. Consequently, when I showed my special civilian passport to the smartly uniformed Irish immigration officer, he looked sternly at me and said, "Oh, *Lieutenant* Fairbanks! *Navy* lieutenant, I think." I smilingly shook my head and nervously mumbled a denial. The Irish official courteously asked me to follow him into his office in the back, which I did with, I hoped, equal politeness.

Once inside, he shut the door and asked if I'd like a bit of Irish coffee. I declined. He smiled and confided with a wink, "Don't worry, Lieutenant Fairbanks. I won't do anything to any of you. You see, I was an officer in the British army myself—the Irish Guards in fact—and was invalided out after being wounded at Dunkirk. When I got better, I came home to Ireland and got a job with immigration here at Foynes. Hell, old chap, I'm collecting my British pension regularly! Come on! Let's have your autograph and *then* let's have a drink." I complied. We shook hands and chatted for a few minutes before I took off again.

Our next stop was Gibraltar, in a few hours. Gib was fascinating. A junior official from the governor's office was at the airport and apparently thought I was a VIP. He gave me a guided tour of the great fortress—both outside, where the apes scamper about, and inside, where it's so big there are military cops directing traffic on crossways on different levels. I was told there were stored munitions, ordnance of all kinds, communications and air-conditioning systems, plus enough food, drink, and fuel to sustain thousands of troops for many weeks, even months, should the place ever be besieged by an enemy. It was a stunning experience.

From there to Algiers. I checked in with Lieutenant Julie Boit, Hewitt's flag secretary, who sent me over to the same boss I'd had at home—Captain Bob English, head of the Planning Section. I was given the impressive-sounding title of Special Operations Planning Officer. Next—where to live ashore? At first I was billeted in one of the officers' Quonset huts, but I later decided to follow the lead of some permanently Algiers-based U.S. Air Force staff characters who rented permanent flats in downtown Algiers—a surprisingly (to me) large modern French colonial city. A friend of a friend of a friend introduced me to Captain Clif Lord, a young, energetic American air force officer who, with U.S. civil servant Charley Moffley, had two or three army and navy officers sharing his rent. He offered me a small outside room in the rambling apartment at 108 rue Michelet if I wanted it. I did. I kept some gear in our suffocating tin shack back at headquarters, high on the hill outside town, but for what I needed daily this was fine.

I had barely settled in when I learned that work had started in preparation for the next major landing—Sicily, code-named Operation Husky, the first invasion of Europe proper. The paperwork occupied our whole staff. My "diversion baby," the newly formed Beach Jumpers task group, or BJs, had gone far from Algiers headquarters and me. The officers, men, boats, and gear were all based in Bizerte and Ferryville in Tunisia, many miles away. The outfit's oddball martinet skipper Captain S., his small staff, his good-sized crews and maintenance men, a couple of temporarily attached squadrons of PT (patrol torpedo) boats, medium landing ships, landing ship tanks, air-sea-rescue craft, and assorted small craft were all at the new secret Tunisian base. They also had mountains of electronic gear, loudspeakers, prerecorded sounds (the noises of the beaching of landing craft accompanied by voices of every imaginable American and British accent calling out orders, reports, and replies), radar-jamming and stock deception equipment, smoke-laying equipment, rockets, torpedoes, machine guns, bazookas, and small arms. I was distressed to be so detached from a group for which I had been responsible, but regulations stated that those in operations could not be on staff. The reason was that if, for instance, a staff member was captured, he would risk compromising and endangering a whole force because he knew too much. In my case, I was the only American anywhere who had had practical experience in all this hocus-pocus. Hence I had to prepare, with help, the special operation plans for future tactical deception operations. Meanwhile the operational group went ahead with its training in Tunisia.

Originally it had been intended to test the expertise of our American Beach Jumpers against an enemy target even before I arrived. The minute Italian island of Pantelleria was suggested. Not only was it an obstacle to most transmediterranean sea traffic, but it was also potentially in the way of Operation Husky, the invasion of Sicily. Then the high command decided that instead of a preliminary diversion off Sicily, it would be better to simply smother the little island fortress (crammed as it was with artillery and nearly one hundred German and Italian aircraft) by bombing it for *five straight weeks*. When this was done and British troops finally landed, more than ten thousand groggy defenders staggered out of their shelters and gave up. The only British casualty was a Tommy who got bitten by a donkey. Both recovered.

Saturation bombing was surely an effective method of persuading tiny Pantelleria to surrender, but *we* thought that our kind of deceptive tactics would have been cheaper in the expense of lives, time, and money—not that any one of these considerations was other than an expendable of wartime. But there was no debating this after the event, and so I arranged to be ordered to fly down to Tunisia for my first visit to our special operations base in the Bay of Bizerte. I was very pleased to see "my" outfit once again and all those eager young volunteers I had recruited. They were now fully equipped, trained (many as specially commissioned sonic and electronics experts), and

rehearsed for what they called "tricky trials with deceptive decibels."
I shared their natural disappointment at not rehearsing under fire. I
did manage to kindle their enthusiasm by hinting that I had been in
on the initial planning for an even bigger show—not too far off!

I still couldn't bring myself to like their commanding officer, Captain S. His rasping voice, exuding all the charm of a rattlesnake, still
scratched ears. I had a disturbing report about him from his exec,
Lieutenant Arthur Bryant, a handsome muscular young fellow from
Hawaii who was no relation to his historian namesake.

Art's speech and manners clearly suggested a background many
notches higher than that of his captain. But Bryant knew naval rules
and regulations governing insubordination. He had considerable responsibility himself, so it was to be some time before he could do more
than hint (privately to me) at what he called "personnel problems."
Meanwhile we agreed between us to ride along with Captain S. for the
moment.

Back in Algiers there was disappointingly little work for me to do
aside from making friends in the British army's top-secret A Force.
There was already an American army major on their staff. This small
group was always personally cordial, but their own security rules,
despite my very special letter from Admiral Hewitt, remained too tight
for me to penetrate their setup very far. As I later learned, this was
quite proper.

Among old friends and familiar faces that I found unexpectedly
in wartime Algiers was the American polo great Jock Whitney,
who was forever going into romantic rhapsodies about his love for
his new bride, Betsy. Jock was a specially commissioned lieutenant
colonel and aide in the Office of Strategic Services (OSS). This
semi-independent intelligence organization did not enjoy the unlimited goodwill of the regular military services because it seemed to
them—not without some justice—to be almost a law unto itself, an
organization of special intelligence-gathering and counterintelligence
spy operations. Somehow they managed, despite a paucity of professional military support, to do much good work. But occasionally
they just got in the regulars' way.

Despite the nightly blackout, I did manage to see something of
wartime Algiers. My part of the big flat I'd rented was small indeed.

But the rest of the almost unfurnished apartment was really quite spacious, and Clif's PR job for the fly boys allowed him ample time to entertain clusters of rich Algerians and French civilian colonials— and their pretty girlfriends. Most of the guests were connected with oil or shipping, some with routine spying. Evenings were too often so hot and muggy that our only relief came from a temperamental air conditioner augmented by big fans suspended from the ceiling. They moved so slowly that the flies and mosquitoes seemed not to notice and just rested there. The guests tended to dance and generally raise hell until far too late for the neighbors, the police, and me, who had to report shortly after dawn each morning. Our host, to whom I paid an appropriately small rent, seemed able to make his own rules. Most of us in the Allied military establishment began our workdays early in order to get a lot done before the pervasive Algerian heat wilted us altogether.

On one night of almost unlimited revelry, our host had invited a spectacular-looking female guest. I recognized her from a recent cover of one of the biggest weekly magazines. She was not quite what I would have imagined from her picture because she was at least six feet three inches tall. As I am six feet, I felt somewhat overwhelmed by this picturesque French colonial Amazon. With little advance notice she indicated that she wanted to speak to me privately in my room. I found that my French small talk was becoming increasingly awkward. With so much hot, sweaty hustling about in the big rugless room, the loud music, and the high-pitched French chatter, any hope that I might have had of quietly slipping into my little room to hit the sack and get some undisturbed sleep was useless. I therefore resigned myself to just sit and listen to her amiably, in a corner of the apartment well away from the old piano—and not in any gossip-provoking cell of a room like mine.

It soon developed that my striking giantess had something special in mind. She very matter-of-factly paid me extravagant and embarrassingly personal compliments. I mimed a modest "Tut-tut," waving a deprecatory hand. She hadn't known till a bit earlier, she said, that I had been a *"grand vedette du cinema."* Then she came to the really punchy part of her confession. She allowed as how she was a keen devotee of sadomasochism. As I tried to look clinically interested, she began to unbuckle her chic leather belt. She said she would dearly love me to *whip* her bare back—for starters. I thought at first that she might be an undiscovered comedienne, looking for a postwar movie contract. So, stalling for time, I confessed that despite my presumed sophistication, the idea of that particular kind of carnal fun and games had never really appealed to me, nor frankly had I ever considered experimenting with it. I then added, rather apologetically, hoping I wouldn't sound too stuffy, that I was married with a young family at home. She waved all that aside and levelly continued asking if I would at least "try the reverse, *par example?*" Would I "submit" to her giving me a hearty thrashing? By this time most of my poise was in stuttering disarray, but I mustered just enough to reply, in my best Maurice Chevalier Montmartre-slangy French, that I absolutely *hated* pain of any kind—from stubbed toes to dentists!

She looked at me condescendingly, smiled with pity, and shrugged. We rejoined the still noisy indifferent group in the middle of the room. I slipped away soon after that, wearily locked my door, and slid into a bemused sleep.

Chapter 6

Sɪᴄɪʟʏ–ᴛʜᴇ first major part of Europe to be invaded by the Western Allies during World War II–has commanded the attention of countless histories, reports, and biographies. I will set down only a few ringside impressions, as my participation was only a smidgen more than minimal. I saw it from a near distance most of the time and close up only as seldom and briefly as I could get away with in obedience to orders.

Task Group 80.4, the designation the planners gave to my gang of Beach Jumpers–I never really thought of them as other than "mine"– had had their original quite large diversionary mission reduced to virtually nothing more than a series of nuisance demonstrations to be executed on the western flank of the main assault. It was decided (by very senior and therefore cynical planners) that these little diverters were too limited in their capabilities to make much difference to any large and alert enemy; they were all right, perhaps, along the North African coast, or for limited commando or ranger raids, but for a *big* operation? They'd "be in the way!"

Before midnight on July 10, 1943, as the invasion armada plunged its way through heavy seas and winds and drew to within a few miles of its destination, still undetected, the signal came to slow down. The gale continued and the landings of both the Americans and the British seemed doomed.

I had been assigned to Admiral Hewitt's command on the head-quarters ship, USS *Monrovia,* having come aboard when she sailed from Algiers. General George S. Patton, who commanded our American land forces, was also aboard. My job was rather ambiguous in that I was to keep an eye on reports from our Beach Jumper units on their errands of annoyance up the west flank, and somehow help the beachmasters once the actual waves of landing craft had begun on the designated beaches. At this point I had no idea how I would do this.

There was little to see yet, but I could tell from working on the plans that this was a gigantic operation, the largest ever attempted. What no one yet knew was that it was to remain, even after the later Normandy and South of France landings, the biggest amphibious invasion ever recorded anywhere at any time. More than three thousand Allied ships and crafts were involved in establishing, under fire from enemy sea, land, and air forces, no less than *seven* Allied divisions (two more than would land in Normandy in less than a year). They were to be put ashore at seven different places on Sicily's southern and southeastern coasts in the initial assault.

The U.S. Navy had assembled 580 ships, transporting 1,124 landing craft, while the British to the east, under Vice Admiral Sir Bertram Ramsay, had 795 ships and 715 landing craft, with a standby task force way to the north composed of battleships, carriers, cruisers, and destroyers, some making another strategic feint off the Greek coast.

By dawn's early light, the winds and seas had subsided, and the first assault waves began to come in to shore. I had little to do on the *Monrovia.* By radio I kept track of our Beach Jumper Task Group 80.4 and stood what I thought were unnecessary watches on behalf of the admiral's staff alongside the *Monrovia's* captain, his exec, and other juniors. I also kept a curious but useless eye on the decoded messages of progress made by the other commands and groups, including the British force to the east.

A short while before we set sail from North Africa, I happened to pick up an oblique description from a British planner of a very high more-secret-than-top-secret deception plan that had been put into operation some weeks before. This very earnest and diligent character assumed that I knew "all about everything." I'd had an inkling of the basic idea, months before, back at Combined Ops in London, but didn't take it seriously at the time: A young, good-looking, unclaimed corpse in a London morgue was dressed in a British officer's uniform, given a name, and had an imaginary career recorded. Then special letters were put in his pockets along with his ID and other papers. After all that, it was arranged for him to be washed up on some part of the Spanish Mediterranean coast. The papers, addressed to Eisenhower from the Imperial General Staff in London, hinted at a future Allied landing in Sardinia—instead of Sicily. The whole story was published and later made into a movie, under the title *The Man Who Never Was*. The person who dreamed up this complicated, morbid, but brilliant move was a peacetime lawyer, a friend of mine, then attached to Mountbatten's Combined Operations, Lieutenant Commander Ewen Montagu. As planned, the body of the poor unknown soldier was found by German spies in Spain, and the Luftwaffe gradually moved a number of its aircraft to Sardinia. When our attacking force was finally reported to be at sea by enemy spies and scout planes, Sardinia was alerted first.

My other lightweight duties were to "liaise" with particular army commanders and their aides, keep all the war correspondents on board happy, and look the other way when they broke out their own smuggled booze (of which, very occasionally, I gratefully accepted a few shots). I was also charged with briefing those who were due to land in one of the earlier assault waves about what to watch out for. Most of the time all was tense and quiet. All, that is, except the wind that kicked up the sea so gruffly that the idea of turning back was at least briefly considered.

While the navy brass became increasingly silent as we plowed slowly on, General Patton sent word he wanted to see me in the admiral's empty cabin, off the bridge, topside. He was very genial— quite contrary to the "blood and guts" image he had so carefully cultivated. But what did he know of me, I wondered? He said he had worked for days on his personal message to his men to be read out on the troopships just before the landing. He explained that he wanted to "inspire" them, and he thought my theater experience would provide him with an expert opinion. Then, in his ill-fitting high-pitched voice, he read out his go-get-'em message. I said I thought it wonderful. And I suppose it was, in a rather corny, melodramatic way. But even if it wasn't, I was far too flattered to think of criticizing it. Anyway, I doubt if I, gutless as usual, could have.

The Axis powers had stationed formidable forces on the large island of Sicily—about a quarter of a million ground troops alone. Their eight hundred aircraft spread out from Sardinia, the mainland, and Sicily and could seriously hamper our assault. The Italian fleet, whittled down but still potentially powerful, was smarting angrily since great chunks of it had been defeated by British cruiser squadrons, most spectacularly in the Battle of Taranto. Indeed, it was this famous action that immediately won the British commander, Admiral Sir Phillip Vian, a second "battlefield knighthood," news of which was flashed to him on the king's behalf. It also earned him a classic felicitation from his superior, Royal Navy Admiral Sir John Cunningham, who signaled him: "TWICE A KNIGHT AND AT YOUR AGE—CONGRATULATIONS!"

As we came closer to the Sicilian coast, the great invasion fleets of the Allies slowed down to minimize the white phosphorous wake trailing the hundreds of ships, already rolling most unpleasantly in the capricious sea. It was just after midnight on July 10, about three hours before the first wave of coastal landings. Our airborne troops were scheduled to fly over later and come down well inland. The British used mostly gliders and dropped paratroopers before dawn. Our first wave came mostly in transport planes. They ran into previously unpredicted high winds that blew them way off course—so much so that several flew directly over our invasion fleet. Our sailors, nervous, frightened, and trigger-happy, began firing at them—and kept on despite the shouted orders to *"Cease fire!"* Far too many couldn't stop—or, for one reason or another, couldn't hear the commands. The desperate result was that during this early part of the invasion our own naval antiaircraft guns brought down more of our airborne troops than did the enemy. The survivors of the original 3,400 Americans who parachuted down were scattered all over southwest Sicily; few survivors were anywhere near their targets. The British had even more tragic luck. Of the 144 fully loaded gliders that took off, half were released prematurely and fell into the sea, drowning all their occupants. Of the 87 men who did land near their target, all but 19 were killed or put out of action. But these few held their bridge objective for hours until the main landing forces caught up and relieved them.

It was to be expected that the closer we got to the coast, the more alert and fierce enemy defenses would become. As we finally hove to, the larger landing craft carrying the first waves of men slithered up to shore behind a heavy protective artillery barrage from our warships, which were moving slowly but far enough away from shore to be beyond the range of the enemy's stunned coastal defenses. As the morning light intensified, some of the enemy's aircraft began looming in on top of us from inland bases, in ones, twos, and widely separated threes, very low at first so as to stay undetected that much longer. Others, later, would come on us from very high, adding to the confusion of the inexperienced sailors manning our shipboard antiaircraft guns. The enemy made very few hits at first, but there were far too many near-misses that concussed the sides of our ships most unpleasantly.

Several of our ships were badly damaged, but the first ones sunk were the destroyer USS *Maddox* and an LST liberty ship. Then another liberty ship loaded with ammunition was hit and blew up, nearly knocking *us* out at the same time. Twenty-three more of our own transport planes were mistaken for enemy aircraft and shot down into the sea. A more heartening moment came when we saw the first waves of infantry getting ashore with surprisingly few casualties. The second wave didn't have it so easy as enemy defenses, until now sporadic, began to get the range.

Each assault wave of infantry and vehicles was taken in by the navy's amphibious landing craft. They made for a specially assigned beach, marked by our beachmasters (a Combined Ops innovation). These hardy souls went in as the "second of the first," marking off areas signaled by frogmen who swam ashore as the "first of the first." It was the job of the beachmasters to ascertain and mark their position, stake out the width of each designated landing beach, and then as soon as possible mark their stretch of beach with large square-colored boards stuck in the sand: for example, "Red Beach," "Blue Beach," "Yellow Beach," and so on. Each landing-craft skipper was assigned a particular beach where he would discharge his troops, back off, and return for another load—all in the face of increasing enemy fire and pileups of bombed, damaged, or beached craft.

Our staff operations officer noticed that one beach in the most hotly contested Gela section was clearly marked with a blue and yellow card, but no one was landing there. In fact, the beach was clear of everyone— even the beachmaster. Efforts to contact someone—anyone—in the naval landing party by hand signal or radio were unavailing; there was too much banging, booming, vehicle clanking, and men shouting for me to separate the sounds or hear any one thing.

The operations officer, seeing me standing about on the bridge doing nothing, angrily ordered me to get the British staff liaison officer, Lieutenant Commander Gerald Butler, to take the standby landing craft in to shore and "see why the hell nobody's using that beach over there. They're crowding and clogging up all the other goddamn beaches!"

"Aye, aye, sir," I stuttered, and hurried away.

Butler was cheery, easygoing, and experienced. He had been on the commando raids to Narvik in Norway and St. Nazaire in France. I felt confident going in with him. We signaled up the staff standby landing craft. The enemy ground fire didn't even bother with us—one solitary LCP (landing craft, personnel) lumbering in on the flank—alone!

Our LCP scrunched up onto the sandy beach, the ramp was let down, and Butler and I jumped knee-deep into the water and stumbled to dry land. Finding no one at all on this fine stretch of beach, except one wrecked and deserted LCT (landing craft tank) lying on its side in the shallow water's edge, the two of us began waving at the beachmaster of Yellow Beach, just to the right of ours, about a hundred yards or so eastward. We tried to wave him over to us, but his only reply was to wave back, calling us to *him*. Oh, the stupid jerk! *Bang!* A shell exploded behind us, and we flopped facedown in the sand. When we looked around we saw the damned thing had gone off too far away to hurt anyone.

By now both Butler and I were steaming with anger at the stupidity of whatever beachmaster was designated to stand where we were but was somewhere else, letting so many extra men and so much materiel, landing craft, and equipment pile up, contributing to more confusion and targets. Sharing a will-to-win type of indignation, Butler and I trudged together as swiftly as we could over the soft white sand, preparing to give the nearest beachmaster (a lowly ensign) absolute hell—on behalf of the admiral, of course! Ignoring the occasional forays of planes attacking our ships and the enemy artillery firing from inland on all the beaches, we began our remonstrance of this poor stupid twerp. But he interrupted, shouting almost hysterically, *"Sir! Thank God you're okay. You've just walked over a mine field!"*

We had no ready response.

The Allied advance proceeded slowly but inexorably on all fronts. We on our side had three principal coastal towns to secure. They were, reading a map from left to right, Licata, Gela, and Scoglitti. On the whole resistance was sporadic, and great clumps of Italians came out of their burrows, hungry and terrified, with hands held shakily aloft. We had the most difficulty at Gela, but concentrated naval gunfire and our impatient infantry gained the day. About midmorning, and many assault waves later, the order came from on high to "send in the AMG crew." The Allied Military Government crew was composed of several large teams organized to administer the civilian population centers in the areas we intended to capture from the enemy. Back in Algiers, we had many of these multilingual teams in training. With us over here, we had one big Italian-speaking crew and the British had another. Our AMG team was led in to shore by Colonel Charles Poletti, a specially commissioned former lieutenant governor of New York.

This gang landed on various designated beaches along the front and, as the enemy slowly retreated, made its way to the coastal villages and towns. There the AMG soldiers unrolled great proclamations—printed in Italian—and pasted them on walls everywhere. The posters boldly announced to the local populace something like:

ATTENTION: TO THE BRAVE PEOPLE OF ITALY: YOU HAVE AT
LAST BEEN LIBERATED FROM THE HEEL OF THE TYRANT BY THE
OVERWHELMING ARMED FORCES OF THE UNITED STATES OF
AMERICA AND THE UNITED KINGDOM OF GREAT BRITAIN AND

THE BRITISH EMPIRE! OUR SOLDIERS, SAILORS, AND AIRMEN HAVE
DEDICATED THEMSELVES TO BRINGING YOU REAL FREEDOM—A NEW
DEMOCRATICALLY ELECTED GOVERNMENT. . . ."

Signed: On behalf of the Allied Forces—
D. D. Eisenhower, General, U.S. Army, Supreme Allied
Commander—Mediterranean.
Sir Andrew Cunningham, Admiral of the Fleet, Royal Navy,
Commander, Naval Forces—Mediterranean et al.
Sir Harold Alexander, General, Commander of Combined Allied
Forces—Mediterranean.
Sir Arthur Tedder, Air Marshal, C.A.F., Air Chief
Marshal—Mediterranean.
Carl Spaatz, Lieutenant General, Commander, Allied Air
Forces—Mediterranean.

The battle had moved well inland by this time, and more and more
of the local population began to creep out of their cellars and hideouts
like gophers to see if the land was clear. Little by little, neighbor found
neighbor and parents called children. They began to look about and
check on how far the war had gone inland by guessing at the carrying
power of artillery cannonades. They saw the posters, and calling
friends to join them, stood about in groups, then shrugged and wandered off in varying directions.

This seeming lack of interest by people for whom that morning too
many Yanks and limeys had been killed, wounded, or captured was
incomprehensible. These Sicilian coastal folk just glanced briefly and
indifferently at the notices and went on their way. Eventually a few
of us asked the junior AMG officer, who seemed to be in charge of
poster-pasting under Poletti, about this desultory welcome to the "gallant liberators." The lieutenant shrugged with an air of finality and
said sadly, "We just found out that nobody around here can read."

My bit part in the invasion of Sicily was at an end and I returned to
Algiers. The BJ group, T.G. 80.4, returned to its base in Bizerte.
Although intercepted enemy reports had noted their presence and
alerted the defenses on that coast, their course was too far offshore to

be seriously threatening. Contrary to orders, the weird Captain S. continued around the western side of the island before bringing his specially equipped PT squadrons back to base as directed.

The strategic deception plan had been wonderfully successful as the enemy was unable to decide whether Sicily, Sardinia, or Greece was our principal objective until we were all well and truly landed.

The next major job for the Allies after Sicily had been "liberated" was to knock Italy itself out of the war and push the Germans as far back as possible. We hoped they would be forced to withdraw some divisions from the Russian and Balkan fronts as well as from the English Channel and the French and Italian Mediterranean coasts.

While the British and Commonwealth forces of Field Marshal Montgomery's Desert Rats were to climb up from Sicily through the "heel" of Italy, the main Anglo-American assault was to be about one third up the other side of the "boot" at Salerno, a small town with fine beaches backed up by mountains, south of Naples. Once this force on the west joined up with Monty's gang on the east, they were to press on over the high uplands to capture Naples. The old saying "See Naples and die" was soon to take on a literal meaning.

Certain elements now seemed to favor our cause. Mussolini had been overthrown and dismissed by the King, whose power he had originally abrogated. Field Marshal Albert Kesselring, the brilliant German commander in the south (Rommel was by now in the north of Italy), had strong forces that could be brought forward to resist any Allied assault in the area. He also had, so we heard, a big reserve force in the Naples area and even more just north of Naples. Nevertheless, our amphibious "devious deception" group—augmented on land by the magicians of A Force and, unknown to us at the time, the top-secret strategic deception team in London—was charged with so "threatening" enemy forces in and north of Naples as to discourage further reinforcements at Salerno.

We had practically finished enlarging static optical deception by now; that is, developing dummy tanks, landing craft and aircraft, artificial airfields, and harbors. We did continue to employ masses of fake radio signals in breakable codes, or uncoded "panic" messages. We were well equipped to jam the enemy's radar and to so fool it that a few of our PTs and small craft could appear on their radar screens as much bigger ships. We still projected accurate recordings of the sounds of boats gathering for a big amphibious assault over varying distances and behind thick smoke screens.

Our planes were equipped to drop strips of silver paper or tinfoil that blanked out or deceived radar screens. In a word we deliberately behaved like so many Davids attempting to fool a mass of Goliaths, even a little.

The Beach Jumpers' chief staff officer, Lieutenant Art Bryant, continued in vain to lodge official protests against the seemingly mad Captain S. Each time Bryant wrote a "correct" report of complaint, the captain refused to pass it on, though he was by law required to do so. Bryant grew desperate—on behalf of our Special Ops Beach Jumpers, the PT squadrons, and landing craft crews. Captain S. certainly seemed mentally unbalanced when he confided that on the next operation for T.G. 80.4, we must arrange to get lots of casualties or else we'll never be recognized by the top brass. . . . And Bryant told me quietly he had no doubt that the captain would do just as he proposed. It was therefore up to me to stretch, evade, or otherwise circumvent navy regulations, jump the complaint past intervening authorities, and go straight to my bosses, Captain Bob English and Admiral Hewitt. I believed it was worth the risk.

I came clean with Bob E. and made broad hints to the admiral. It worked. In the end Captain S. was declared on the verge of a breakdown by the senior staff medical officer and ordered to report to a naval hospital back home. Unbelievably the "old school ring" mutual-protective network, loyally supported by graduates of all service academies, then worked again. A few months later, Captain S. was discharged from the hospital, declared fit, and given command of, I believe, a transport ship in the Pacific.

Meanwhile Captain Charley Andrews, an experienced old crony of Admiral Hewitt's from Annapolis days, a wonderful, swaggering hearty who had been passed over for commodore and/or rear admiral, was named as a replacement. Andrews was a slightly tubby, handsome "good ole boy" (Newport, Rhode Island variety) called back to active duty but without an important assignment—until now. It was explained to him that I, though still a mere two-striper lieutenant, actually had some practical knowledge of how special operations worked, but not the rank to assume command of a naval task group. Therefore it would be necessary hereafter for me (and my own unofficial small staff of real specialists and experts) to prepare the tactical cover plans, coordinate them with the British hush-hush deception A Force, and be attached to Captain Andrews as his operating chief staff officer. This was not an "official" job at all—it was strictly against custom and required another stretching of standard operating procedures. Thankfully, Captain Andrews, though at first stern and very much in command, soon warmed up and we became—despite a disparity of years, rank, and experience—the closest of friends.

In fact we were so close that Bryant and I were sometimes obliged to get him out of off-duty trouble. Once, after a few too many at an Allied officers' club in Bizerte, there was a free-for-all and the Shore Police (comprising ordinary bluejackets and one ensign) put the suspected participants under arrest. Captain Charley challenged the puny young arresting officer, but before this could blow up into an ugly situation, Bryant and I made impassioned pleas on our new skipper's behalf. I even heard myself protesting that our gallant captain had just come back from some hair-raising operation and was lucky to have survived. As anyone could see, he had been given the Purple Heart as a result of having been wounded and . . . Our plea worked, and we managed to get our captain back to quarters, where he still vehemently bellowed and snorted his protests at the "nerve of that young pipsqueak." What I later heard from his most enthusiastic booster, the foreign correspondent assigned to our group—the great John Steinbeck—was that the "wound" I'd referred to had been caused by a bit of falling plaster from the roof of a bombed house in Oran, weeks before. It had ripped the seat of his trousers and caused a superficial cut and some bleeding on his backside, which the local navy medics swabbed and bandaged. But as the building had been bombed by the enemy, his wound was indeed the result of enemy action, which, according to regulations, qualified him for the Purple Heart. I hope Steinbeck's story was true; it made dear Charley even more the colorful old pirate he always seemed.

* * *

Our T.G. 80.4 was enlarged considerably for this assault on the Italian boot—Operation Avalanche. Captain Andrews commanded the group from a destroyer, the USS *Knight,* itself skippered by Lieutenant Commander Ford, and we had as distinguished company two Dutch gunboats, the *Soemba* and the *Flores.* They were hospital-clean and experienced, brave men served aboard them. Also in our formation, scooting way around the main attack force, heading north, were six American PT boats, eight British MGBs (motor gun boats) and MTBs (motor torpedo boats). All were fully equipped with our gadgets, as well as with rockets, flares, and very fine gunware. We also had some small landing craft in our group.

In the meantime the British had another amphibious group that, by coincidence, was commanded by my old Combined Ops chief at HMS *Tormentor,* Captain Derek Wyburd. This group was mostly concerned with landing Lieutenant Colonel Bob Laycock's commandos in a spot from which they could get at the Huns from the rear, high in the hills above Sorrento, to help if need be. And by God help became most desperately needed in a day or so. Just their presence served to augment the impression of more impending action by the Allies in and above the Naples area.

Intelligence had informed us that the German commander Field Marshal Kesselring intended to hold Naples as strongly as he could and would keep a whole division up his sleeve north of there—near the Gulf of Gaeta—ready to come to any needed rescue farther south. It was to threaten that whole area and discourage the Germans from rescuing their forces at Salerno that we made such conspicuous fun of our deception. We suspected, but could not know for sure, that just a few hours before our Allied forces were due to land at Salerno, Italy's Field Marshal Pietro Badoglio's secretly signed surrender had been announced. The result for the Italians was a mixture of panic and relief at being "out of it," more or less. The Germans were furious but quite cool. Their political leaders may well have been maniacs, but their commanders led a well-trained and stubborn soldiery. They did not panic. Far from it, they resisted our landing with such fierce determination—aided by the saucer of hills behind the assault beaches—that for several days the success of our invasion of mainland Italy was in terrifying and bloody doubt.

At first our group passed well out beyond visual land range. Then, as we slowed down and headed for the Pontine group of small islands off Gaeta, west and north of Naples, our sonar watch called to the skipper on the bridge that he had a submarine on his screen. The ASDIC also started its terrifying banshee screech, and Captain Andrews told the destroyer captain to order "action stations." The whole task group slowed down and manned their guns, awaiting further orders. The image on the radar appeared not to move—to be "lying doggo"—so the skipper ordered a torpedo fired at it. It hit and exploded on target. But the image remained on the screen. It was less than a mile away and there was moonlight high and ahead of us (thus saving us from being clearly seen in silhouette). A command was given to fire at it with our six-inch guns. Still no visible score or damage was done. Then suddenly the *Knight*'s exec rushed up to the bridge with a chart and a hooded flashlight, calling out, *"Sir! Look! Look at this chart!"*

Captain Andrews and Lieutenant Commander Ford looked. Andrews swore a great baritone curse. "Hold everything! That's no sub! That's a goddamn *rock*—sticking out of the water! *There it is. On the goddamn chart!"*

Everyone returned to his regular post. Our remaining worry was whether our stupidity had been noticed by the enemy on shore several miles away to starboard. We crept on silently through the early night.

Our task group was now slowly closing in on the small isle of Ventotene, the key to the Pontine chain outside the Gulf (more like a wide crescent) of Gaeta. Gaeta was near the main base for the German forces of the area.

Ventotene served as a strong offshore radio communications center for the Germans. It also boasted bothersome coastal artillery defenses with, according to our intelligence reports, a skeleton defense garrison of royalist and antifascist Italians. They were very probably ready to call it a day once they heard the news, openly broadcast for the first time that very night, September 8, 1943, that their government had surrendered and Italy was out of the war.

Any conquest of Naples itself, or end-run assaults to the north of it, would necessitate neutralizing these islands lying like little guardians above it. This applied even more so to the nearer, much larger islands of Capri, Procida, and Ischia, sentries to the Gulf of Naples.

As we slowly moved through the calm waters about a half mile offshore, we began projecting false and confusing radar signals. The *Knight,* behind great clouds of smokescreens, projected a prerecorded demand over our powerful loudspeakers that Ventotene surrender. The broadcast stated that an Allied fleet of ships was offshore preparing for a large-scale landing on the mainland. The islanders were instructed to signal their surrender within ten minutes by sending up three white rockets from the headland near their coastal batteries. A failure to respond would be met by shelling.

In fact the two Dutch gunboats and the *Knight* were indeed at their action stations, and gunners had slammed their first shells into the breeches of their five-inch and six-inch guns, already aiming at the Ventotene town and its outer defenses. When the ten minutes had expired and no sign of any kind was noted from shore, we played one last recorded warning of five minutes—supported by staged background sounds of men shouting, anchor chains rattling, and all kinds of appropriate noises, including nonexistent airplanes. We then shot up a lot of fancy skyrockets to light our targets. When the last second of the warning ticked by, we let loose a couple of salvos, deliberately short of their mark, rather like going "Boo!" in the dark. Then within seconds, we saw three great white rockets soar into the sky and loop down. A chorus of cheers came from our ragtag "fleet."

Captain Andrews wondered who should go into the little harbor first to make certain we were not being tricked. I began to make some sort of suggestion about procedure, and Andrews leaped to the conclusion that I was volunteering. It was *not at all* what I had in mind, but I hadn't the nerve to back out, particularly as Steinbeck insisted on coming along in another boat. So with self-assured bravado I clambered into a waiting whaleboat to case the joint accompanied by three amphibious Beach Jumpers.

Preparing to follow right after us in a landing craft of their own was a small Office of Strategic Services gang led by an old peacetime friend, Navy Lieutenant Henry Ringling (Buddy) North (one of the heirs to the Ringling Brothers–Barnum and Bailey Circus) and Captain Frank Tarallo, a career army officer of Italian descent.

I had my tommy gun at the ready and my commando dagger stuck in my belt for good measure as we putt-putted into the small harbor.

We came up quite close to a German motor longboat, its swastika-emblazoned naval ensign still flying aft. As our coxswain turned our boat's searchlight on it, a German soldier, clutching his tommy gun, suddenly jumped out of the shadows of the boat onto the quayside. Immediately a great bomb blew up his boat. He barely managed to escape the explosion. No one was hurt, but the repercussion knocked us back down in our whaleboat.

I was not a little taken aback by our welcome, but as we got closer to the nearly wrecked German boat, I made a jump for it and, without thinking, ran up the jetty trying to catch the Jerry, who was fleeing into the night. Buddy North also bumped ashore, but he and his squad went in the other direction. I could see no one else about, but I did hear all too clearly the differing sharp cracks of rifles, pistols, and machine guns. They were probably firing at random, but it felt as though I was their only target.

I had had training for possible close combat on a beach, but once *really* ashore, in a small old Italian village amid narrow streets, in the dark, with invisible enemies shooting at me, I thought this was no place for a *sailor* to be.

What should I do to get on from here? Then in a silly, ridiculous flash, I recalled Gary Cooper ducking a tough hombre's bullets in the night. Coop had flattened himself against a wall and slid quickly along it toward his target—or away from it. I couldn't quite remember the movie. All that mattered was to cling to the side of the building. I took some pot shots at something without being quite sure what it was and was irritated when some shots came zinging back at me seeming, by contrast, to be quite sure what *I* was. None of my own old movies called for this sort of maneuver.

I circled back to the quayside and found several of the local *Fascisti* militia already gathered to surrender. Other boats came in cautiously—one carrying the gutsy John Steinbeck—and landed our fellows and the few from OSS. One of the "Eye-ties" (Italians) who spoke with what sounded like a phony stage accent told us that there was a political prison on the island and all the inmates had just been released. One of those freed turned out to be a well-known politician whom Il Duce had put away. This man soon came running up, tears cascading down his cheeks, embracing and kissing me and any other

Allies he saw. Hurriedly piecing more bits of reports together, we found our intelligence had been most unpleasantly wrong; there were not just the surrendering Italian militia but about four hundred stubborn German coast artillery troops at the other end of the island, busy reporting our "invasion" on their radio and preparing to fight it out.

By this time I had had more than enough of bangs followed by the unmistakable twang of bullets, luckily missing me. Nor did I like it when Captain Andrews, after ordering our ships to fire at the far ends of the island, instructed me to take a few men and set up defensive pickets at what we grandiosely called "strategic points." These led down to the quay—now a bustling place where bluejackets were trying to round up and guard the relieved and chattering Italians. By that time we had little choice but to maintain our bluff as long as we could.

One trusting local Italian ran up to report that there were signals being flashed from the neighboring island of Ponza, asking us to come over and rescue them as well. I forcefully insisted it was a trap and we should refuse to answer. A few days later we were told the signal was urging us to come quickly as Mussolini was there, en route to Sardinia. At first I could have kicked myself for being so stupidly suspicious, but then we heard even *that* was a false report. I never did know the reliable truth, but I remained pretty certain that "Musso" had long since come and gone.

There was a stalemate for an entire day as many (though not all) Germans, who suffered only a few casualties, were still holding out. One Luftwaffe snooper flew over us but was shot down. Presumably all their other pilots were over Salerno. We stretched our few inexperienced sailors and soldiers as far as we dared. By the next night of random exchanges of shot and shell, our bluff had worked and about four hundred Germans trooped down to surrender. I think a couple of British LCTs took them back to the Salerno area and transferred them into a bigger tub, en route to a POW camp in North Africa.

Our victory made Captain Andrews so incredulous he decided he would quietly accept his preferred shot (or two) of whiskey, which one of his trusted subordinates had more or less smuggled aboard. When our whole group in other whaleboats had bumped its way inside the small harbor and the *Knight* had anchored outside, Andrews sent word that he wanted the local Italian "authorities"—police, militia, and guards—to send their commanders down to "sign a surrender paper and give us such ceremonial swords and military flags as they had." He then instructed Frank Tarallo and me to type up a formal surrender document while he went below to take a "badly needed nap."

The so-called "Commanding Officer of the Axis Armed Forces of the Islands of Ventotene and San Stefano" and his assistants, having hurriedly decked themselves out in semblances of uniforms and holding their full-dress swords so as not to trip on them, clattered down to the quayside, and ceremonially awaited our pleasure. Tarallo spoke to them in Italian, promising God knows what and threatening dire alternatives if they didn't comply. The poor *Ventotenesi* were obviously mystified. Tarallo spoke a slightly American-accented, North Italian dialect, and our shaking local captives spoke only the southern Neapolitan dialect. But both could read, and the rest of us remained as solemn as we could while they obediently scribbled their names to the "surrender."

There was more adventure the next night. John Kramer, a very senior lieutenant and one of our leading Beach Jumpers (a bit of an overage, sloppy old boy whose trousers were always drooping) lived up to his reputation as one of the bravest of the brave. In peacetime life he was the reverse of the educated slouch he appeared. Bryant and Steinbeck told me he was a nonconforming member of Philadelphia's Main Line. He persuaded Captain Andrews to let him take one of our PT boats into or near Gaeta and give the natives and lookouts a bit of a fright with a few of our tricks. Steinbeck went with him, contrary to all regulations (he took off the war correspondent identification on his sleeve). Had he been captured and discovered, he could have been executed under international law. He knew all that but preferred a tommy gun to his notebook, and in he went. They fired a few rockets into the night air and came back.

The effect of their hit-and-run trip was hard to determine at once, but subsequently we were told the combination of events had put all the area's defense lookouts into a real tizzy. By noon the next day, Ventotene and the Pontine Islands had been secured, the jails emptied, and the political prisoners released, making temporary room for as many of the captured and surrendered German and Italian soldiers as possible.

We left a few craft behind to support the Dutch gunboats guarding our island conquest. They would also continue, by one means or another, to imply further Allied assault. By radio we requested more craft and men to take or threaten the other islands in the area, but too much was going badly with the main assault to spare anything.

On the Salerno beaches the situation had become so desperate that U.S. General Mark Clark was nearly frantic. Monty had been moving more slowly than predicted from the other side and had not yet joined up. The Krauts meanwhile had brought the famous Hermann Göring Division and a tank brigade into the battle. These not only further separated the Americans from the British so that one of our bombers mistakenly—tragically—dropped bombs on some of the Scots Guards (one young officer I had known was, he told me later, lucky that he only lost a leg), but blasted their way to within two miles of the beach. A desperately worried Clark told Admiral Hewitt that he feared our land forces must leave Salerno as soon as possible and that preparations to reembark should be initiated immediately. Hewitt calmly declined, replying that *his* orders were "to establish the army ashore" and that was precisely what he intended to do. Meanwhile the Luftwaffe bombers, which were attacking the invasion fleet day and night, for the first time began using their frighteningly successful radio-controlled "glide" bombs. Several ships of the Allied invasion fleet were put out of action. Some lesser craft were sunk. No one could yet fathom a defense against this sinister new weapon.

After Hewitt had ordered all combat ships of our task force to open up on the enemy forces on shore, firing remarkable hits on moving enemy tanks and armored cars, he dispatched a message to Admiral Cunningham in Algiers asking urgently for heavy naval reinforcements.

Our previously mocked Beach Jumper and diversionary efforts as decoys had, up to now, worked well, inasmuch as we had so confused the enemy in and above Naples that it appeared they dared not move their last division-sized reserves down to Sorrento and over the hills to the Salerno battle area. Now, though, the risk was that having very probably sniffed a rat, they *might* risk committing whatever they had left in the area.

Then, early the next morning, as in some corny boys' adventure yarn, just as the pressure on our troops ashore was becoming really intense and the destroyers and cruisers were having to get ever closer to shore in their unusual duel with the enemy's land-based armored vehicles, what seemed like great twelve-inch and sixteen-inch shells from somewhere out of sight began exploding in the German ranks. We soon learned they came in reply to Hewitt's plea for rescue. Several Royal Navy warships were boiling up over the horizon from North Africa. Naval gunfire had by this time become very fierce and accurate. The Italians, having rid themselves of Mussolini, were now being led by the young, popular, pro-Allied Prince Umberto. They quit the Nazi partnership and came over to our side, thus accelerating the German decision to withdraw—just nine days after the first assault. They were badly damaged, though far from defeated yet. During that same short period our U.S. forces had suffered more than 3,500 casualties just on the beaches. The British score was even worse, showing a loss of 5,500 men! The enemy casualty lists were not always reliable, but their losses were believed to be much less than ours.

Before I made my way via PT boat back to Hewitt's command ship in the main assault area to report our achievements, someone sighted an Italian torpedo boat (called a MAS boat) coming toward us from the Isle of Capri. It was flying a large white flag. As it drew nearer, word came over a loudspeaker that they sought "a U.S. Navy Lieutenant Fairbanks." I wondered what on earth . . . ? The answer came soon. The Italian officer had a note for me! It was from the Duke of Aosta, nephew of Italy's then king, Victor Emmanuel III, and first cousin to Crown Prince Umberto, with both of whom I had, with official approval, begun to surreptitiously correspond after we knew Italy was going to either quit the war or join us. As the Italian royal family was strongly anti-Nazi and antifascist, but powerless, I had realized that no immediate reply was possible. And now Aosta was telling me that if we came quickly, we could take the lovely Isle of Capri. The Germans, who had used it for their officers' rest and relaxation, were moving out from one end, and we could move right into the other by the main harbor. To help us, he offered me, of all people, his command of the marvelously fast and efficient Italian MAS torpedo-boat fleet. He himself was obliged to remain behind as a cover.

With some embarrassment on my part, we took these splendid squadrons under our wing and in an effort to have them prove their "honesty," I accompanied them as they led us through the many mine fields around the Bay of Naples and back to Capri. I made a point of being "correct" and encouraging to the group's officers. With Admiral Hewitt's approval, Charley Andrews and I absorbed them into our task group. It all eventually led to the new King Umberto II (whose father, Victor Emmanuel III, had abdicated) awarding me the Italian War Cross for Military Valor, with star. Among other familiar exaggerations, the citation referred to my "comprehension of the delicate situation which was created after September 6. . . ."

Few of the belligerents noticed us as we slid toward Capri in single file, like a line of strange iron seabirds emerging from the pandemonium of the combat area. In doing so we just barely avoided the latest enemy bombing and shelling attacks that hit some three of our ships.

The leading Italian MAS boat had sped ahead around the back of Capri and alerted the civilian population to our imminent arrival. By the time we got there and slowed down to about five knots, it was late afternoon. Now the only noise apart from the distant thunder of battle and our task group carving the sea was sudden cheering that came from the people living on that high historic rock. The residents, dolled up in their brightest, lined the shore, the huge rocks, the village above, and the winding paths, waving colored hankies. It looked for all the world like a spectacular scene in an old operetta or movie musical.

I have likened so many memorable moments in my life to their theatrical counterparts. As usual I seldom succeeded in facing up to earthly reality. My shipmates and I could scarcely believe the peaceful sunset sight in comparison to the war's slaughter only a few miles behind us.

Shortly after we settled in on Capri the British Combined Ops group, commanded by my old *Tormentor* skipper, Derek Wyburd, joined us. He was in the leading LST (landing ship tank) and was followed by a flock of landing craft and MTBs. Derek still claims he and his gang arrived before we did that day, but if so, we never knew they were there when we tied up alongside.

Later Andrews and others reported my so-called bravery in such glowing terms that I was eventually awarded the Silver Star Medal—a decoration that can only be won in combat action. It then ranked only below the Navy Cross and the Congressional Medal of Honor. I actually received it months later, and when I read the citation, I thought it so damned exaggerated and embarrassing that if I had had a bit more integrity I would have declined it—respectfully, of course (hoping they would insist on my keeping it). But I accepted it grate-fully.

It was the first award of its kind that I knew of to be given to someone from my profession. Deserved or not, I was as pleased as Punch! And I assumed my family would be too. One thought that I remember with crystal clarity flitted through my head briefly: Too bad my father was not there. He might have been quite pleased with me. Or, fretful second thought, would he have been put out because *he* hadn't done whatever it was?

The citation read in part:

> The President of the United States takes pleasure in presenting the Silver Star Medal to Lieutenant Commander Douglas Fairbanks, Jr., . . . for conspicuous gallantry and intrepidity of action . . . and courageous conduct under the most trying and dangerous conditions . . . during the amphibious assault on Italy. . . .
>
> Efficient and untiring in the performance of duty, Lieut.-Comdr. [then Lieutenant] Fairbanks [also] rendered valuable service in the formulation of important plans for mixed Allied operations of a highly technical and complex nature . . . later, while attached to the staff of a Navy Task Group Commander, he volunteered to accompany the two combat units in a motor whaleboat, leading the landing force ashore against the enemy-held island of Ventotene. . . . Having landed, he courageously led an armed reconnaissance of the town and environs and established important picket positions despite explosions and [being] exposed to enemy rifle fire, thereby contributing greatly to the successful accom-plishment of the missions.
>
> The exceptional courage . . . fearless leadership . . . and outstanding skill under fire displayed by [Lt. Cdr. D. F., Jr., USNR] were in the highest traditions of the United States Naval Service.

Being based on Capri, out of range of enemy guns, was a welcome intermission from the worst of the battle. Our days were dedicated to sleeping, replenishing frayed nerves, eating, and snooping through the elegant villas left behind intact by their glamorous owners. One notable example of our misbehavior was when I and a few other brutes made our way up to Edda Mussolini Ciano's big, empty house. As I had met her and her foreign secretary husband, Count Ciano, in London in the thirties, I persuaded myself that I had a special variety of entrée. We just walked in, shrugging off the shocking example we might set if caught, and looked around. The only things of any interest to us—and these were fascinating—were the piles of family photograph albums that contained snaps of "Papa" and family, friends, and off-duty *Fascisti* officials.

I later regaled my fellow house invaders with tales of the extra-young-man-for-dinner-kind-of-friendship I'd had with the international society beauty Mrs. Harrison (Mona) Williams—later Countess Bismarck. We calmly walked to her villa, opened a back door, and went in. Unfortunately for our curiosity, she had wisely removed most of her best things, including bibelots and pictures. Looting was certainly not on our agenda, but we were admittedly keen to trespass just a little and have a look at all we could. To our later and greater shame, after we learned that Mona's cellar was still open, well stocked, and untouched, we made frequent return pilgrimages to her lovely place for our own wine-tasting sessions. We managed to convince ourselves that we were thus better fortified for the nuisance raids we were to carry out later that night.

On one of these evening outings, our dear old sea dog Captain Charley (as we now called Andrews behind his back) decided we should, if possible, fine-point the Germans' coastal gun emplacements around the Gulf of Naples. Arguing more from concern for my life than for the Allied cause, I tried (but failed) to persuade him that our intelligence already had all that kind of information. But Charley's buccaneer spirit was excited by the Brits' excise-free scotch, and brushing me off with a "you're no fun" gesture, he sent for the commander of the fast and powerful British motor gunboat squadron attached to us.

Lieutenant Richard Greene-Kelly was one of those dashing real-life prototypes of the heroes I had sometimes pretended to be in my movie past. This laughing, bearded character would, when lying in wait for enemy E-boats or coastal supply craft easing down the Italian west coast, refrain from firing at them from a half mile to a mile away as American standard operating procedure demanded. Instead, Greene-Kelly slipped up in the dark, right alongside the enemy and, followed by hand-picked members of his crew, all armed with tommy guns, jumped aboard the enemy craft, taking prisoners when feasible and then sinking their ships. He himself rarely carried a gun at all. Instead, he scared the bejesus out of the enemy by yelling like a wild Indian and waving an old razor-sharp cutlass! What's more, he became murderously adept in its use. Once, some time later, during the frustrating drawn-out Anzio deadlock farther north, he pulled his trick once too often and was killed. His last of several decorations for bravery was posthumously presented to his family by his king.

But on this particular late afternoon, Greene-Kelly delightedly agreed to take Captain Charley on a thoroughly nonregulation, fast-paced tour of the Gulf of Naples. I tried to disguise my inner quaking, reluctantly joined Captain Charley aboard Greene-Kelly's MGB, and we zoomed off.

Naturally we succeeded in inspiring some reaction from the shore, luckily ill aimed, and marked the approximate spot of the gun flashes on our chart. We had heard earlier from one of our 150 well-hidden OSS troops on the Isle of Ischia that German tanks had been seen carrying out their threats to shoot whomever they saw in the streets of a Neapolitan suburb as a reprisal for the civilian killing of a Nazi soldier. Charley was intent on personally confirming the town's punishment. But as we started to come closer to shore, the aim of the German (formerly Italian) Coast Guard defenses got too accurate—even for Greene-Kelly! So we turned tail and at flank speed scooted back to Capri.

Over the hills, south of the Sorrento Peninsula, the biggest, bloodiest battles had begun at last to favor us, while our little decoy group continued, with diminishing effect, our diversions and threats.

Back down in Salerno, as the Allies slowly and bloodily pushed the enemy back over the hills leading to Naples, we had a few more chores to perform. One required the occupation of Procida, another island in the gulf. But we were out of troops. The British groups came and went and came again, but our own Task Group 80.4 had established our presence on a total of nine islands; protecting them were a dozen OSS and navy signalmen on the Pontine group (including Ventotene), after clearing it of all Germans and leaving the Italians to work along with our fellows. There were fifty men on Procida and sixty-six on Capri. We were very short of men, and soon we would be short of food and drinking water. I therefore sent a message, via Derek Wyburd's British group, still in port with us, to Colonel Bob Laycock—a great, heroic commando who was destined to succeed Dickie as CCO—asking if he could lend us a few squads of his men for a night or two. His reply will never be forgotten: "WE PUSHING OVER THE HILL TONIGHT. ALREADY SO SHORT OF BODIES EVEN OUR COOKS AND DRIVERS SHOOTING THEIR WAY ACROSS WITH THE REST OF US."

On one of the smaller diversion-job nights I was sent to recover an Italian navy chart purporting to show the location of mines laid in southern Italian ports. A captured Italian admiral had said the chart was in his villa, way behind the German lines—so far behind in fact that there wasn't a Nazi within miles. The only risk was that someone with residual empathy for the old regime might report our presence. About four or five young Beach Jumpers followed me. We slipped out from our PT boat into two rubber boats and paddled as silently as possible close to shore. We lowered ourselves into the water, and as I was senior by half a stripe, age, and frogman training, I led the last few paddling yards. We had been well briefed as to the whereabouts of the admiral's villa. It was a nice holiday cottage, quite near a small village, close to a port full of fishing boats. So far, so good.

Well, only partly good! What we hadn't been told was that the admiral's "empty villa near the sea" was surrounded by an eight- or ten-foot stucco wall that shone white in the moonlight. There was only one entrance off the street, a large wooden gate under an arch. The back door was too close to other neighboring houses that might easily be disturbed. But the bolted gate was high, and any attempt to break it down was bound to invite local attention. I whispered that it would be quieter if we just climbed over the wall.

I could see by the way the BJs settled silently back on their heels that they were thinking that if there was any wall climbing to be done, *I* was the one to lead the way. After all, hadn't they seen me climb higher walls than this in lots of prewar movies, and single-handedly spike dozens of armed villains with only a handy cactus or a rusty nail? And hadn't they heard of my dad and his even more fearless and nimble ways? In something shorter than a flash, I determined that inasmuch as there was no fixed rope disguised as a vine, no foot or handholds, nor any experienced propman handy, it was most unlikely that I could, if I failed to make it the first time, have unlimited, unassisted tries at getting up and over that wall. I'd be damned if I'd make a bloody fool of myself for these kids by falling ignominiously on my backside for the greater glory of my country. So in a most self-assured whisper, I said the risk was too great and we should break down the front gate instead, just as first planned.

It was infinitely easier than I had at first supposed because the gate was not locked after all. We just walked in silently. The villa was empty—of people and almost all furnishings. The admiral's charts were just where we were told they would be, in a big old wooden box that also held masses of dusty books, two croquet mallets, a couple of hoops and a ball, a game of Bola, an old spyglass, and one tennis shoe.

With the charts in the grip of a responsible j.g., we slunk our way back through the sleepy little town toward the beach. About two unevenly cobblestone streets away, we jumped at the sudden sound of air-raid sirens. This was most unexpected. We had forgotten that part of the overall diversionary plan was for our own aircraft to drop a few bombs on this faraway part of the coast to make some gullible Kraut suspect we just might be softening things up to make a big "end run."

The town woke up within moments. Frightened villagers rushed into the streets in night clothes, scrambling toward safe cellars. In no time our little squad was part of the group of sleepy, scared townsfolk. After the doors to the shelter were safely closed, someone lit a couple of candles. At first no one paid any attention to us. I guessed that to them all military men looked alike, and our blackened faces and scruffy khakis inspired no curiosity. Then they heard us murmuring to each other in English. As the bomb banging continued faraway outside, one of the unshaven locals broke the contrasting quiet inside in a rasping Italo-Brooklyn accent: *"I know 'oo y'arr! You arr Dawglas*

Fayerbanksa!" I was more than a little surprised that in the prevailing circumstances he recognized me for someone I had been more than two years ago, but felt like no longer. He went on angrily, "I'a have-a-bona to picka wit you!"

It occurred to me that our shared danger might have inspired comradeship. But no such luck. His was not a friendly recognition at all. He barked on, telling how he had once owned a movie theater in Brooklyn, but the United Artists Company (*"Ooneita Arteesta Corporazioni"*) had charged such exorbitant rentals for their films that he had gone broke and was forced to return to Italy–"to *dis!"* He waved eloquently at the bombing outside. I protested that it was not I but my late father who was a partner in United Artists. But it was all to no avail. He refused to listen to my explanation and went on holding me to blame for his forced repatriation. My snickering young charges and I were extra relieved when the ack-ack stopped, the all-clear sounded, and we could get back to the beach and our waiting boat. Celebrity recognition is not always so flattering.

She was leaning against a wooden rail by a path at the top of the highest spot in Capri. One of our sailors seemed to be reading to her. She appeared somewhere between sixteen and eighteen, attractively fresh and unspoiled. I had seen her when she came across the Bay of Naples on a hot afternoon a day or two before with her family. They came with bundles and bags in a large rowboat, slowly and laboriously propelled by two husky boatmen. One of our bluejackets on watch had spotted them earlier through his binoculars. They seemed to be coming from somewhere near the Amalfi area. To our lookout's surprise, they were not fired on from the mainland, but made their way peacefully over calm water in the humid afternoon air.

When at last they pulled up to the dock, they were assisted ashore by a couple of locals. Aside from the men at the oars, the boat's passengers were one weak and tired oldish-looking man, his worried, bedraggled wife, and the young girl–their daughter, I assumed, whom I was to see again on the top of the hill. The old man turned out to be one of Italy's–one of the world's–greatest modern philosophers, Benedetto Croce. It seemed that he had been successful in persuading the local German authorities to allow them to leave the nonstop bombing and fighting in Naples and go to Capri, now occupied by the Allies and out of the mainstream of battle.

My always lively curiosity was stirred to find out exactly why this pretty young girl, Croce's daughter, was listening so intently—and happily—to an American sailor reading aloud. As I strolled inconspicuously near, part of my wonder was answered. The rest came later. Apparently the young Croce girl spoke no English but had a devotion to the works of Shakespeare, *in Italian*. She had always wanted to hear those classic verses in their native tongue. The bluejacket, his white cap way back on his head, spoke words that were almost as unfamiliar to him as they were to her, but he stammered slowly and manfully on. She, her eyes closed, a faint smile on her lips, just kept leaning against the rail, transported by what her ears' imaginings had made newly beautiful. It was a lovely sight. Here a few kilometers from horror was a new reassurance, of a kind often lost in the shuffle, that life and beauty and poetry and civilization were not only worth preserving, but were actually *being* preserved.

Chapter 7

IN THE middle of September I visited one of our Beach Jumper units
making random raids along Yugoslavia's Dalmatian Coast. There on
the island of Vis, our men—mostly navy plus a group of first-rate OSS
army "smugglers"—were based alongside British MTB squadrons and
a group of Combined Ops commandos and "special operations executive" toughies. This international-interservice group's mission was to
pass seaborne supplies along to Tito's forces ashore and prey upon all
enemy coastal shipping and small land bases. Because of the fierce
Yugoslav resistance and the mountainous Balkan terrain, the enemy
depended on such coastal shipping.

The little island of Vis was well equipped for the group's use. Its
small deep-water excuses for harbors were comparatively easy to
defend, and as one of a chain of islands, it was not far from where
supplies for Tito's followers were landed. German bombers raided
Vis occasionally but created little damage (there was nothing much
there except the boats, scattered peasants' and fishermen's houses, and
us). This backwater of the European war was a disappointment to the
grand and magnificent old pest, Admiral Sir Walter Cowan; having
been retired soon after World War I, he must have been four score
years if he was a day. But now, in 1943, he had somehow got fobbed
off onto Lieutenant Colonel Jack Churchill's (no relation to Winston)
resident commandos. In his day he had been a colorful and eccentric

senior naval officer. Once during the Russian Civil War of 1917–19, Cowan was ordered to anchor his Royal Navy cruiser squadron off Archangel's shore defenses, prepared to protect British and/or Allied citizens. The admiral, so the story went, got bored when there was no action. One day he just turned his guns on the Russian coastal defenses and opened fire! His superiors in the Admiralty, on being informed of this unauthorized petulance, quickly relieved him of his command, but the action itself, fortunately causing no casualties, was forever afterward referred to as "Walter's War."

The old codger *loved* war! In 1939 he pestered the life out of the service chiefs, begging to be put on active duty again, despite his age. Eventually, with naval insignia on a Western Desert Army battledress uniform and so many medal ribbons that they were said to rise up his chest and back down over his shoulder, he reported to the Eighth Army in Egypt. They got tired of his grumpy quaintness and allowed the Italians to capture him. The Italians, feeling sorry for him, sent him home with an escort. He continued to complain—not just because he wanted to be in the forefront of battle, but because he hated returning to his wife in England! He had been married to her for over forty-five years, but though they lived together, they didn't speak to each other. They would communicate through their butler, a former marine who, for example, relayed messages given from one end of their dining table to the other.

Old Cowan carried his misogyny everywhere, even to Vis, and when he spun yarns in the old peasant house that served as our officers' quarters and mess hall, he shooed the uncomprehending local housekeeper out of the room. Each time an air raid began and everyone headed for the cellar shelters, the old admiral ran out to the jetty, stood on the end of it, and hoped to be "killed with my bloody boots on—in action!" Finally he got his wish and was, everyone hoped, pleased to learn on reaching the Great Battleship in the Sky that he had been posthumously awarded his second Distinguished Service Order—the oldest recipient ever!

I had myself come over to Vis from the Italian Adriatic port of Bari, where I had stayed the night in a waterfront *albergo,* getting slightly sloshed on Yugoslav wine with one of Tito's officers. I asked the guy if he was a communist, royalist, Chetnik (a Serbian guerrilla), or partisan. "I only poor farmer," he sadly explained. "In mountain—not give goddamn about nodding and noboddy! One day man stick gun in stomick, say, 'You are Chetnik! Come along!' So I say nodding and go 'long. Few weeks lader, I try shoot Cherman, or someting, when man come up, also stick gun in stomick, say 'You are partisan! Come!' So I come! Again annoder man stick gun in me, say, 'You are Chetnik.' *Boga mia,* I dunno *what* da hell I'm!"

Early the next morning before daylight, I set off across the Adriatic to Vis in one of our PTs that had several Nazi kills recorded on its windshield. I was coming to help plan some newfangled tactics for our combined groups and also, on Hewitt's order, to help Jack Churchill receive Yugoslavia's "boss-man," Marshal Tito. It was announced that he was coming over secretly in the dead of night to thank a few representative Allied officers for helping to get supplies ashore and attacking enemy coastal shipping.

When the day dawned and Tito had landed, four Americans (including me) and five British from our base at the other end of the island crowded aboard two old jeeps and bounced painfully along the dusty excuses for roads. The ride was made more uncomfortable by Admiral Cowan's (Sir Walter's) insistence on coming along too—just "for the interest," he said.

Along the way, Jack Churchill and I teased each other about who would get what by way of a decoration from Tito. I insisted that he, a lieutenant colonel, would surely get a big gold star on a blue ribbon around his neck, whereas I, a marginal U.S. Navy lieutenant, *might* get a little "gong" hanging on a green thing with a rosette. On our arrival at a small farmhouse, we were ushered in and briefed. Our small group of Yanks and limeys snapped properly to attention as the head man with his entourage and a threatening Alsatian dog came in. A man behind Tito held a large open box that presumably contained our decorations. Jack and I nudged each other and stifled giggles as Tito, competing with his almost equally unintelligible interpreter, droned on about the deep appreciation of the Yugoslav people for the "inestimable help" of the Anglo-American Allies, etc., etc. Impatiently we kept trying to peek into the box behind him. Finally, the Great Man said that what he had to give us was a "poor and inadequate symbol of thanks," but it was all they could offer at this time. With that he signaled for the box to be brought forward, and then, after the nine of us stepped smartly one pace forward, he presented each of us with *two tins of Yugoslav anchovies!* I kept mine to give to Mary Lee on my next home leave—not just because I was so thoughtful, but because I hated anchovies.

Jack Churchill was another of that colorful breed of warriors from much the same mold as Greene-Kelly—always cheery, ever dauntless. Just to be different, Jack sometimes led his gun-toting men on night raids with no other weapon for himself than a bow and arrow with which he was singularly adept. I was told he would also sling his beloved bagpipes over his shoulder and on occasion, as his own personal "cock a snoot" gesture to stunned Nazis after a raid, he played the pipes from his boat as it slipped back into the dark sea night.

While on that almost forgotten outpost of Vis for just those few days, I helped plan one small raid while some of our BJs created minor diversions north of our main show. When the raid was over, the dawn became our signal to withdraw. Our guys got into their boats, moving at a maddeningly slow speed so as not to create visible white wakes. As they purred out to sea, I stood on shore with our local BJ commander, a lieutenant from Pittsburgh, behind a small hillock, just low enough to peek over the top, checking to be sure everyone else got off and away before we ourselves could leave. Our main worry was that among the British the only one not accounted for was Jack Churchill.

The Germans, not being exactly sure where we were, fired blindly at us. Occasionally they'd lob over some kind of mortar shell. Finally my BJ sidekick and I began to think that either Jack had been killed or we had missed seeing him board with his men. I decided we, too, must get to our boats quickly—and silently! We had been standing, literally, shoulder to shoulder, and as he'd been silent, I turned to ask if he agreed. He couldn't answer. The top of his head had been blown off. Because he was so well balanced and my shoulder was partly supporting him, he was still standing. I stepped away, too shocked to react immediately, and he fell forward on his face, against the hillock. Presumably it was some oblique form of hysteria, but when I realized that I had not so much as a speck of dust on me, I began to laugh a little to myself. How horribly ridiculous he looked with half a head.

I went on with getting aboard my boat and away. I didn't have any remembered reaction until the next day. Then the macabre ghastliness of my friend's hideous end and my own totally untouched escape became a conscious event. I went out and puked. I shook and wept and puked again.

Once out to sea, those of us aboard my PT voiced our deep worry that Jack Churchill had "had it." But just as we were beyond range of the beachfront guns, we heard—very dimly, very distantly—the faint melancholy wail of a lone bagpipe. It was Jack's signal to us that he was alive. In fact, he had been captured. But it wasn't long before he escaped and returned to his men and the action he loved.

At the end of September I was ordered to Cairo, supposedly to help plan the tricky evacuation of British, Greek, and American OSS troops from Greece's tiny Dodecanese islands of Leros and Cos, off the Turkish coast—north of Rhodes and a hell of a way from Egypt. As the Germans had taken (but never conquered!) most of Greece and these last Allied and Greek army holdouts among the islands were no longer considered defensible, an operation to bring the men back to Egypt was ordered. Years and years later, old Niv, with Greg Peck and Tony Quinn, made a movie called *The Guns of Navarone* that was said to be based on this operation at Leros-Cos. The real operation was a tricky but relatively small one. Furthermore there was absolutely no need for me to "advise" anyone, as the whole thing had already been planned before I arrived by Britain's A Force, virtually the inventors of modern tactical deception.

Because there was a lull at our Algerian headquarters until we moved all staff personnel to Naples, it became an unofficial leave for me. It was hoped that I would learn more about the deception racket. I was also given a delicate, off-the-record errand. This was to very discreetly reassure King George of Greece, now based in Cairo and preparing (or hoping) to lead the remnants of his forces back to his classic kingdom of the Hellenes, that the United States and Britain would continue to support his cause—*provided* that his people voted for his return and that he agreed to support a democratic form of government.

It was a wonderful, though necessarily brief, visit. The bestiality of war is rarely a constant thing. Even the poor bloody infantry, the "dogfaces" who usually get most of the worst of it all, were given occasional respite. So now in Cairo, the flashing nightmares of our actions on the edges of the Battle of Salerno and my too-eventful trip to Vis behind me, I had an enviably good time—playing, sightseeing, learning, and doing the minimum of work with a surprising number of friends.

Early one morning some of them took me on a jaunt to see the Sphinx and the pyramids. I viewed these ancient wonders with heart-beats high in my throat. Like others during the millennia before me, I could only stand and stare. Then some of us, like other sucker-tourists, got aboard some filthy camels that their drivers were hiring out. Major Max Niven (Niv's older brother) got on one, and as it was led away, rolling this way and that, Max held on to his saddle as if the ride were a cross between a slow-motion bucking horse and an erotic indulgence. Finally he called out for help to dismount because, as he shouted for all to hear, "If this keeps up, I'll have an *orgasm!*"

I suppose some vestigial sense of duty ought to have disciplined my hours, but I found it quite easy to enjoy almost everything. It was certainly a change from anything else I could remember. I gave brief attention to political business after Greece's King George told Hum Butler (his British aide-de-camp) he wished to see me. Accompanied by his faithful aide and confidant, Colonel Levidis, the king was his usual pleasant and tactful self. He was concerned that our State Department did not seem to be giving his country's cause enough support. His informants had reported that we were encouraging the communists and republicans as much as we were encouraging those wanting a return to constitutional monarchy and parliamentary democracy. Although I had not been given much inside knowledge, I tried to persuade him that Secretary of State Hull's office had told me to reassure him that we were wholly on his side and doing all we could. I think now, in retrospect, that whereas both we and the British did indeed prefer his restoration, we were actually ready to help any group that would fight the Germans. In Yugoslavia we deserted Mihajlović, our original choice, and switched our support to Tito, a communist, because his soldiers were killing more Nazis. Later in

France we learned that the various leftist groups usually proved to be the most effective of *La Résistance*. And so it went.

Philip Astley, once Gee Lawrence's fiancé and later Madeleine Carroll's husband, conniving with Max Niven, Hum Butler, and Henny Oakshott, insisted I go with them to visit some amusing Egyptian ladies who often welcomed Allied officers in a big apartment with illegal booze and "jolly jokes." I didn't want to appear stuffy, but I realized I must be damned careful to stay out of all trouble not expressly ordered by the U.S. Navy. Sometimes, though, I went along anyway.

A huge, villainous-looking Alsatian dog sleeping on an ornate Turkish rug was being petted by a woman I assumed was our hostess. A bit self-consciously, she introduced us to her four girlfriends, using a silly alias when she got to me that was accepted without question. We all settled down for drinks and bawdy stories. The ladies were not madly seductive but rather pleasant hostesses.

Suddenly loud male voices were heard from outside, coming up the stairs. The ladies panicked. They hurriedly explained that the voices were variously their husbands and boyfriends, who would not really approve of their entertaining foreign officers. Fatima (our chief hostess) whisked us hurriedly out of the room and into a kitchenette, where we were admonished to keep very still. As we five, clearly on the defensive and embarrassed, quickly shuffled out of the way, the great Alsatian roused himself and, recognizing the men's voices too, wagged an anticipatory tail.

In the kitchenette we were as quiet as paralyzed mice. Finally Philip whispered, "This is bloody intolerable! Five officers huddled together in a bloody kitchen because of some jippies [rude wartime slang for Egyptians] calling on their birds! What the hell! Let's bloody well walk out, and if they dare to fight us, we'll oblige the bastards!"

We agreed, and following the handsome Colonel Philip Astley, marched defiantly out, ready for anything. The ladies giggled nervously, but Philip, keeping his British cool, marched up to one of the men with an extended hand and a smile, saying, "Good evening, my name's Astley! These are . . ." and he rattled off all the names *except* mine.

The Egyptian men reacted with unexpected geniality despite their bewilderment. All of a sudden one of them called aloud to his companions, *"Looook! It's Douglas! Dooglas! Look! It's Douglas Movie Star!"* I froze and my companions groaned. The ladies took another, closer look at me and squealed. The other men rushed over gleefully to pump my hand, slap my back, and cause consternation with my A Force chums.

This sudden commotion aroused the Alsatian, who began to snarl and, assuming I was a threat, charged me. One of the new arrivals yelled at the beast to stop and grabbed his collar, just barely restraining him. The girls let loose another kind of scream, and Philip wisely shouted for us to "get the hell out of here!" With that he pushed me forward toward the door while he and the others formed a protective rear guard. We all beat the best retreat we could, the dog pulling his master with him, snarling and barking and clearly wanting to take a huge bite out of my retreating backside. Once clear, I thanked my friends for their comradely protection, and we returned to our quarters for a nightcap and a deep sleep.

The planning for the evacuation of Leros and Cos proceeded, though the operation was not successful until the following summer. I, for my part, spent a day visiting Major Jasper Maskelyne's "dirty-tricks factory" at the Abbassia Experimental Station, went sightseeing, and drank at the exclusive Mohammed Ali Club (where the Egyptian pashas and gentlemen still wore the red fez and had never *heard* of American Shriners), and with Prince Aly Khan at the Gazine Sporting Club. Best of all during my hectic week's visit I was grateful for new and replenished old friendships, and finally returned to Algiers by way of storied Tripoli and Tunis (Carthage) to await new orders. They were not long in coming. But first there was some news that made me pleased as hell. I had been promoted to lieutenant commander, to date from October 2 just past. Somehow the word went out in a routine ALNAV announcement, but nobody told me.

Naples was the next Allied Mediterranean headquarters, but I was just as glad to receive orders to go to London first for conferences on the forthcoming operations. We would leapfrog up the Italian west coast to the Anzio assault, followed by the recapture of the French islands of Elba and Corsica. Then on to southern France. FDR and Generals Marshall and Eisenhower were strongly in favor of these plans as a necessary prelude to easing the pressure on the forthcoming

Allied landings in Normandy. But Churchill stubbornly insisted that it would be at the *very* least another year or more before we would have sufficient men or means for either assault. He thought that badly bleeding Russia, now on the verge of collapse, clearly could not hold out long without some relief. Old Winnie pleaded—with great emotion, it was said—for us not to delay any longer but rather to keep pushing our way up through Italy and the Balkans, and into "the soft underbelly of Europe." He insisted that this would be both quicker and cheaper than landing in force in southern France—in lives, money, and materiel. Our American leaders disagreed with his arguments, overruled him, and went ahead preparing for the two French invasions as speedily as possible.

I remember having read that old family friend Charlie Chaplin had been, for the first time in his life, making public speeches and urging a "second front," berating the Western Allies for the delay in relieving the terrible pressures on the Soviets. When I saw him on my next trip home, I'm afraid I got very angry and asked, "What the *hell* do you think you're trying to do?"

His reply was a shy, self-deprecating smile and, "Oh, I know! You're right! I *was* foolish, wasn't I?"

I half melted.

While Allied headquarters staffs were busily planning the move from Algiers to Naples, I flew off in some rattling old DC-3 to London en route to home! There were some disappointingly brief refueling stops—the first at the fascinating Marrakesh, in Morocco. But soon after taking off again and leaving the African continent about three hundred miles behind, a conked-out engine necessitated our immediate return. This would have been greatly appreciated had I not let a very bad cold degenerate into a high-fevered flu. Fortunately for me, the senior Allied medical officer for the Mediterranean (a British general) was a fellow bucket-seat passenger. Detecting my flushed face and shivers, he ordered me on his "supreme medical authority" to stay behind in the Villa Taylor.

This required special arrangements because the villa, built by and belonging to old Mrs. Taylor of New York (mother of playboy Bert and playgirl Dorothy [Taylor] di Frasso), was—and is—a famous place. It is a near-perfect example of a most luxurious Moorish house with beautiful gardens enclosed by high walls. The inside had marvelously designed "Arabian Nights" bedrooms with great adjoining baths complete with such glamorous touches as huge sunken tubs that would have made C. B. deMille envious. Indeed, it was all so classically special that old Mrs. Taylor offered it, and the Allied high command accepted it, for the exclusive use of ailing diplomatic and military brass. Luckily the place was at this time empty of such bigwigs. Only the colorfully accoutered Moroccan household staff remained, slippering silently from one marble or tiled room to another. I was added "off the record" to its list of temporarily privileged inhabitants.

I was not all that ill for more than another day or so. Therefore, after wobbling into the fabled town of Marrakesh to buy slippers for Mary Lee in the storybook Medina bazaar and peeking into the famous Marmounian Hotel, I had to go flying on my way. But not without again noting to myself how unbelievably lucky my whole life had been—so far. I took Churchill's dictum "Survival is all!" as my own shield, always realizing, however, that the shield could fall. After more fuel stops en route and scary warnings of enemy planes on the prowl (my dear old partner-in-mischief, Leslie Howard, had recently been shot down coming home from Gibraltar to the U.K.), we set down first in Prestwick, near Glasgow, and then flew on to London where, on November 29, 1943, still sniffling and woozy, I reported to our navy headquarters.

Awaiting word about passage home, I rang up friends and lunched with Edwina Mountbatten, A. V. Alexander (the First Lord of the Admiralty) and Noël, who was just back from another trip to "imperial outposts," entertaining troops. My flu punished my once bushy-tailed spirits and a new, but luckily brief, high fever of 104 degrees assailed me. I muttered regrets to sudden invitations from "Chips" Channon, Emerald Cunard, and Sybil Colefax, all indefatigable flibbertigibbet party-pitchers through peace and war.

By midweek I was well enough again and by the weekend was ready to go to lunch for the first time in a year with Niv and his new, lovely "English rose" of a bride, "Prim" (Rollo) and their brand-new baby son, David Junior, at their pretty country cottage. I then drove on in a tiny rented car to Larry and Viv's equally small, equally postcard cottage, close to Korda's big London Film Studios, hard by the village of Denham. The mad bonging of village church bells at Sunday Evensong was a spiritual sedative. Their houseguest was Bobby Helpmann, who had survived all air raids and was still dancing. As the Oliviers had no staff and did all their own cooking and cleaning after long days at the studio, they welcomed relaxed weekends with pals helping out. After extended chatter, I remarked that Larry must truly be dedicated to his filming of Shakespeare's *Henry V* to have such a funny-looking, sixteenth-century, soup-bowl haircut. He came back at me by asking how *I* felt because "to be frank, old man, *you* look like an Oriental spy!" Why? Because, he explained, I was turning "rather yellow!"

My merriment ceased as soon as I looked in the mirror. By God, the whites of my eyes were indeed getting yellow! Autosuggestion? I cared not. I immediately began feeling nauseated and hurried to the Olivier loo to be sick. Larry insisted on driving me back in my car to London, where I checked into the navy's medical department. The medics there confirmed the assumption that I had jaundice. ("Drinkin' outa them dirty Eye-tie cups," guessed the medic on duty.) Into a military hospital I weaved. The first diagnosis was confirmed and I was given certain unheard-of (by me, anyway) medicines and all the hard-sugar candies I wanted.

As I improved and was no longer a threat to the other patients, I was moved into another room which I shared with Lieutenant-Commander Ewen Montagu, a peacetime lawyer and naval reservist who had also been with Combined Ops. We talked about all manner of things—the war, current gossip, and our particular ailments. Outside our windows, plunking hand organs, ululating bagpipers, Colchester shellfish peddlers, Spanish onion hawkers, and rag-and-junk collectors made the bleak early winter at least sound like spring. My old staff boss at Combined Ops, RN Captain Tom Hussey, came along to visit, with USN Captain Elliott Strauss and my boyhood-in–Central Park playmate, Johnny Schiff. I got get-well messages from Admiral Stark, Larry, Niv, Ivor Novello, and Dickie Mountbatten.

A cable, however, suddenly got me in real but happily only brief trouble. It was from Mary Lee! It so happened that after Victoria's birth, Mary Lee began to have terribly uncomfortable enlargement of some glands under her arms. Being frightened, she had understandably postponed an operation to remove them for as long as possible. Finally, she had the worrying job done and sent me a cable reading, "ARMS OPERATION SUCCESSFUL. ALL WELL. LOVE, FOO."

Greatly relieved, I whipped off a cabled blessing. Next morning, however, I had a visit from two officers—one from Scotland Yard and the other from the USN Intelligence Section. They wanted a detailed explanation of the sort of *"arms* operation" the intercepted cable referred to.

On December 9, 1943, I was still in the dreary military hospital and would give my thirty-fourth birthday no more than a passing nod. After listening to odd bits of conversations, my roommate, Ewen Montagu, had not unreasonably assumed I knew much more about all sorts of secrets than I actually did. I was not at any pains to disabuse him of that assumption. In fact, I probably encouraged it with knowing looks and smug smiles. Since my teens I had practiced giving false impressions of expertise in many an obscure subject. Montagu, hearing vague bits and vaguer pieces of my slim relationship with Brigadier Dudley Clarke's A Force in the Mediterranean and about our Special Operations and Beach Jumper groups, let a word or so out about his recent successful contribution to the victory in Sicily of Operation Mincemeat—the super-deception operation later known as *The Man Who Never Was.*

By the merest chance this was the very first time my recurring suspicion that a top-level strategic deception planning group actually existed was verified. Bit by bit, over the next months, I was to learn more. The group was called by the innocuous cover name of "The London Controlling Section" and was headed by a well-known peacetime banker, Colonel Johnny Bevan, who was answerable only to the War Cabinet. Eventually, despite the utmost security measures to preserve its secrecy, I gained a small measure of Bevan's confidence, largely because he hoped that *I* might have enough high-level clout to persuade our American Joint Chiefs of Staff to cooperate in strategic deception planning and operations.

One of our generals said he felt such sophisticated deception was "dirty and unfair"—an echo from a World War I incident when the British broke the German code and passed on the information that the Kaiser's Germany planned aggressive action against the United States.

The story goes that our then Secretary of State Henry Stimson declined to accept the British communication, reportedly saying, "No gentleman reads another gentleman's mail." The result was said to be the sinking of the *Lusitania* and the loss of many American lives. (Of course, this seems incredible in today's climate of "dirty tricks.") Actually I did not so much as hint at or pretend to any special influence, but the idea persisted that I had entrée to high places, and so I was encouraged to "influence" anyone I could in Washington on my home leave following my discharge from the hospital.

Before boarding my boat train at Euston Station on the evening of December 13, I stood in the raw, damp cold, outside the gates to the trains, watching the familiar scenes of farewell as if I were a disembodied spirit. Here were the smothered weepings, the chins-up, thumbs-up reassurances, the desperate last clinches, the waves and the blown kisses, and the poor young kids with lives to lose and no one to wish them good luck. I still remember my own sloppily sentimental eyes getting blurry and my relief that no one noticed.

Fog, the night bombing of rail lines up ahead, and the priority of troop trains heading for God and the generals knew where, so delayed our overcrowded sit-up-all-night ride to Glasgow that the roughly eight-hour trip took more than twelve hours. On arrival a rusty old tender breasted up to dockside and took a load of us out through the piercing damp to Cunard's *Queen Mary,* the giant liner lying at anchor in the roadstead just beyond.

This trip home was one great chase after another. U-boats kept signaling our course and we, with our astonishing speed and ability to read their codes, continued playing a "dodge 'em" game up and down and across the Atlantic.

By far the wittiest of my fellow passengers was RNVR Lieutenant Lord Stanley of Alderly, accurately nicknamed "Dirty Eddie." Erudite, poetic, brave, handsome, but studiously unwashed, he was a commander of LSTs and en route to Newport, Rhode Island, to sail one of them back to England. On arrival, he took some leave to see old American friends and, as it happened, met my stepmother Sylvia. Despite his grubbiness, he was witty and attractive, and as Sylvia adored the idea of having a title again, they married. After an extended compassionate leave he returned to the wars, and Sylvia, for now less bothersome to our family, stayed on the East Coast. Her faithful maid who had never ceased calling her "milady" now continued with greater confidence.

My own home leave was sweet but too short. I had just a week or so to recuperate in Newport with Mary Lee, adorable, solemn Dabby, and teeny-weeny, ever-laughing Tory—all squeezed into a small rented white clapboard colonial house. One day I managed to drive over to Watch Hill, an hour or so away, to show Mary Lee the grand old Sully family manse, Kenneth Ridge, where I had spent so many childhood summers. This lovely sprawling estate had belonged to my mother's family until her father lost his fortune as the King of Cotton. Now it was a Catholic convent rest home, and the missionary nuns who lived there gave us a sweet, bubbling welcome. In return, I signed some autographs and showed them some long-forgotten secret panels behind which old plaster copies of Greek statues were hidden. I was happy to see that the romantic statue of the kneeling Indian remained down the road where I had bicycled so often.

I was still a bit shaky on our trip down to Washington for a few days before I had to return to Algiers. My efforts to convert any upper-echelon brass hat to the idea that a special section devoted to strategic deception should be considered an integral part of war planning were disappointing. My first handicap was my relatively low rank—an important consideration in the military fraternity. A further, tiresome obstacle was my continuing identification in D.C. as a former movie celebrity. The Washington "Chairborne Brigade," though friendly enough in informal encounters, continued to make private inquiries as to whether I'd ever had any *real* sea duty or seen any *real* action. One well-known Washington-based admiral harrumphed over a lunch at the Metropolitan Club to Arthur Krock of the *Times* (who told me about it later) that if "that Fairbanks guy was given a high 'combat-only' decoration like the Silver Star, the navy must have lowered its standards to the level of the other services!"

In the end I did find one or two tolerant and interested high staff officers who reacted well to my "cause," but even they thought it would be some time before the Joint Chiefs of Staff would bother to listen to anything "too subtle." They were, by tradition, too attached to conventional warfare.

* * *

My leave over, I flew back to Algiers and the most awful soul-freezing cold I had ever experienced. After seeing and feeling the wet soaking through the Algerian plaster or stucco walls where I shivered in bed beneath a small mountain of coarse dirty-brown GI blankets (themselves quite undryable), I concluded that North Africans must promise themselves each winter that when summer next appears they will somehow seal their houses against the annual extreme damp cold to come. Then, when summer does happen along, it is so terribly hot and humid, and sleep becomes so elusive, that there is no energy left to invent something to ward off the coming winter cold until, as for centuries past, it is once again too late. An Algerian big shot actually admitted to me their habit of postponing everything except sex and moneymaking. Since the decline of the great Moorish era, this has always been the case.

After our various combined and special naval groups had peppered the still resistant Italian coast and the Allied land and air forces had battled their guts out, our leaders believed we had done enough to soften the enemy up, even though we had not pushed much closer to Rome. Consequently an amphibious assault, under the command of American General Truscott, was mounted against the beachfront environs of Anzio, about thirty-five miles south of Rome.

The landing itself, toward the end of January 1944, was at first a surprising success. (Though our Special Operations Group helped to confound enemy defenses, we took more credit for it than we actually deserved.) The Germans, momentarily stunned, pulled so far behind the lines that a couple of our war correspondents took a jeep and drove unhindered and unchallenged all the way to Rome and back. Nevertheless as no reconnaissance was launched and German whereabouts remained unclear, our commanding generals agreed it was too risky to follow up their initial success and our troops were told to dig in where they were. When the Germans discovered our timidity, they moved back and put up such a stubborn defense from then on that Anzio became—instead of the pushover it almost was—one of the longest, bloodiest (and most fiercely criticized) battles of the Italian campaign.

I got ashore at Anzio a few times without serious incident, but was always shocked anew by the horror of unrecovered bodies—Allied and enemy—some already decaying but almost all lying rigidly and indiscriminately in grotesque indignity. I was usually too busy to allow myself time to reflect on the vulgarity of violent death, or indeed to overfear it. I think I was always more frightened of being wounded, or even of being captured and tortured. I was certain that if I were subjected to severe pain, I would blurt out any secret my punishers wanted. But there were also many silent lonely moments when I wondered why I was there at all. Was it just because I was personally outraged by the massive use of ruthless military force by our enemies? And, if so, was I all that brave? Certainly—emphatically—not! I knew I was a closet coward who would settle for the intention rather than the act. Would I not have better served the cause by being a supporting celebrity at home, speaking publicly and making movies? Was I now just showing off by getting so irrevocably involved in the shooting part of warfare—and if so, who really cared? My family would think me wonderful whatever I did. Mary Lee would be proud of my dedication, but would prefer that it be at home with her at headquarters—probably Washington. Mother would think the whole war was being directed by her son. My father might have been proud; I couldn't be certain. Since he did much better for his country during World War I by selling several millions of dollars of Liberty Bonds than by joining anything, he might *not* have been so very pleased with me after all! And, lastly, what possible difference would I make to *any* resolution of the worldwide conflicts? None!

A temporary distraction from this useless self-pity that I can still recall was one day finding a broken bottle in a ditch beside the road to Rome. It lay near a few bits of what had once been a whole German soldier. Still stuck on the bottle was the torn remainder of a label that read: DEUTSCHES SCOTCH WHISKEY. I was never able to find a full bottle or learn what in hell it tasted like.

Chapter 8

I WAS GLAD to move to Naples. For the past year and a half I had seen enough of North Africa. Except for those two ends of the Muslim Crescent, Morocco and Egypt, I had no particular wish to revisit it. Many people and places had charm and were interesting, but many of the very dirty poor of the cities had a singularly shifty manner toward foreigners and cruel ways toward each other. The hotter the country the more flagrant these evils seemed. The most repellent were found, as in parts of India, behind the poor but colorful casbahs or bazaars. Too often parents could be seen offering temporary leases of their young children's bodies. Children as young as twelve or under openly proffered their scrawny little selves for small remunerations—sometimes for only packs of cigarettes. In a few cases I had seen, from Algiers to Cairo, how swarms of flies had so infected the honey-smeared eyes of strapped-down babies that they would, according to plan, grow up blind and have flourishing careers as beggars.

These incidental sideshows—the sight of which, to be fair, could be avoided—were gladly left behind when early in July 1944 we finally moved all the gear and personnel equipment of the whole of the U.S. Naval Forces in the Northwest African Waters and resettled in and near Naples. Poor Naples! So much of the city was by now a shambles, but so were so many other lesser towns. Some cheered our entry, but too many of the desperately underfed just looked on impassively.

Since the very first entry of the Allied military into Naples, at the end of October 1943, there had been a massive effort to make the city work again.

Now I was flying back and forth between Algiers and Naples to help make logistical arrangements for the final July '44 move. By midwinter 1944 all the thousands of corpses—military and civilian—had been disposed of. The worst-damaged buildings were blown up and the rubble cleared away. Deep potholes in the roads and streets had been patched. Some food was arriving, and though a third of the city's population had either fled or been killed, the remainder clawed out or begged for a living. Transport, electricity, and sewage were once again working, though not perfectly.

Most of the Italian warships in the harbor, badly damaged and leaning against docks, had to be towed away or sunk to make room for our ships, those of the nonmalevolent, curious, generally good-natured conquerors. It shocked me later to learn that our ships anchored in Naples harbor daily dumped enough surplus food and garbage overboard to feed the entire Neapolitan population for several days.

Because the great harbor and environs of Naples were European, it was a less alien-seeming place to all of us than Algiers. The Italians of the north, however, tended to sneer at it as the place where Africa begins—a description not at all appreciated by the Neapolitans. But to those who were to be based there for the next several months, it was beautiful, colorful, noisily poor, filthy, musical, and long-suffering. The music was, as travelers had noted for centuries, constant and pervasive.

On my second day there I found an old man quietly weeping beside the remnant of his narrow three-storied house soon after one whole side of it collapsed, as if exhausted. All his modest furnishings were now in full view. On the first floor I happened to spot what seemed to my untutored eye a large undamaged stack of fine porcelain. He offered in choked broken English to sell it to me for a tiny sum—for "anything!" I can't remember what I paid him, but I couldn't afford more than much too little. Later I found it had been a fine Capo di Monte dinner service and centerpiece that the Empress Josephine had given to the queen of Naples. How he got it I didn't ask or ever know, but whatever it was, my conscience whispered that I had probably shortchanged the old geezer, so I went back to pay him more. I was too late. He had died a few hours after I'd left him. As he had no known family, the rest of his house was soon looted by street urchins.

Not everything was gloom or drama. The USO had sent touring shows, plays, and star players wherever our men could be reached. In places like Naples, our sailors, unless shore-based, were naturally unable to see very much live entertainment. Occasionally I would hear that some old peacetime colleagues were coming through, but each time I was away on one of our little "nuisance raiding" forays. Once Mary Brian, a friend since we were about fourteen in the silent film *The Air Mail* and later in *It's Tough to Be Famous,* came to Naples to entertain the military. Now she was a beautiful lady who clung happily to her Texas accent. Her troupe only stayed a couple of days, but I was lucky enough to take her to dinner on one of the evenings. Next day I learned how many gibbering young officers suddenly claimed to be my best friend and wanted to meet her. Too late! The troupe had moved on.

My favorite land-based playmate in Naples (when time and duties allowed) was Philip Astley, newly transferred from Cairo and now wearing the small red tabs of a full colonel on his lapels. He was in charge of British army public and press relations. In strict secrecy he also operated as one of the "skullduggery" planners. Philip had followed up a silly suggestion I made to him in Cairo to form an informal group of like-minded characters to be called "The Cad's Club." They would have an undesignable but classically *describable* (in old heraldic lingo) coat-of-arms of "Everything rampant, and anything couchant." Astley now added his own bawdy idea—a badge or sign of membership in the form of short swagger sticks for members, to be covered, he insisted, with skin from the private parts of a rhinoceros.

When in mid-March of 1944 the venerable Mount Vesuvius grumbled and burped and spewed forth rivers of molten lava, Philip and I decided one late afternoon—after what he called "rather one or two too many beakers, old bean!"—to go up close to have a look. As we approached the immediate "disaster and danger" area, our jeep was stopped by a British military policeman. No one, he advised us, was allowed beyond that point. The molten lava had already descended and overtaken a couple of villages on Vesuvius's slopes, and many refugees were desperately trying to escape the slow, implacable inferno as it swallowed everything—even whole towns—that stood in its inexorable path downhill.

But Philip was determined and, wrongly assuming that my curiosity and fascination were as keen as his, sternly reminded the poor young soldier of his red-tabbed colonel's authority and said that I, his guest, was the "U.S. Navy's Official Liaison Officer for Disasters" and we were going to proceed despite the lad's orders. And we did.

Our jeep rattled uphill past streams of frightened, heavy-laden refugees until we came to a place that would obviously be engulfed by burning lava very soon. We parked the jeep, took a few extra gulps of whiskey from Philip's hip-flask, and climbed up to the flat roof of a house at the very edge of the village, the far end of which had already been swallowed up.

"Isn't this great?" we kept saying to each other excitedly between sips of Scottish mother's milk. The atmosphere was almost intolerable, the lava burning the very air around us as it piled up to a certain height, then spilt over and began to build up again, always moving its way slowly downward. Soon we noticed it coming down the streets on both sides of the line of houses. Ours was the last in its path. Suddenly we heard a loud CRA-A-A-CK, and felt our little building shudder. There was no doubt our rooftop was due to cave in and be swallowed up in minutes. Philip and I sobered up in a flash. *"Christ!"* said my gallant colonel friend to me, his terrified young pal, "Let's get the hell out of here!" With that we turned and leapt from one rooftop to the adjoining one—reminding me (afterward, you may be sure) of my rooftop hops in *Gunga Din,* filmed a lifetime of six years ago. In minutes, still intact but a little torn and very messy, we jumped into his jeep and careened down the side of the mountain. Then, well away, we each took turns with the flask in our shaky hands.

A few days after this asinine episode, I had occasion to take a PT boat out to Capri and meet with Vice-Admiral Hewitt's immensely popular chief of staff, Rear Admiral Spencer Lewis, USN, from, I promise, Calvert-on-the-Brazos, Texas. After our meeting we stood on the isle's summit and through our binoculars watched the continuing streams of lava still slowly creeping down Vesuvius. We were more than twenty-five miles from the volcano's fire and billowing smoke, yet we could see evidence of its ashes at our feet, blown over by breezes. A famous letter from Pliny the Younger to his father in Rome, about two thousand years ago, described in rich detail the dreadful tragedy he'd seen and what happened when the hot ashes suddenly fell upon ancient Rome's popular and opulent summer resort towns of Pompeii and Herculaneum. The volcano reminded us of how unselective and impersonal nature can be. To relieve the tense, awed silence I turned to the admiral and half-teasingly mumbled quietly, "Well, Admiral, you can't tell us you have anything like that in Texas!"

Lewis, his quiet drawl accompanied by a sly half-smile, answered, "No, son, we haven't. But the Dallas Fire Department could put it out in ten minutes."

We returned to Naples and the eruption ceased after a few more days. Today the hills around the crater have houses and farms on them once again.

The personal, individual lives of Allied military personnel were more or less cut off from the city's distress. Those ashore were billeted in hastily restored Italian army barracks, hospitals, and patched-up remains of schools or public buildings. Most officers, except those on ships, were billeted in various hotels or rooming houses. Mine, the Parker's Hotel, was up a steep, winding road and, though small, was actually quite nice and often clean. Most of the more regular senior officers objected quietly that I, a brand-new reserve lieutenant commander, was being billeted in the same little hillside hotel as they. But since I had "Top Secret" planning duties and a small staff (still, thank God, composed of Jack Watson, Ernie Wehmeyer, and a couple of others) at headquarters with another irregular job of occasionally going to sea on actual operations, I had to be close to the center of things. Also, since I had to dash hither and yon on occasion, I was temporarily allowed any old spare jeep I could find from the motor pool. More accurately, my small privileges were not so much allowed as tolerated.

Realizing the irritation my presence caused and that it was made worse by my few extra liberties, I made a conscious effort to be both overly respectful and sickeningly charming to my official betters.

When the hot, humid weather began, however, and our regular long cotton khaki uniform trousers seemed to make us sweat more, I inspired fresh criticism by occasionally borrowing part of the British hot-weather kit of khaki shorts (whites for dress-up), like those that Boy Scouts once wore, and open-neck, sleeveless shirts with USN rank markings on collars and shoulder boards. These were cooler and better than ours. Eventually even Admiral Hewitt agreed to this dress in that climate and officers of his command were permitted to wear the same—except in battle, when long sleeves and trousers were obligatory in order to minimize possible flash burns.

About twenty miles north of Naples, the new "Supreme" Headquarters of the Allied High Command in the Mediterranean was now situated in the great Palace of Caserta, originally the Palace of the Kings of "Naples and the Two Sicilies," and a smaller (not by much) edition of Versailles. Each story was about fifteen or twenty feet and the Yanks—unaccustomed to much climbing of stairs—hated having to go to some general's or admiral's office where no elevators existed. It also convinced us that eighteenth- and nineteenth-century courtiers must have had the very muscular legs and lungs of athletes.

Not far off, but closer to the sea, lay the bitterly and stubbornly contested and tragic Benedictine abbey of Monte Cassino. The Germans fought so fanatically well there that they halted the major Allied advance up the boot of Italy for many months. I drove up one day with Jack Watson to have a look, from a distance of course, and arrived just in time to witness the latest repetition of one of the worst accidents to befall any side in any war—the mass killing of our own troops by miscalculation. Allied aircraft rained masses of bombs down on our GIs and British Tommies. It was—and the memory still is—too horrible to contemplate for longer than it takes to write of it.

Before leaving Algiers permanently for Naples, I had somehow learned about a few of the preliminary strategic deception plans for the future Big Show, the cross-Channel invasion of France. Now I could easily guess that we in the Mediterranean were to be at least a part of the smaller part of two invasions of France—one from the U.K. and one from the south.

A most famous victory roused the Allied world when, on June 5, General Alexander announced that Allied troops had taken Rome, the

Eternal City. It is hard for a modern young person to appreciate the symbolism represented by that conquest. Many years later, an arrogant Roman lady was being very condescending to General "Alex" and, after needling him for being a foreign general, asked if he had ever been to Rome before and if he knew anyone there. The gentle general answered modestly in the affirmative. The *grandissima contessa,* with seeming surprise, said, "Oh, how is that?" Alex replied icily, "Because, madam, I conquered it!"

Very early on the sixth of June the vast fleets of the Allies, jammed with soldiers, sailors, marines, weapons, mechanized vehicles and all, burst ashore on the coast of Normandy in France not far from where William the Norman sailed to conquer England nearly a thousand years earlier. The surprised but desperate enemy defended themselves fiercely, selling every yielded yard for high prices.

Months earlier I had been asked by Bob English whether I wanted orders to go to England and be in on Operation Overlord, with only some nominal adviser-observer duties, or to stay in Corsica for Anvil (the code name for the invasion of southern France), where, in addition to heading up the amphibious diversion plans, I would actually take tactical command of a task unit within the old Task Group 80.4. My indecision lasted for seconds only. I saw immediately that for me to join in Overlord was only to be able to say, "I was there." Of course it was tempting, but to be a useless extra observer would not really be satisfying. I wondered briefly if I could do both–fly up for Overlord and, if still in one piece, fly back as soon as possible, do my bit for the Elba invasion, and then pick up the planning and rehearsals for the Anvil operation against southern France, due to be launched about eleven weeks later, on August 15. I got no further with that idea, as Bob English said, "Too irresponsible! Choose one or the other!"

All our BJ units, plus American and British MLs, LCPs, PT and MTB squadrons, had been transferred to Corsica, the majority to Calvi, some to Bastia. My "Chief Everything" (mostly communications), Jack Watson, supervised most of the moving job. Shortly after getting settled, we learned that our next important assignment was to help the French Bataillon de Choc–newly reformed from their forces in North Africa–to recover the island of Elba. It was not really a terribly vital objective to anyone but the French. However, to them its repossession was a matter of raising national morale and the waning prestige of French arms. It was, of course, where Napoleon spent his first exile and from which he later escaped to begin his Hundred Days of restoration as emperor.

Just as I was leaving Naples for the main Corsican air base in Ajaccio, I was shocked to hear that my old friend and adviser on my 1941 South American mission for FDR, Hutch Robbins, had been shot down flying to Sardinia. As I took off in a small navy plane, the type usually used for transporting a few passengers and small cargoes, I gulped down a couple of antijitters sedatives. I was the only passenger. As there were no seats, I sat on some blankets on the deck, leaned against a large stack of mailbags, and dozed off. The next thing I knew there was a terrific jolt—like a crash. In fact, a crash was exactly what it was. I could feel and see that our plane had upended on its nose. The pilot and his sidekick were strapped in but badly cut up. I was saved from all harm by the cushioning of the mailbags I'd been sleeping against. When fire fighters rushed to douse the flames from the engine, they were astonished, but no more than I, to see me crawl out of the wrecked nose-down fuselage not even bruised.

On landing near Bastia, the plane's brakes had failed, and we had overshot the short field and dived headfirst into a ditch at the end of the runway. As I'd been asleep, I hadn't had a chance to be frightened, but I did manage to whisper quite a few prayers of thanks for weeks afterward. I also gave some thought to how long my lucky life would go on being lucky.

The commanding French generals were as distrusting of our Special Ops usefulness as our own commanders had been. In fact, when I first signaled a request for special air transport to get me to Corsica in a rush, some hopeful wit radioed British Admiral Sir John Cunningham's headquarters to ask, "Is Air Command carting Fairbanks over to look for his Corsican brother?" I tried to keep from showing my smug gratitude when the admiral signaled back, "I know of no more urgent business in Corsica than that we have commissioned Lieutenant Commander Fairbanks to do." Ahem!

The Allied naval forces in Corsica were under the command of Rear Admiral Tom Troubridge, one of whose ancestors served under Nelson at Trafalgar. On June 17, 1944, amphibious forces were to land the French troops on rocky Elba's south coast. But four hours earlier—H minus four, or about 2:00 A.M.—I was to lead our group of fully equipped and armed PT boats to a specific area on the north coast, hoping to pull at least a part of the island's defense to us and away from the real assault area.

I led the motley squadron as slowly and quietly as possible toward shore so as to get our team of commandos and saboteurs into rubber boats and paddling toward land, unnoticed by the Germans. It was the most delicate phase of our assignment, as we had to approach fairly close to shore. We knew that in the hills high above there was a battery of six-inch enemy guns and large searchlight emplacements.

Once ashore, our troops flashed an infrared signal that all was okay. As they began to climb up and over the side of the great hill, we began our firing, smoke-laying, rocket launching, and prerecorded sound effects. This brought a murderous barrage down upon our heads that, due to our heavy smoke layers, was happily inaccurate. Our subsequent action report stated: ". . . gunfire with tracer bullets flying seemingly everywhere but where our boats were. . . . Flashes of more large caliber guns were noted—probably 140 mm—firing seaward from the mountain above us. . . ." Once our radios told us that most of the French forces in the south had landed and dawn disclosed our tactical duplicity, we withdrew and lit out for home.

The fact that the Bataillon de Choc had got ashore and up into the hills before the Germans realized that they had been duped was another small but important prize. On the other—and sadder—hand, once the battle had been joined, the Germans, whose defense forces were larger than expected, inflicted dreadful losses on the ultimately victorious French. A few of the German prisoners were captured in cement pillboxes, actually chained to their machine guns and unable to run away. They just stopped firing. One hung his dirty white handkerchief on the muzzle of his gun.

The next day, we were all assigned to help bring the bedraggled, haggard prisoners off Elba and over to Corsica. The French troops— worn out, bone-tired, dirty, hungry, but triumphant—were ordered to line up just as they were for an inspection by their famous, ruthless commander, General de Lattre de Tassigny. I daresay they would have mutinied had they had the strength. As it was, one unshaven, disheveled poilu nearly fainted. When de Lattre saw him, he not only gave him a ruthless tongue-lashing but said he would send him, as "punishment," to the Chad, the mercilessly hot North African French colony. I myself saw the end of an intelligence "interview" with a German prisoner whose unsatisfactory answers to military questions won him hobnailed kicks in the groin—after each one of which, I was told, he fainted. I didn't wait around to learn whether or not the French intelligence officer found out what he sought to know.

Jolly Admiral Troubridge whispered to me the week after Elba that the French were recommending me for the Croix de Guerre, and with a palm attached to the ribbon as an extra distinction—won only in combat.

As soon as I could, after Elba, I set about working out details for our largest diversionary plan so far and for my command of a sizable operational unit. The principal and ultimate strategic aim of Anvil was to relieve enemy pressure on our forces in Normandy: to attempt, after a great amphibious assault, to swing inland to the north and envelop the Nazis in a huge pincer movement.

Anvil's main landing was to be carried out by three (later a fourth) American and four French divisions (taken from General Alexander's forces in Italy). Nearly three quarters of the Allied air forces in the Mediterranean were also to be moved west for the new plan. This not only infuriated Churchill further but deeply distressed General Alexander, the "truly great strategist," as MacArthur called him. But there it was.

Actual landings were to be between Fréjus/St.-Raphaël and St.-Tropez/Ste.-Maxime. The enemy's dilemma, which Allied planners intended to intensify, would be where to concentrate their main defense. Movement along so much of the Côte d'Azur could be made only on a small coastal road through towns, or one of the other *corniches* that wound around the high hills behind. Or they could go way inland, circle around, and come out again. The ultimate target of the Anvil landings was the Marseilles-Toulon area and the question for the Germans was how best to defend it.

All our local diversionary plans, coordinated with London's overall deception plans, were intended to suggest at first that we might land in northern Italy, near Genoa. Actually, the main thrust was to be far to the west, in France, between St.-Raphaël and Bormes, behind the Isle d'Hyères.

The first stage of our diversion plan was to land a group of French commandos at a place called La Pointe des Deux Frères, between Cannes and Nice, at about four hours before predawn H-hour. They were to move inland, do some sabotaging, and raise general hell in the area. We at sea were to carry out some desultory coastal bombardment. Then as the main armada, just arrived, was to begin debarking troops, we were to scoot behind them to an area between Marseilles and Toulon called the Baie de la Ciotat. After darkness the first night we were to pull out all the stops—with some help from the air forces—in our efforts to suggest another major landing right there.

The naval craft assigned to us were an almost comically patternless force. There were first two small British gunboats, the *Aphis* and the *Scarab,* brought halfway around the world from the Yangtze River in China, mounting just one big six-inch gun and a few antiaircraft guns apiece, four RN MGBs (motor gunboats), twelve USN PT boats, and one American destroyer, the *Endicott,* commanded by the colorful swaggerer Commander John D. Bulkeley. He had won our highest wartime award, the Congressional Medal of Honor, in recognition of his command of the "They Were Expendable" squadron of PTs that took General MacArthur, his family, and staff safely out of threatened Japanese clutches in the Philippines to Australia in 1942.

It had been one of my more foolish conceits not to ask any of our Special Operations Group to do anything that I hadn't done, or at least tried to do myself, whether it was climbing ropes or even swimming underwater as a frogman. When we were making diversionary plans for Anvil and working out both fake and real parachute drops, I decided with dry-mouthed reluctance that I must learn to parachute. So far, I'd resisted, as the idea terrified me. But I went out to the parachute school anyway. There the instructors were in great towers, and there were the small planes used for troop training.

I swaggered up to the instructor, my heart beating most irregularly. He told me what to do and when. I got fitted out, strapped up, and taken aloft—very sympathetically. But when the big moment came, I just plain chickened out! (Shades of *The Air Mail* back in 1923.) I didn't burst into tears this time, but my tongue was as dry as the Mojave Desert, and my resistance to being pushed was as the strength of ten. Finally, I said to hell with it. I'd write the plan as first envisaged and let the para-boys jump as directed. And I'd never be so goddamn "noble" again!

The whole of our Task Group 80.4 was now commanded by the serious and efficient Captain H. C. Johnson, who, though newly assigned to this sort of command, took to its unorthodoxy quickly and well. My own subcommand consisted of the two RN gunboats, a squadron of USN PTs, some air-sea rescue craft, and a small flotilla of amphibious raiding craft.

Early on I had located the exact targets of our two gunboats' bombardment. I took care—disgraceful care—to avoid hitting the houses of people I knew. Instead, I pinpointed what I was pretty sure would be empty railroad stations, post offices, beachfront cabins, and the like. With luck in our not-too-accurate markmanship (from well offshore, in the pitch-black dark, with only two or three radars in my task unit) we *might* hit one or two targets.

Jack Watson had carefully prerecorded a lot of meaningless chatter between American aircraft pilots to be broadcast by one single air force plane dropping strips of tinfoil as our new device for radar-jamming, called "window." A more sinister but very effective bit of lethal gadgetry was dropping hundreds of dummy paratroops in the hills near Toulon. When I ordered them, I suggested they be made in different sizes—normal, half-size, and very small—so that when they were dropped from a plane, the ground observers' perspective would (at least at first) make it seem as if the large ones were closer and the smaller ones proportionately farther away. On being thrown from the plane, those wrapped-up rubberized dummies automatically inflated. Then, inspired by ideas from the Far East, I requested that all the dummies be booby-trapped.

Thus on August 14, D-minus-one day of Anvil, the several units of our task group would set out from different ports hours before the main attack force, as if going toward Genoa. After one big group made this feint—for the benefit of German radar and spy planes—they would converge in two sections at precisely planned times, all well before midnight.

During the last few weeks of preparing for this operation, I thought I had somehow contracted a new (to me) sort of venereal disease. I couldn't imagine how such a thing could be, because I had not had any adventure that could conceivably expose me to such a fate. Still, I was less worried about the illness per se than about the regulations, which clearly warned that anyone who knowingly possessed a communicable illness or disease must immediately report to the medical officer and then be relieved of his duties until cured or the medical officer authorized a return to duty.

I was frankly terrified. In a week or so, I would have my chance to actually command a small naval task unit during a major amphibious landing. I had privately persuaded myself that this operation was without real risk, but could be—if it worked—a spectacular thing to bring off. I dreaded a negative medical report.

I decided to improve my friendly relations with the young base medical officer. One night I scrounged some rather bad bourbon, got him quite tight, and then swore him to secrecy. When he warmly though woozily agreed, I confided my fears to him, adding that whatever his diagnosis, I must go ahead with the assault (now re-code-named Dragoon, as someone feared the name Anvil had been compromised) because only I knew how to execute the details of the plans I had written.

It was a bald-faced lie, of course, but it worked. The young doctor promised to pass me somehow. He saw me early the next morning. At his instructions, I stripped and showed him the evidence of the illness that had kept me awake with worry for several nights. The young doc took one look and began laughing. I controlled my indignation and questioned his untimely hilarity. "Because," he laughed, "you have no disease, sir, you're just lousy! Somehow, from a dirty toilet seat or bedsheets, and the shortage of baths we've all had, you've picked up a bundle of lice and they've made all those itchy spots on you. Here—take some of this stuff and put it on. You'll be rid of 'em in a day." He went on laughing. I almost wept with relief!

The collective tension of our group could not have exceeded mine. We received coded messages that the several task forces, a plodding military-laden argosy, had already left their different ports and were even now converging on their planned rendezvous points prior to the clashing of arms on the southern French beaches.

I led one of our ML and PT squadrons to a point where we were to put the first Free French troops ashore in their still-captive country. One of our frogmen swam in to the beach. After a seeming age of waiting, we picked up his infrared signal light through our special goggles. The light was to direct us to the spot at which we were to send our eager Frenchmen ashore. From there they were to go rapidly inland to sabotage road, rail, and telephone-telegraph equipment.

The brave young French—or "Froggy-Frogmen" as some called them—eagerly waded ashore. It was too dark to see them, but we heard several severe blasts coming from their direction. We slowly pulled back out to sea, contenting ourselves that the noise indicated our Frenchmen were doing their job quickly and very well. The next night we received the sickening news that the infrared signaler had somehow got himself way off the place where his regimental pals were supposed to come ashore. Instead, we had landed them right on a big, freshly laid mine field. That explained the first explosions we had heard. The losses suffered by that small gallant group were dreadful: more than half. But they did cut a crucial coastal supply road.

Not knowing of this immediately, we turned back out to sea and swung well in front of the main oncoming invasion fleet until we reached the other or western side of the assault front. Our task unit chugged closer to our target area, the big Toulon naval base and its environs, in particular the Baie de la Ciotat. Our group's protective destroyer, *Endicott,* carrying our task group commander, Captain Johnson, deliberately stayed about fifteen or twenty miles away, though ready to dash to our help if necessary. The main assault landings had already begun, as planned, very early in the morning of August 15, only shortly after we had passed in front of them. It was now—I remember this better than so many things—between 3:00 and 4:00 A.M. that same morning. We began firing our best salvos into designated targets, and our PTs and very fast ASRCs—air-sea-rescue craft—fired their beach-barrage and heavy-smoke rockets.

This immediately drew a gratifying reaction from shore as the enemy, clearly believing we were a powerful force about to land, opened up on us with heavy but ill-aimed fire. Soon the whole area lit up and then as quickly went dark; star shells roared in the sky trying to illuminate us. Searchlights flashed along the coast and inside the Baie, east and west. Twenty- and 40-mm shells flew from all directions and burst near us. These were followed by huge flashes from 88-mm, 105-mm, and 240-mm near-misses. Some of our craft reported minor damage, but that, "for the moment," they said, was all.

Despite the risk of mines—we knew their general locations–I ordered our gunboats, the MLs, and ASRCs to maneuver as close inshore behind smoke as we dared. Then we started up our sonic and radio tricks. Between 4:00 and 5:00 A.M. we withdrew, hoping to be out of clear sight by the time it was full daylight.

We earnestly hoped that our simulated threats were being supported, not only by prerecorded chatter from our aircraft, but also by the "rising up" on a broadcast signal of the much-vaunted French underground, *La Résistance*. We had heard so much about its size and potential for so long. But when it was time to call on them, our Free French liaison officer admitted their number was not so large as predicted, and the best disciplined and organized ones were, alas, the communists. He also told us sadly that the original resistance groups in the Netherlands, Belgium, Denmark, Norway, and Luxembourg were, in proportion to population, the best and most reliable.

As soon as I could, I transferred my command from our leading PT to the *Aphis,* the senior of the two British gunboats. I did so because its skipper, a reserve lieutenant commander, was an older, very experienced ex–merchant ship's master who knew infinitely more about everything nautical than I ever would. I was still theoretically commanding one small unit–a section only of our bigger task group–but the *Aphis*'s skipper was right there to advise and correct me whenever I made a mistake.

At daybreak on the morning of the fifteenth we could see in the hazy light the other gunboat, *Scarab,* astern of us, and then, tagging along in loose formation, our slightly scattered flotilla of MLs, raiding or landing craft, several of our PTs and ASRCs. At 5:40 the *Aphis*'s radio crackled and squealed with a call from one of our ASRCs. It had had a breakdown, and was now under attack from two big enemy ships and asking for immediate help.

This was a brain-rattling moment. Our intelligence had assured us there were no enemy warships left in Toulon or the Baie de la Ciotat. But, goddammit, here they were! Two of them! They had already disabled our leading ASRC, equipped with our best secret electronic gear and some rockets. She was now lying dead in the water, partly aflame but still firing defensively as best she could.

I sent a PT to rescue her and ordered both our gunboats to turn about and engage the enemy ships as soon as possible. At first we could see only two small specks about four or five miles away with flashes from their guns coming at us. At ten minutes past six, precisely, we opened fire on them, still not knowing what kind of ships they were. Earlier, we had radioed the *Endicott,* requesting—nearly *begging*—her to come quick and help out. In case they cared, we also radioed Admiral Hewitt's HQ ship, USS *Catoctin.*

Our returning shots, not well aimed, were wide of their targets, but we pressed on nonetheless. The Germans began to bang away at everyone, so it seemed, in our group. I ordered the MLs to screen us as best they could as we closed first to less than two miles and then down to one.

The big, very old six-inchers on both our gunboats were getting so hot that our gunnery officer said we must allow a bit more time after what he called, with a smile, our cannonading, to cool down. The early exchange of fire had indeed been violent, and the *Scarab,* still astern of our port side, noted about fifty straddles and near misses in those almost endless few minutes. Then the Nazi gunfire became even more intense and accurate. As the leading ship in the group, we were their principal target. We were now close enough to see that the two ships trying to destroy us were both slick and fast. A fresh radio report told us that one of them had just been identified by a U.S. naval air scout as a small former Italian (now German) destroyer-corvette-type ship, the U-Jäger *Capriolo,* and the other as a large armed converted yacht, the *Kemid Allah.* Too late, we learned that each mounted three radar-controlled four-inch guns, plus torpedoes, and were capable of between twenty and thirty knots. *We* could, sometimes, with luck in wind and tides, push our broad-bellied gunboats to about ten knots.

When it became foolhardy to get closer, I signaled a couple of our still-screening small craft to circle around and lay a very thick smoke screen. While that was being done, we led the rest of our little group into the middle of the smoke and made wide circles inside. We were like a couple of ducks leading our little ducklings around and around.

The *Aphis*'s skipper and I decided in an exchange of shouts that there was no sense in slugging it out any longer. Both the *Aphis* and the *Scarab* had had their radar shot away. Since our radio was still operating, we sent further frantic word to Captain Johnson and Commander Bulkeley in the *Endicott*: *"For Christ's sake hurry up! We're in a bloody pickle!"*

Since we could no longer fire our big guns except at intervals of a couple of minutes, we fired antiaircraft guns just to make trouble. Most of the electric power on both ships had gone out minutes before. Soon after, we saw the *Scarab*'s radio antennae being shot away, then minutes later, our own went. Compasses, too, had been struck out, one by one.

The great skipper of *Aphis* was so very calm that he might well have been in a peacetime exercise with harmless firecrackers exploding. I made no bones about being terrified but, as was often the case, my fright disguised itself with a forced show of high, good spirits. Others often thought me cool and calm and—sometimes—even funny. Usually only I knew my lighthearted banter was my particular form of hysteria.

With shrapnel bursting around us like steel confetti, we continued to lead our little pack of moving targets in great figure eights. Some of our ships sustained damage but, thank God, none of our people did. Continuing to disguise my terror while still on the *Aphis*'s bridge, and supposedly in command of our task unit, I deliberately kept dropping things on the deck—my helmet, or binoculars, for example—behind the ship's canny captain. This meant, of course, that I would have to bend down and pick up whatever it was in the shameful hope that the next bits of flying metal would hit something or someone besides me!

But where in God's name (the international object of many different appeals and some blame) was Captain Johnson? And the *Endicott* with skipper John Bulkeley? Our gunnery officer shouted above the din that our big main battery had now cooled enough to begin firing again. Though our smoke screen had helped hide us somewhat, it couldn't hide us from the enemy's radar. And as the Germans were causing more damage to all of us, there seemed no point in continuing to hide behind the smoke. We had long since lost our bearings and didn't know where the hell we were. The captain and I agreed, when we could hear ourselves shout above the din, that we might as well come out into the clear and shoot at anything until rescue came.

The men were marvelous, beyond praise. They went about their jobs efficiently and shouted jokes at each other. The cooled-off guns were reloaded and more shells were ready to be shoved into the breeches.

The next problem was that we didn't have a clue as to how to get out of our goddamned smoke screen. I wanted, if possible, to get around to the rear of the German ships, thereby hoping to cut off their easy escape to Marseilles or Toulon. Suddenly we saw a thinning of the smoke and headed for it. Once in the clear I saw we were going at right angles across the bows of the two enemy ships, which were still keeping a fair distance from us. I can't say how far away they actually were. They had visibly slowed down and were nearly abreast of each other, still firing, though not, it seemed, as much as before. Now, by the purest chance, we had come out of our bloody smoke screen and performed the classical naval maneuver of "Crossing the enemy's T," a more or less self-explanatory description of naval choreography that was said to have happened in battle no more than twice since Nelson and Trafalgar. But as this was a minor scrap between minor ships in a "sideshow," no one cared. Because they were heading for us, they could only fire with their forward armament. We, on the other hand, were coming across and in front of them and could fire on them from anywhere.

I don't know if I gave the next order to fire or not, but I got the credit for it. I honestly doubt that I was thinking very clearly, though someone was. And with our very first salvo, shooting point-blank at the *Capriolo,* with neither our radar nor targeting devices left, we made a direct hit! The *Scarab* made a very near miss that was said to have damaged the enemy destroyer's plates. To our shocked surprise, the other enemy ship—the old converted armed yacht—seemed to hesitate momentarily, as our first target began visibly to list, as if in the first throes of sinking.

Stunned by our accidental success, we saw great flashes and explosions all around on first one and then the other enemy ship. By God, again like the old stories of the cavalry to the rescue, our fast guardian tin can, *Endicott,* came pounding in, her several five-inch guns blazing.

Once more, good old dashing John Bulkeley, the "sailor's sailor," did the spectacular thing. First, after orders to "Fire when ready!" from Captain Johnson, he finished off our own already near-mortally wounded victim and then proceeded to blast the second one out of the water.

The smaller craft of Task Unit 80.4.1 went busily about picking up as many as they could of the enemy still able to swim in the calm, oily, and very messy water. The gunboats, designed only for river water, had shallow, nearly flat bottoms, with no more than three feet of freeboard, so they joined the rescue party.

I was standing, weary and relieved but still excited, on deck when a German lieutenant commander (we knew his rank by his one remaining shoulder marking) was pulled out of the water by the strong regular Royal Navy hands of our ship's CPO. It is international naval protocol and custom that, on boarding any naval ship, anywhere, officers and/or men of any military service or rank are first supposed to salute the quarterdeck and then, after routinely requesting permission to come aboard, to exchange courtesy salutes when such permission is granted.

In this case, the German skipper, after being pulled aboard, dripping and angry, turned and gave the Nazi salute, the stiff right arm Heil Hitler! On seeing this, our CPO, an old cockney sailor, unceremoniously lifted his foot to the German officer's middle and pushed him right back into the sea. He then called down in his richest "gor-blimey" accent, "Naow, none o'that there 'ere! You come back up and do it proper-like—or back in you bloody well go agayn!"

The German got the gist of the lecture and was hauled aboard, furious. But this time he gave the proper salute and went below for later interrogation by the *Endicott*'s intelligence officer.

The whole of Dragoon went exceedingly well. From scattered parts the invasion fleet had converged and another hell was let loose on schedule and according to plan. The Germans' "Mediterranean Wall" had several holes in it and their coastal defenses were hampered. To thwart them further, our diversionary tactics, though little noticed by historians, were on the largest scale so far and proved very helpful. In fact, it was a fatal two days before the Germans knew for certain where our main thrust would be. We had pinned down another complete enemy division. We were, on the whole, very well satisfied with our sideshow part in the victory. The Nazis had originally moved in several divisions of infantry and over two hundred big coast defense guns to protect the falsely threatened Toulon, and Baie de la Ciotat area, with almost the same amount to defend the port of Marseilles from the sea. (Both were eventually taken from the landward side.) In fact, forty-five more German coast artillery batteries were spread along the Côte d'Azur, some even camouflaged as cabanas. Mine fields on land and in the harbors were all over the place and sharp-pointed poles were erected in fields to impale paratroopers (French workers deliberately dug such shallow holes that most fell over at a touch). When our multisized inflatable rubber parachute dummies were discovered to be booby-trapped, the Berlin radio squealed and protested at the "inhuman, bestial" methods of the "evil" Western Allies! We knew that they knew we were coming—but they didn't know where. The great pincer movement did work, and the main attack in the north continued, expensively but steadily and victoriously.

Chapter 9

THAT, AS far as I could tell, was the end of my war in Europe. I was greatly overrewarded for my actions during the past few months. This is not said out of any old Gary Cooper–John Wayne manure-kicking, aw-shucks modesty, but my own view of just deserts. I was very grateful for my newly promised symbols of official recognition of services rendered, whether deserved or not. The French, for instance, told me they were going to add to my Croix de Guerre (after Elba) by making me a Chevalier of the Légion d'Honneur (military division). (This was for landing the first French troops returning to France, and the order was to be signed by "Le Grand Charles" de Gaulle himself.) They did so with a nice ceremony in July 1945 when I was back in Washington, D.C.

About the same time the British sent a message that "the King had approved a recommendation from Admiral Sir John Cunningham, via the Admiralty," that I receive the Royal Navy's very special Distinguished Service Cross, only to be won in combat, for the Mediterranean diversionary operations carried out in collaboration with British forces. Most gratifying of all was a fabulously exaggerated account of my activities with our own U.S. forces, for which Captain Johnson hoped—and even predicted—I would get the Navy Cross. This was very honestly far in excess of whatever I might have deserved, especially in view of my really "scaredy-cat" wish to run away.

However, as it turned out, the navy's award board determined that if they gave such a high decoration to a movie celebrity, "the Navy would be criticized for seeking cheap publicity," and so settled on a combat Legion of Merit decoration to which they added a bronze *V* for valor.

Many years later Admiral Hewitt said: "It appeared to me that [Fairbanks] was constantly trying to contribute the maximum toward winning the war, and making good as a naval officer, while avoiding any appearance of capitalizing in any way on either his own or his father's reputation as an actor. Fairbanks's service throughout was distinguished and a credit to himself and to his country. I was happy to have him with me."

Some days after our troops began taking over Marseilles, street by street, that August of 1944, a missing friend suddenly reappeared. Jock Whitney, the handsome millionaire and high-goal polo player, showed up after having first been captured and then escaping. With no clearly defined duties and the temporary rank of lieutenant colonel, he had been driving a jeep through the port city's back streets and inadvertently found himself behind the slowly retreating Germans. On being captured, Jock was whisked off to be questioned by the enemy's local intelligence officer. According to the story as I heard it, Jock's monocled interrogator began, "It says here you are John Hay Whitney of New York, yes? Are you also known as *Jock* Whitney?" Jock nodded nervously. The German looked up and smiled. "You don't remember me? I played polo against you in Long Island about five years ago, and outside of London before that."

Jock by then recognized his captor, but hesitated to do more than nod. The German then winked and whispered that he would arrange for Whitney to escape from the train taking him away that night, along with the Germans' favorite English jockey, who had been captured from a British unit during the landing battles.

The enemy officer was as good as his word. The Yankee colonel and the limey jockey "escaped" and reported back to headquarters the next day.

By the end of August 1944, I had taken sad but grateful leave of my gang: Jack Watson, Ernie Wehmeyer, Arthur Bryant, Tom Curtis, Norman Hickman, and the other members of the original BJ Group. After a few days' stopover in London, where the awful V-1 buzz bombs had now been replaced by the really fearsome V-2 rockets, I was back in hot, humid, beautiful Washington. There I was temporarily assigned to the Strategic Plans Division, connected with the Psychological Warfare Division under the Combined and Joint Chiefs of Staff. I had no idea how long I'd be there before being shipped out again.

Having once mocked flashy awards as being too often cheaply or politically won, I now began to look on my own personal awards not so much with my usual cynicism but as personal passports to a wider range of military acceptance. In fact, only a short time after we had settled back into Washington war life, I was officially notified that Captain Johnson's recommendation for my award after Dragoon was approved. With Mary Lee in tow, I appeared at navy headquarters for the small ceremony when Assistant Secretary of the Navy Artemis Gates pinned the decoration on me. Mary Lee wore a proud sunny look all day.

Washington friends helped to find us a handsome house for a reasonable rent on exclusive Massachusetts Avenue. What was left of my share of my father's inheritance had been considerably depleted by now. But whatever still dribbled in, when tickled up by my naval pay, along with a part of Mary Lee's cautiously invested income from her divorce settlement from Hunt Hartford, proved just enough for us to live conservatively, though in style. We entertained moderately but well. No doubt some sniffed, considering the grim reports of war still going on around the world, that it would be more becoming had we chosen a more modest base. Perhaps we should have, but we were so relieved to have weathered fortune's blizzards without harm and to be restored to each other intact that we decided to ignore the snipers.

Mary Lee and our two little girls were reward enough for everything. Dabby, always very affectionate, was now willful, serious, and as stubborn as her parents. Mary Lee's mother, Nancy Epling, was as ever the calm, slow-moving, quick-thinking, unreconstructed rebel who never gave in to the "damn Yankees." My mother, Beth Whiting, was her same loving and extravagant self. My stepfather Jack had not worked since the summer of 1943, when he had played in Noël's *Design for Living* in Cleveland.

Having no terribly demanding duties, Mary Lee and I could now and then slip off to Hot Springs and nearby Boxwood Farm. It had been so very long since I'd played the gentleman farmer that I savored every spare hour in that magical valley.

At first Washington seemed unreal. There were no air-raid sirens, no bombed-out buildings or casualties, and not even serious rationing. It was a city so elegantly intact that those of us who had seen the bleeding and wreckage of other cities felt as much guilt as gratitude.

As Germany reeled to bloody defeat and Hitler rang down his Wagnerian curtain, the great concern of the United States was how finally to defeat Japan. Despite Admiral Nimitz's recent phenomenal victories, MacArthur's Caesarean communiqués, and the accounts of Mountbatten's sweating forces causing the most enemy casualties, that nation's people seemed impervious to fear. To invade the Japanese homeland would mean 50-percent Allied losses on the landing beaches, according to a consensus of Allied intelligence. I was not in the least keen to go out to the Pacific, even if we were winning. I had come home safe from the European fracas; I decided now to make myself as useful as I could—but here at home.

A major Allied advantage had been dangerously compromised when Colonel Robert Rutherford McCormick, the famed anti-Roosevelt isolationist publisher of the *Chicago Tribune,* printed the true story that we had broken the Japanese top-secret code. This was a shocking breach of security and it was even rumored that the government was considering charging him with high treason in time of war. But the powerful McCormick was not even reprimanded. It was believed that taking any action against McCormick would have been tantamount to admitting the story was true and thus would oblige the Japanese to devise an entirely new secret code. It was therefore decided that the White House and the Pentagon must issue a vigorous denial. A famous comic strip was hurriedly redrawn and distributed via the *Tribune*'s syndicate so that its hero appeared to be helping to break an enemy code, thus saving Allied lives. Stories were then spread abroad that this fantasy cartoon had been used by McCormick to boost his paper's circulation. Then, in order to counter the damage and to persuade the Japanese that we had *not* discovered their secrets, we took a step almost too dreadful to recollect. When the latest decoded message disclosed an imminent Japanese plan of attack, we deliberately did nothing to forestall it. The ruse worked. This dreadful but necessary plan, which allowed many American casualties just to prove the McCormick *Tribune* story wrong, was carried out in the hope that such a decision would save many more lives later.

The whole episode was deliberately slanted away from public curiosity and smothered by an avalanche of other news, but at such heartbreaking cost. However, it did inspire me with an admittedly wild scheme which, if it worked, could bring about a Japanese surrender.

The plan, in the form of a top secret memo, was prepared in January 1945. After the war was over, it was discussed in a number of war histories and reminiscences—not as anything major, but rather as a small, offbeat episode. Unfortunately, few remembered the details of the plan very well, so some of the later accounts of it were nearly unrecognizable.

The essence of the idea evolved after I recalled that many years before, my father had, during one of his trips to Japan, made a good friend and golf partner of Prince Konoye, a relative of the emperor and a former prime minister. Pete also met the emperor a few times when he was still Crown Prince Hirohito. And, in fact, Pete gave him my pony when I was seventeen. As a result of their partly Anglo-American education, both the emperor and Konoye were suspected of pro-Allied leanings. In addition, I had heard authorities on Japan confirm information leaking into the State Department that the strong-willed dowager empress, though as constitutionally powerless as her son, was discreetly very influential and secretly as opposed to his government's war policies as he was.

It occurred to me that we should arrange a super-secret contact with the dowager empress by some mad, thoroughly unmilitary hook or crook. She, in turn, would persuade her son, the emperor, first to protect himself and then to personally broadcast to his people that "in view of the imminent probability of more Japanese lives being needlessly lost and the nation subsequently wrecked," he would declare his unconditional surrender. This would be followed by a major coup d'état.

Meanwhile, a conspicuous distraction designed to precede the emperor's courageous gesture was a nearly indispensable part of the plan. An American submarine would surface off some remote Japanese coast and a small party of high-ranking American officers would come ashore and demand a parley with Japanese officials or authorities of equal rank, to assure them of our determination to invade at any cost. But in order to avoid further needless slaughter, we would give them a certain limited time to consider sending us notice of surrender.

There was no doubt in anyone's mind, including my own, that the plan was zany and inspired. But, I insisted, if every link in the chain leading to the dowager empress was made as secure as the ingenuity of our top cloak-and-dagger boys could arrange, I reckoned the remaining risks were worth taking.

My immediate superior, Captain Dupre, was, while amused, frankly sympathetic to the plan, as were some new and unexpected allies. The first was Cecil Lyons, whom I first met on my trip to South America for FDR in 1941. He put me in touch with his father-in-law, who had been one of our most distinguished senior diplomats, the former U.S. ambassador to Japan Joseph Grew. Ambassador Grew laughed but also applauded the idea, particularly as he had been a proponent of a diplomatic rather than a military end to hostilities. Grew commended my plan to the assistant secretary of state for Japanese affairs and the chairman of the committee for formulating surrender policies, Eugene S. Dooman. He also did some aggressive lobbying on the plan's behalf among the service Chiefs of Staff and their advisers.

Johnny Bevan, over in London, also supported the idea, despite its more fantastic aspects, but as the Pacific war was thought by the military in Washington to be our exclusive responsibility, we declined as many offers of British, Australian, and New Zealand assistance as we could without inviting a break.

We knew that the Japanese economy was suffering, their military situation was deteriorating on all fronts, and their recent losses in the Pacific and Burma had been very serious indeed. We also heard that influential groups had begun to discuss a vague peace settlement that would save face.

But how to actually reach the inner imperial circle—to create and maintain a discreet line of communication? I proposed a whimsical idea that we start with someone in the Vatican and then, through other devious means, forge the next loose link with someone responsible and trustworthy in a neutral country like Sweden or Switzerland. From then on there would be a continuing chain of secure contact links, zigzagging out of Europe, into the Mideast and eventually, with help from a thoroughly trustworthy and sympathetic diplomat, we would make this most careful, catlike approach to the Japanese emperor. This last diplomatic link would cover his tracks all the way and select only those closest to him in sentiment and rank to make the first tentative hint of the ultimate plans.

Suddenly, my irregular proposals to win a major war without another major battle had to be laid aside when I was brought down with a combination of ailments said to have originated in the Mediterranean. I had amoebic dysentery, which brought on a severe allergy affecting my legs and feet so I couldn't walk without debilitating itching and/or pain. This was compounded by another pneumonia, my fourth or fifth, and a bad case of trench mouth, all of which combined to put me in Bethesda Naval Hospital for six weeks. Afterward there was a short, agreeable, but maddeningly ill-timed convalescence in Palm Beach, Florida. When I returned to duty I found that absolutely no action, nor even any serious thought had been taken by the Chiefs of Staff, so I started over again to lobby every person of influence who might lend a willing and helpful ear.

I was disappointed but not surprised that our Joint Chiefs sniffed impatiently at my plan. I was told that when they learned the identity of the author they sniffed again. Perhaps they were right. We will never know. Japanese willingness to discuss a cessation of hostilities had already been signaled to us via intermediaries from, among others, Vatican circles.

Soon after, secret information reached Washington from a Scandinavian diplomat that a reshuffle of the Japanese cabinet was about to be ordered by the emperor. The diplomat proved right. The Japanese ambassador to Germany, General Hiroshi Oshimoi, had been captured in Germany by the Allies. He indicated he would be prepared to mediate with new Japanese authorities. But interservice rivalry was still so keen that we military lowlifers who got wind of this development were merely informed that the U.S. Army was well aware of several peace plans that had originated in the Navy Department. Thereafter they forbade the navy access to the Japanese diplomat in the POW camp where he was said to be held.

I next employed my (I hope discreetly practiced) old habit of pushing my way to the topmost boss I could find. Assistant Secretary Gene Dooman, still my best supporter, enlisted the interest of Cordell Hull to get an audience with FDR himself—recently returned from his last Allied conference at Yalta in the Crimea. The president was such a professional charmer that I couldn't know for certain if he was really intrigued with my idea or merely being friendly to a young supporter. But we did meet briefly and he did promise to check on it and instructed his secretary, Missy LeHand, to make a date to talk about it again on his return from a badly needed rest in Warm Springs, Georgia.

Our meeting was set for the afternoon of April 13, and I was to come into the White House by a special entrance in order to avoid the press. There was no question in my mind that FDR needed some serious rest in the meantime. He looked haggard, and his manner was noticeably less vigorous than when I had last seen him, just before I went off to war in October 1941. I had heard some gossip suggesting that he had been less effective than usual at the Yalta meeting with Stalin and Churchill. In fact, it was widely whispered that old Winston, war-weary but a devoted and loyal partner (who had already been overruled on strategy several times by FDR), complained bitterly that Stalin had been promised far too many political spoils from a defeated German Reich in return for joining the war against Japan.

But the air at that political altitude was too rarefied for me. I knew hardly more than an odd hint of something here and there. I do recall, however, that Winston was supposed to make another of his trips to Washington in the near future and that one day Mrs. R. took me aside and, assuming I knew the Old Man well (which, of course, I did not, but I said nothing), whispered to me outside in the hall, "Do tell Winston we're so-o-o looking forward to his visit, but please remind him tactfully that Franklin likes to go to bed *early* and as fascinated as he is with Winston's stories, he just cannot stay up late. Winston *must* find someone else who'll sit up all night with him."

I smiled, nodded politely, took my leave and, of course, never passed the message along.

While the president was away, I managed to meet Vice-President Harry Truman, a fine, no-baloney midwesterner whose job gave him prestige but neither power nor influence. Dean Acheson, then an under secretary of state, complimented me on my "ingenious plan" but was discouraging about its acceptance. Needless to say, I did not know the military had other, more devastatingly lethal, plans to end the war.

Not long after this, on April 12, Mary Lee and I attended a large afternoon reception in the attractive garden of Senator Warren Austin, later to become the first head of the American delegation to the United Nations. Suddenly we heard the shocking news of the president's death in Warm Springs.

The death of Roosevelt was a deeply emotional blow not just to the United States but to our allies and supporters everywhere. The news was heard around the world by ordinary people in a pall of disbelief. Ironically, it preceded the unconditional surrender of the Third Reich by only about three weeks and the signing of the United Nations Charter by less than three months. Everyone worried and wondered—what next?

Harry Truman was next. And it was he who was to preside over the great victory celebrations of that year of our Lord, 1945. The unfancy butt of big-city wise-guy jokes took the reins of government into his hands firmly and wisely.

Victory in Europe—V-E Day, May 8, 1945—was the day when people cheered and wept for as many reasons as there were people involved. Mary Lee and I were part of the joyful, tearful fragments of the explosion into the streets of our capital city, around our White House and almost everywhere.

Jim Forrestal, our first secretary of defense, had examined various plans to end the war with Japan and dismissed mine in a brief memo declaring: "On the whole it may be said that the extreme, difficult and hazardous means proposed by Commander Fairbanks are entirely unnecessary to convince Japanese leaders that they are on the verge of defeat."

One of the U.S. Navy's Japanese experts, Captain Ellis M. Zacharias, had an equally unconventional plan to end the war. Captain Zacharias, whom I had known when he was chief of staff in southern California's naval district, was well known for his contrariness and independent views and had suggested contacting the enemy's military chiefs. Forrestal clearly favored Zacharias's plan as originating from a "professional source"—but even it was, in his opinion, "impractical." Both were turned down by the Joint Chiefs of Staff.

There was an interesting sequel to this episode a few years later when I got a "private and confidential" letter from a Commander Farago. He had once been Zacharias's aide in all matters involving psychological warfare. Zacharias, by now retired, recorded his abbreviated version of our efforts:

> One of the plans, proposed by Douglas Fairbanks, Jr., the distinguished motion picture producer and actor . . . His idea was to establish direct contact with a group of influential leaders gathered around the Dowager Empress who indicated their willingness to discuss peace with us through members of a neutral legation in Tokyo or elsewhere.
>
> Commander Fairbanks . . . developed the plan on his own initiative, to end a remarkable wartime career on an exceptionally gallant note . . . and he seemed to feel certain that [the men around the Dowager Empress] could be persuaded to act on our behalf. . . . Although prepared in minute detail . . . this plan was vetoed as "fantastic." Fairbanks may be interested to learn that Op 16 [Zacharias's Psychological Warfare Section] tried to get approval for his proposal. We regarded it as perfectly feasible if properly executed. But there were more important endorsements to be obtained and they proved hurdles which such a plan could not scale in the myopic pessimistic Washington of 1945. . . .

Reluctantly accepting the cold-water dousing from my superiors, Dooman encouraged me to rewrite still another idea in "officialese." Consequently, my next top secret memo—this time marked "For Dooman's eyes only"—included ideas for a draft text of a proclamation by the United States, United Kingdom, and Chinese heads of state (or government) to the people of Japan. The basic idea was that a Japanese agreement to postsurrender peace terms would be more generally acceptable if we were to agree to retention of their emperor as head of state.

To Gene Dooman's quiet surprise and my silent astonishment the plan, this time with no authorship attached, was first approved by Secretary Hull and Ambassador Grew, who then showed it to President Truman on May 28, according to the records. The president said he would accept it providing the Chiefs of Staff, headed by General Marshall, concurred. This was the document that might be called the preface or the protocol which President Truman and Secretary of War Stimson took with them to Potsdam and showed to Prime Minister Churchill. It emerged practically unchanged as the preamble to the later Potsdam Declaration on Japan. What was then regarded as the essential paragraph included the words ". . . the establishment of a responsible government of a character representative of the Japanese people. This may include a constitutional monarchy under the present dynasty. . . ."

I was fully aware at the time that I was neck-deep in swirling waters, but I was certain there was at least some hint of merit in my proposal— if only because there was nothing suspicious about it and it accorded with other ideas being propounded.

More than six years later, during the long-delayed proceedings of the Senate's Judiciary Committee in September 1951, dear Gene Dooman was asked the "how and why" of the whole background of the Potsdam Declaration, outlining the Allied peace terms for the Japanese.

MR. DOOMAN (to the Committee Chairman): This paper, then, was taken by Mr. Stimson [the secretary of war] to Potsdam. I arrived myself at Potsdam on the thirteenth of July, and I was told by Mr. McCloy, who was then there, that Mr. Stimson was in active discussion with Mr. Churchill with regard to that document. . . . It was then telegraphed to General Chiang Kai-shek, and on July 29 it was promulgated then as the Potsdam Proclamation to Japan, and it was on the basis of that document that Japan surrendered.

May I also add, for the benefit of—I do not want to take credit that really belongs to somebody else, but I would like to put on record here that the preamble to the Potsdam Declaration was taken from a document prepared by Douglas Fairbanks, who was then in the Navy Department in the Psychological Warfare Department.

THE CHAIRMAN: *Douglas Fairbanks?*

MR. DOOMAN: Douglas Fairbanks. I would like to make acknowledgment, if I could, of his contribution to a paper which, after all, is part of history.

MR. SOURWINE: You are referring to the *movie actor?*

MR. DOOMAN: The movie actor.

MR. SOURWINE: Father or son?

MR. DOOMAN: Son.

MR. SOURWINE: Douglas Fairbanks, *Jr.*

MR. DOOMAN: Yes.

Someone later reported a barely audible "Good God!"

Some months earlier I had been promoted to full commander, and now I wasted no modest gestures of protest when invited to have my photograph taken in my first "brass hat." Then Mary Lee joined me in her Red Cross uniform and I did get more gratifying official recognition in the form of the rare and highly prized British Distinguished Service Cross awarded for "Conspicuous Gallantry in Action" by the Royal Navy. It was pinned on in the king's name at an impressive ceremony at the British embassy by Lord Halifax.

Later on the U.S. Navy decided unofficially that the other two services had given out so very many Legion of Merit medals that the value of the decoration had been "downgraded" to a routine award for outstanding or otherwise worthy staff and/or administrative duties. Therefore the department ordered it to be worn *after,* or below (rather than above), the Silver Star. However, to preserve some of its former symbolic value, those won in combat had a bronze *V*–for valor–attached to the ribbon. So that was what happened to what was initially meant to be my highest combat award. Nevertheless, I was very moved and grateful, if still a bit distrustful of it all.

One day in the latter part of July 1945, Captain Dupre, soon to be made a rear admiral, asked if I'd like to go out and join Mountbatten again. He was now at his South East Asia Command Headquarters, in what was then called Ceylon (now Sri Lanka). Word had been passed on that I might be useful to him in a liaison capacity. I suspected it was a way of getting a gadfly out of the Navy Department's thinning hair. The orders—considerately called a suggestion by Dupre—were for me to go to Dickie for the invasion and recovery of Singapore and Malaya, then on to Chungking for a reason I never did know, and from there to Okinawa, where I would help with various cover and deception plans for the projected invasion of Japan. I was also to command a tactical group, a task unit, as in the Mediterranean. The British representative member of the Combined Chiefs of Staff, Admiral Sir James Summerville, had already written a charming letter of introduction to the British navy's commander in chief of the Far Eastern Fleet, asking him to put me in touch with Peter Fleming and his cloak-and-dagger people because I was "in on nearly everything." I was also to coordinate the tactics of the amphibious diversions.

Dupre was concerned about me and my currently vacuous duties in Washington. I had not dared say anything to Mary Lee and I was allowed some days to think about it and decide whether or not I wanted to be "ordered" abroad again. It was clear it would be only a matter of time before Japan was brought to heel.

In June our fliers had begun a series of massive bombings of Japanese home targets, dropping great blockbuster bombs around the clock. I silently wondered what I would be allowed to do.

We went to New York, where Jack had ended his latest tour and Mother was complaining, saying she had no more Sully heirlooms of value to sell. Though she knew I had little myself to spare these days, she would ask, weeping sometimes, "If it's at all possible, dear . . . ?" Mother was largely unaware of it, but one of their closest family friends (and Jack's ex-colleague), John Hundley, confided to me that Jack was becoming heavily dependent on drink. He hid it well, but it was shortly to become a worry to everyone.

It had been about two years since I had ceased my solitary support of the Douglas Voluntary Hospitals that Dickie Benson was running in England and turned it all over to the St. John's Ambulance Brigade and the British Red Cross. Somehow, with a small assist from Mary Lee and the sale of a small bit of the remaining United Artists company holdings I'd inherited, I did manage to give Mother and Jack a bit of an allowance for a while.

Johnny Bevan came to Washington from his London Controlling

Section, hoping to somehow persuade our still suspicious Chiefs of Staff that strategic deception actually, provably worked. He had heard from Dickie that I knew everyone in Washington and could be of help in high echelons. It was further evidence of Dickie's exaggerated confidence in his friends.

It had been a hot sticky summer and dress whites were the "after-hours" uniform. I went to Union Station to join Johnny Bevan en route to New York, and the awful humidity made me look as though I had just got out of a pool. Standing at a newsstand, I was jolted out of my sweaty dopiness by seeing my train begin to pull out. I snapped to and ran for it. It was slowly gathering speed. Johnny was already aboard and the Pullman doors were all closed. I jumped on the steps and began hammering on the door. A porter appeared at the glass window above and waved me away, but the train was by now going too fast and I dared not drop off. I banged and yelled and was becoming truly frightened at the prospect of holding on until Baltimore, the next stop, when a passenger, seeing my plight, opened the door and helped a desperately tired, dirty, soaking wet naval officer climb breathlessly aboard. The rest of the trip was celebrated by Johnny and me with cold gin-and-tonics because the Chiefs of Staff had rather reluctantly agreed—at last—to cooperate in planning and executing strategic deception.

I made as little of my very real apprehensions about joining Mountbatten as I could. I told my family only that I was going to "India or Ceylon or somewhere to advise on the planning and to instruct the tactical commanders and the technical and electronic officers." Of course, this last was a dead giveaway, as anyone who knew me was fully aware that I remained as ignorant as ever of the intricate workings of our electronic gadgets and most of our special types of communications. Nevertheless, I put in a bid for Jack Watson to join me and then began the business of packing and taking a last long leave in Newport, Rhode Island, with our two girls, to visit mostly Mary Lee's friends.

In Newport on August 6, I received a telephone call from Mother in New York.

"Darling!" Her voice was clearly anxious. "Have you heard the radio this morning?"

No, I hadn't. "Why?"

"Well, they said we dropped a very big bomb on Japan—the biggest ever, on somewhere called Hiro . . . something. I really don't understand what they meant, so I called you!"

I had heard nothing about anything, let alone a new kind of bomb. "Oh, dear!" My voice was affectionate but condescending. "It's just the air force PR people again. It's the same old kind of bomb—the one we called a 'blockbuster' when we dropped it on Germany, that's all. The papers have to write about something, you know."

Mother was instantly satisfied. She immediately rang all her friends to say, "My Douglas knows everything. It's just the radio and press trying to be sensational. Pay no attention. Don't worry!"

Only the absolute minimum of the highest-ranking people in the land had so much as an inkling of the existence of an atom bomb. I recalled Will Stewart's (one of Pete's closest friends and a noted figure in New York society) exquisite wife, Janet, asking me when we were last in New York if I had heard of a secret something called the Manhattan Project. Of course I hadn't. But that was it!

Three days after Mother's call the press blazed the news that we had dropped an atom bomb—the deadliest, most dreadful destruction ever invented—on another Japanese city. First Hiroshima, then Nagasaki. Few could uncoil their imaginations sufficiently to comprehend what had happened. The Japanese most certainly comprehended. On August 14, they surrendered unconditionally. Nothing on our planet was ever the same again.

Japan had reaped the whirlwind. How many tens of thousands of noncombatant civilians of all ages and sexes were obliterated by those two eradicators could never accurately be assessed. But the war was over, and with a mixture of elation and horror on August 15 we celebrated V-J Day, victory over Japan.

Now I was recalled to Navy Headquarters in Washington. We knew that reservists with the longest service records were first in line for demobilization and that my reserve record, beginning well before our official entry into the war, placed me in a better position to get out than most. Nor would it hurt that I had received several U.S. and foreign combat decorations. But then, after a bit, I began to reflect on what an early return to civilian life might mean, and I flapped a little.

What on earth was I going to do? I had no plans whatever. It is an old theatrical saw—and a political one, too—that one should not be away from the public eye for more than two or three years, at the most. I had been away from my profession for over four years. In fact, except for *The Corsican Brothers* in mid-'41, I had made no movies since *Angels over Broadway* in 1940. There had been no feelers advanced for my services in well over four years. I was due to be let out in an expensive world with far too little left in my poke. I began to consider staying on in the navy as an alternative to conspicuous unemployment. I thought I had no option but to volunteer to remain on duty for another six months. But to do what?

After I'd formalized this decision, I was assigned to the Post-War Plans Division, ostensibly to study the disposition of our conquered ex-enemies. But that would not be back-breaking work, and I had time to seek out other projects.

I hinted to friends in the State Department and to my generous booster Rear Admiral (Reserve) Sid Souers, from St. Louis, the "father" of a super-secret central intelligence group later to become the CIA, that I might welcome an important assignment in diplomatic circles, or in civilian intelligence.

My warm new and uniquely unsought relationship with President Truman evolved gradually. We had two or three long interviews about postwar plans and my former deceptive activities. Once in the White House Oval Office, while giving me a long private lecture on world affairs (using a pointer with a huge hanging map), he began to evolve (it seemed extemporaneous) what came to be known as the Truman Doctrine. Then he smiled and suddenly changed the subject. He reminisced happily about when he was a boy and sat in the gallery of his local movie theater, chewing gum excitedly as he watched one or another of my father's old pictures for, he said, the umpteenth time. Sometimes he described his favorite reading matter—seventeenth- and eighteenth-century history. He envied the English statesmen in those days who only had to bother with Parliament for a very few months in a year and who had time to write wonderful letters on important subjects "in longhand! Here I am, president of the great United States in the twentieth century and I'm so busy being 'chief executive' that I have far too little time to study and decide on matters that affect millions of lives. I only pray those I've assigned to advise me are doing their jobs thoroughly."

I soon got to be very fond of the Boss and became another keen supporter and admirer. I was particularly elated when he asked if I would be interested in a diplomatic assignment. I did say perhaps I would and was very grateful for the query. It was the last I ever heard of it from him. Later on another new friend, Secretary of State Dean Acheson, also dropped hints, but that was all. I knew, as a matter of fact, that no top diplomatic appointment ever went to other than very rich supporters of whatever president was in office. The reasons for this were sound. We did not pay our top diplomats enough to carry the great costs of our largest and most important embassies, so they had to be independently wealthy. Nor had we any system of honors to reward the outstanding good work of private citizens. We could only repay outstanding political services with important foreign diplomatic or government posts.

One afternoon, while my future still hung anxiously in my thoughts, I shared a taxi (an admirable Washington custom) with a gruff-looking admiral. I sensed the old boy giving me sidelong glances and then obviously trying to place me. This was, for me, a long-lost occurrence and provided a twinkle of hope that perhaps I had not been so forgotten as I feared. I tried to look unconcerned, gazing out of the cab's window, chin up and shamelessly posing in the hope that I'd click with him.

All of a sudden he turned and in a hoarse, salty bark said, "What's your name, Commander?"

I beamed my most publicly cultivated smile, replete with professional charm, and quietly replied, "Fairbanks, sir."

"Who?" he bellowed impatiently.

"Fairbanks, sir. Douglas Fairbanks—junior . . ."

The admiral gave a grunt and mumbled, "Oh! I thought it was Thompson. You look like a young feller that was at sea with me in the South Pacific."

With that he turned away. I did the same. Our cab stopped to let me out. I paid my share and slouched away.

* * *

My chances to "make work" increased in direct proportion to the decrease in my duties. I proliferated memoranda for circulation on a profusion of subjects. One envisaged a semiformal assemblage of former presidents, vice presidents, and cabinet members. They would express their views to the administration and Senate of the day when asked to do so, though without payment. These former eminent public servants would always be officially available in posts of honor and usefulness instead of just being relegated to political trash cans on retirement.

Sometimes my memos went further afield, as when they dealt with proposals for removing the potential dangers of a divided Germany by creating a loose German commonwealth, in which both sides would remain as independent as the situation demanded but would officially acknowledge a commonality of cultural roots.

I also thought we should take the lead in organizing a continuing naval connection for "amateurs" by forming a civilian group of ex-reservists called Reserve Officers of the Naval Services (we even got out a periodical of sorts). I further proposed that we emulate several of our allies in maintaining openings for reservists working in civilian jobs abroad to serve as "Honorary Assistant Naval Attachés."

I redrafted a scheme for the national rewarding of civilian achievement somewhat along the lines of the French Légion d'Honneur. Years before, I had suggested something of the sort to Cordell Hull which went into a hopper of similar ideas and ended up as one of the bases for establishing our Legion of Merit medal. However, my argument was that the United States should reward achievements for peace and not just for wartime accomplishment. I was subsequently told that this was one of the determining documents in the eventual creation of the Presidential Medal of Freedom. Alas, this highest national honor has become far less prestigious than originally intended, since presidents pass it around not just to the acknowledged worthies, but also, like pretty presents, to personal friends and supporters.

I was and am a habitual writer of memos and proposals on matters of either major or minor import, quite regardless of my qualifications to even consider the chosen subject. People sometimes find this annoying—as my Beach Jumper colleague Jack Watson recalled in a letter reminiscing about the war:

You were not in the War Room of the "Vulcan" the day that Bob English came instantly to your defense when one of the staffers mumbled a snide remark about you. . . .

English was reviewing some of the possible operations around the Med that were under feasibility review. He ticked them off, and at one point reached the suggestion that a feint be made toward the Balearics, designed to fool the Axis. From somewhere in the room, one of the trade school boys [Annapolis graduates] was heard to murmur incautiously: "Sounds like one of Fairbanks's cockeyed notions."

Whereupon Captain English erupted in a cold fury: "Listen to me, you sonsabitches. While you're sitting on your ditty boxes waiting for the wine mess to open each day, Fairbanks is exploring ways to win this goddam war. I don't care if he submits a dozen plans and we reject them all, at least he's doing what he's assigned to do, which is more than I can say for most people in this room. Now, I don't ever want to hear another word about the so-called Hollywood ideas you find so easy to criticize." Then he proceeded with the briefing.

Toward the middle of my overtime months of duty, I was asked, very informally, by one of the heads of our U.S. Information Agency to discreetly hint to my former film colleagues that they be more "patriotically selective" in the choice of films they distributed abroad. Continental critics and newspapers in the recently liberated countries had complained about the excess of crime movies and those suggesting that however rich and powerful the United States might be, our manners, humor, and moral standards were, at best, immature or coarse. One Austrian critic asked in print if war-ravaged Europe had been "liberated" by the likes of such clownish figures as Abbott and Costello, or if they just represented exaggerations of the American norm. I managed somehow to get the point of the government's query across to friends in the Association of Motion Picture Producers without letting it be suspected that I had been put up to it by the administration. I made it clear, however, that anonymous foreign service officers had said they regretted seeing us advertise our least attractive characteristics so widely.

The only reactions I got were brusque snubs. I was unwilling even to let our government know how some of our movie moguls reacted to the request that we put our better feet forward more often.

* * *

In late November or early December my voluntary extension of duty had about six weeks to go when, out of the celebrated blue, there came a note from my old Hollywood agent Frank Vincent, telling me I had been offered a damned good job. It was the starring role in a big RKO special based on the old Arabian Nights story "Sinbad, the Sailor." Vincent enclosed a huge overwritten first-draft script by John Swift, together with charming notes from Pandro Berman, still head of RKO, from Stephen Ames, the intended producer, and from old colleague director Dick Wallace, with whom I had worked in *The Young in Heart* in 1938.

I knew then for the first time what people meant by saying they "jumped out of their skin." I felt like a preteenager, phoned Mary Lee at the Red Cross in excitement, and after driving out to Boxwood Farm for the weekend settled down to read the first-draft manuscript.

Even if the script hadn't been promising, I would have jumped at it. After all my months of fretting and anxiety, here was an offer to star in a big new color motion picture—still a rarity because of the cost. I didn't even care how much salary I was offered; and what's more, I telephoned Vincent to that effect.

Vincent was as relieved at my acceptance of the offer as I was to get it. He had feared I was too keen on Washington or that I would demand too much money or too many conditions. With these apprehensions in mind, he had insisted ahead of time on RKO's agreement to my having final script approval as well as approval of cast and cameraman. I wouldn't have dreamed of asking for all that, but Vincent knew me of old. He persuaded Pan Berman that I still knew a good deal about film production.

As it turned out, I was delighted with the script in its first-draft form. I did make a number of notes, but to my further surprise, my future bosses were absolutely charming—even about my intrusions into areas other than my purely interpretative one. They agreed with virtually all my suggestions.

The proposed cast was splendid, too. The leading lady was the fairy-tale-come-true beauty Maureen O'Hara. Her naturally reddish hair, perfect Irish complexion, and exquisitely endowed bosom (which she was wisely but discreetly at pains to exploit and which I, ever an untiring student of such anatomical addenda, discreetly admired) may not have been in the least Middle Eastern, but I didn't care. After all, I was not exactly a typical Arab any more than Walter Slezak was even remotely (with his taped-up blue eyes) Oriental. I didn't even care if O'Hara could act. She was so beautiful (Arabian Nights princesses must always be beautiful) that she really wouldn't be obliged to do anything. Every man in the audience would be her eager Sinbad.

For the principal villain, they proposed a young man I'd known before the war. Anthony Quinn was of Anglo-Irish-Mexican parentage and married to an even older friend, C. B. deMille's lovely daughter Cecilia. Tony had always been desperately serious about acting and the theater. This would be a fine opportunity for him to "ham it up" to all our hearts' content. Furthermore, he was a nice, easy guy. I remembered Walter Slezak on the musical comedy stage years before: a very young Austrian, slim and handsome, with a lovely singing voice. Now he was very fat but, as always, a particularly fine actor. My imminent return to a movie career promised to be much more satisfying than I could have hoped.

The move from Washington back to the West Coast necessitated a great flurry of activity. There were lots of RKO-arranged interviews and much publicity, but we never knowingly allowed the children to be photographed for the press. We not only worried about their safety, but also were anxious not to let them feel they were in any way celebrities or "special."

Barbara and Cary Grant had moved out of Westridge some weeks before our arrival, and now we found that we needed to refurbish the house and grounds. Cary had generously given his entire fee for a picture (then about $100,000) each year of the war to the British War Relief and not only performed a good deal of important but unpublicized services for his country but also helped friends in his hometown of Bristol. Barbara, however, had her own ideas of contributing to the war effort: she had ordered our dear old gardener to dig up whatever he could by way of grass and shrubs and bushes and replant it all with potatoes! Now that we were back he was happily restoring the grounds as best he could—trimming the thick, tall, wall-like hedges on the roadside, restimulating the assorted fruit, date, palm, and pepper trees, urging the rose garden to hurry, and repainting the wood folly.

We discovered that the famous Poor Little Rich Girl had kept the furnace heat on indoors winter and summer, resulting in the crackling and buckling of some of our best bits of eighteenth-century furniture. And there were many other signs of thoughtless neglect which Mary Lee was quick to notice. Her eagle eyes found so many that a list had to be made out. Happily, Barbara's lawyers didn't quibble, but some things just couldn't be repaired. It was nearly impossible to get angry with Barbara for long, though. She had been so spoiled that it was not really her fault that reality was no more believable than an old novel or movie—to take or leave as the mood struck her.

As usual, I was spending money before it came in. I began to miss old valet-secretary-man-of-all-jobs Emile's prewar services more and more. Emile was Pete's former valet/butler/secretary who offered his services to me in mid-1938. He thought my life less demanding and more fun than my father's so for a time I had my own Swiss-trained equivalent of Jeeves. He always preferred working for a bachelor so he left me when Mary Lee and I were married. The last I heard of him he had become the postmaster of a tiny U.S. post office in the village of Pacific Palisades (CA). I finally yielded to a compromise whereby Mary Lee took on certain household costs and I did the rest. Because my mother and all her still dependent family had to be housed, fed, and maintained, I was never really ahead of the game, and all too often I was just getting by. However, after an absence of four and a half years we were overjoyed to be back in California. It was just about the New Year of 1946.

The first flush of homecoming was as exciting as we expected it to be. RKO representatives met us in Pasadena and drove us home in convoy out to Pacific Palisades. My adored ex-stepmother, Mary Pickford (now Mrs. Buddy Rogers), organized a charming drinks party with all my nearby family and many old friends.

A day or so after our return I received a call from Darryl Zanuck, my old boss at Warners, now head of 20th Century–Fox. He was a presence on a committee that arranged various sorts of welcomes to those stars who had been away in one of the Armed Forces.

Darryl just exploded with *"Hello there, Jayar!"* greetings. He always shouted. Then he hemmed a bit, and hawed. "Up to last month or so," he stammered through his often caricatured rabbit teeth (my father said they allowed him to eat through a tennis racket), "we've been giving 'welcome home' affairs. Well, you and Bob Montgomery were the first stars to go. But now you seem to be about the last to get back—and, er—and . . . and . . . well, the committee thinks now it would be sort of an anticlimax! And you'd hate it anyway, I knew! You've just been away *too* long. Know what I mean? You understand, don't you, kiddo? Anyway, the damned things are usually a bore— they're really not much!" Then, in a different tone, he added, "Virginia and I want to see you and Mary Lee—and soon. Come to the beach house for dinner, or better yet, a weekend in the desert—down in the Springs . . . I'll get Virginia to call Mary Lee. See you soon, eh? Glad you're back! 'Bye!"

That was my first nonfamily, noncompany reception back to California. I told no one about it at the time. I was embarrassed and Mary Lee was hurt on my account. I would have much preferred to have no mention made of the idea at all than to be asked if I minded not being welcomed home. Still, it was typical.

I was legally obliged to stay in uniform until the first of February, as I was still technically on active duty. It was a bit embarrassing but it was "regulations." Within the first week, I went to the RKO studios for a *Sinbad* conference and was walking down the main "street" to an office building. Seeing a general coming toward me, I automatically saluted him.

"Oh, for Chrissakes! Don't do that!" he grumbled as he passed by. "I'm no goddamn general. I'm an extra in the picture on Stage Five—I don't even know the name of it!"

After my conference, I got a phone call from one of the studio's chief publicity men. He greeted me as an old friend (which I wasn't). "Say, Doug! Great to have seen you, kiddo. You look great, boy. Where'd you get all the 'fruit salad' on your chest? Western Costume Company, I'll bet!" His joke caused him great mirth. "But you know, if I were you, I'd get outta that uniform. Some people might think it's a costume for *Sinbad, the Sailor.*" More loud guffaws for his splendid funny joke. "If it's on the level, people will think you're showing off. They don't like seeing you in it. The war's over, you know! You don't mind, do you?"

I explained that as I was still technically on duty I wasn't allowed to get out of it for another couple of weeks, but he was unmoved. "How'll they know? Who knows from 'orders'? What'll they do to you? Court-martial or something?" He finally gave up with a sigh and a warning to keep out of sight of "the bitchy columnists—like Louella, Hedda, oh, yeah, and Sheila Graham; the three witches are still at it—just for a while anyhow."

The time for the last flag-waving had passed and the welcoming trumpets had been put away. Now we must hide our once-cheered past under dark wraps. Was it just two years ago that I was freezing in damp wintertime Algiers and dealing with my fears on the beach at Anzio?

My childhood friend Genie, ever sensitive to my goings-on, sent me a copy of Kipling's "Tommy," a bitter poem of soldiery, part of which goes:

> For it's Tommy this, an' Tommy that, an'
> "Chuck him out, the brute!"
> But it's "Savior of 'is country" when the
> guns begin to shoot. . . .

Now it was all an anticlimax to be swallowed and forgotten.

Just a few days before I was formally demobilized and permitted, indeed ordered, to wear civilian clothes all the time, Mary Lee and I went to a large dance given in a tent by the skating star Sonja Henie. Mary Lee and I greeted and embraced lots of fine old chums who warmly voiced their pleasure at our return and their relief that I was still all in one piece—a sentiment I fully shared. Suddenly, between whirls, I spied my ex-wife Joan Crawford at the far end of the temporarily emptied dance floor! I hadn't seen her in years. She looked just as glamorous as ever. She happened to see me at the same time and with a loud, joyous yelp of *"Darling!"* that galvanized everyone, spread her arms wide and came clattering across the dance floor. I glanced sidelong at Mary Lee and was relieved to see her smiling broadly (they had never met). I was really very glad to see Joan (Should I still call her Billie? I wondered quickly—I had not called her

Joan), and in a flash I thought she would be one more old friend who would say, "Good! You're back—safe and sound!" Or something like that—a word of real welcome.

As she reached me, I felt the eyes of the entire party on us. She embraced me warmly and then as she pulled back she repeated glee-fully, *"Darling!* I suppose you haven't heard—you don't know—I'm no longer with MGM. I'm with *Warner Brothers* now!"

It was good to be home. Little had changed.

To Be Continued . . .

Index